CAMBRIDGE LI

Books of enduring scholarly value

Polar Exploration

This series includes accounts, by eye-witnesses and contemporaries, of early expeditions to the Arctic and the Antarctic. Huge resources were invested in such endeavours, particularly the search for the North-West Passage, which, if successful, promised enormous strategic and commercial rewards. Cartographers and scientists travelled with many of the expeditions, and their work made important contributions to earth sciences, climatology, botany and zoology. They also brought back anthropological information about the indigenous peoples of the Arctic region and the southern fringes of the American continent. The series further includes dramatic and poignant accounts of the harsh realities of working in extreme conditions and utter isolation in bygone centuries.

Journal of a Voyage of Discovery to the Arctic Regions

Alexander Fisher (d.1838), ship's surgeon on the Arctic exploration ship H.M.S. *Hecla*, was the probable author of the anonymous 1819 *Journal of a Voyage of Discovery to the Arctic Regions*, also reissued in this series. The voyage of the *Hecla* and *Griper* began in 1819, and Fisher's account was published in 1821, going rapidly into further editions (of which this reissue is the third). The intention of the expedition, under William Edward Parry, was to find the North-West Passage. It was unsuccessful in this respect (an account by Captain G.F. Lyon of Parry's expedition of 1821–3 is also available in this series), but Fisher's detailed and lively account claims that the existence of the passage has been so far proved that it cannot be doubted. He describes the people and wildlife seen during the voyage, as well as providing technical details of latitude, weather and currents.

Cambridge University Press has long been a pioneer in the reissuing of out-of-print titles from its own backlist, producing digital reprints of books that are still sought after by scholars and students but could not be reprinted economically using traditional technology. The Cambridge Library Collection extends this activity to a wider range of books which are still of importance to researchers and professionals, either for the source material they contain, or as landmarks in the history of their academic discipline.

Drawing from the world-renowned collections in the Cambridge University Library and other partner libraries, and guided by the advice of experts in each subject area, Cambridge University Press is using state-of-the-art scanning machines in its own Printing House to capture the content of each book selected for inclusion. The files are processed to give a consistently clear, crisp image, and the books finished to the high quality standard for which the Press is recognised around the world. The latest print-on-demand technology ensures that the books will remain available indefinitely, and that orders for single or multiple copies can quickly be supplied.

The Cambridge Library Collection brings back to life books of enduring scholarly value (including out-of-copyright works originally issued by other publishers) across a wide range of disciplines in the humanities and social sciences and in science and technology.

Journal of a Voyage of Discovery to the Arctic Regions

in His Majesty's Ships *Hecla* and *Griper*, in the Years 1819 and 1820

Alexander Fisher

CAMBRIDGE
UNIVERSITY PRESS

University Printing House, Cambridge, CB2 8BS, United Kingdom

Cambridge University Press is part of the University of Cambridge.
It furthers the University's mission by disseminating knowledge in the pursuit of education, learning and research at the highest international levels of excellence.

www.cambridge.org
Information on this title: www.cambridge.org/9781108074919

This edition first published 1821
This digitally printed version 2014

ISBN 978-1-108-07491-9 Paperback

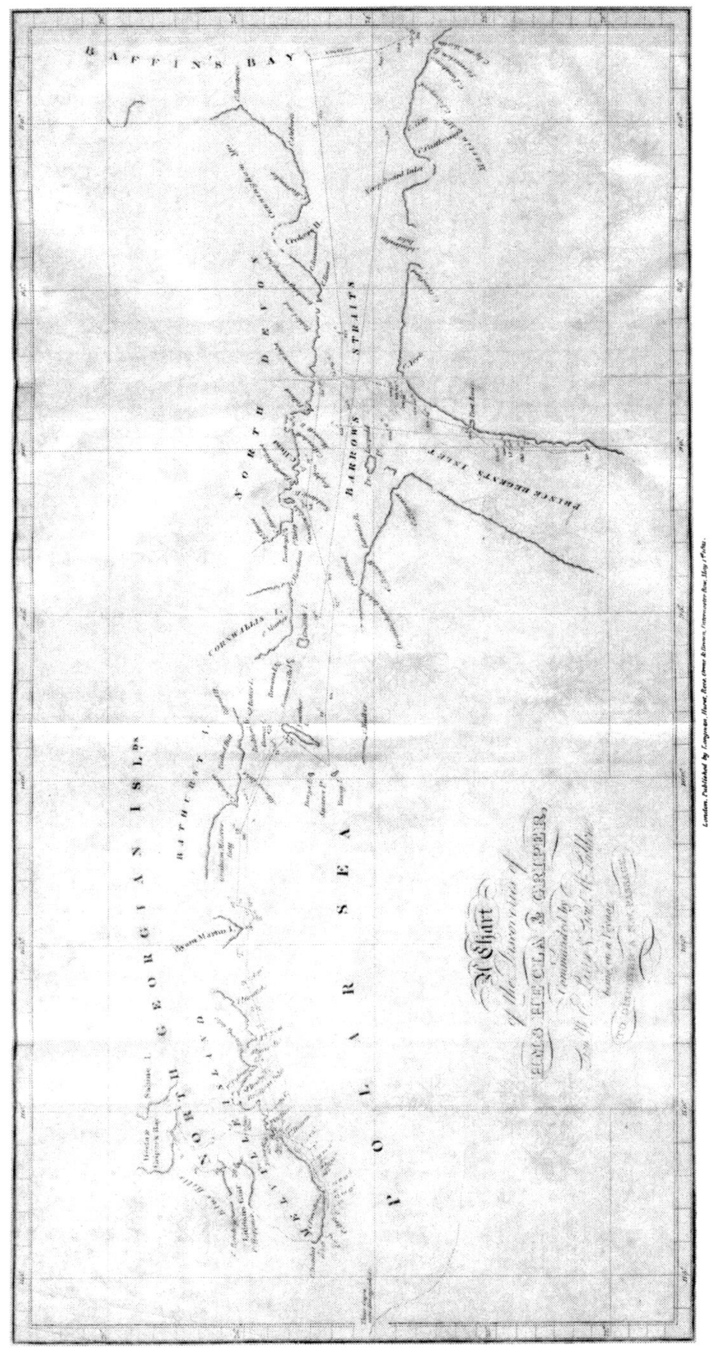

The material originally positioned here is too large for reproduction in this reissue. A PDF can be downloaded from the web address given on page iv of this book, by clicking on 'Resources Available'.

A

JOURNAL

OF A

VOYAGE OF DISCOVERY

TO THE

Arctic Regions,

IN

HIS MAJESTY'S SHIPS

HECLA AND GRIPER,

IN THE YEARS 1819 & 1820.

BY

ALEXANDER FISHER, SURGEON R.N.

THIRD EDITION.

LONDON:

PRINTED FOR

LONGMAN, HURST, REES, ORME, AND BROWN,

PATERNOSTER-ROW.

1821.

Printed by A. and R. Spottiswoode,
Printers-Street, London.

The AUTHOR *being hastily called away to join the new Expedition to the Arctic Regions, has not had an opportunity of correcting the Press, which he trusts will be accepted as an Apology for any Inaccuracies that may occur in the present Impression.*

April 21. 1821.

LIST

OF

PLATES AND WOOD-CUTS.

INTRODUCTION.

The object of the Expedition, of which the following pages contain a brief Narrative, is already so generally well known, that it requires little to be said upon it in the way of preface. Before we sailed on the first Expedition to the Polar Seas, great hopes were entertained, from the reports of several masters of Greenland ships, and other persons, that some great change had taken place in the Arctic regions; in consequence of which they were expected to be found navigable to a greater extent than they had been for some centuries past. From what we saw, however, on that voyage, we had every reason to suppose that Nature is nearly as regular and uniform in her operations there as in other parts of the globe; for our Greenland masters, who had been in the habit of visiting these seas annually for nearly twenty years, declared that they observed no material difference in the state of the ice.

Although the hopes thus raised were in some measure subverted by our first expedition, yet other facts and circumstances, of a more substantial kind, were observed during that voyage, which tended to prove the existence of a North-West Passage in a much clearer manner than the supposititious arguments that had been advanced in favour of it before; for we have reason to believe, from what we saw, that the different wide openings on the north and west side of Baffin's Bay, which were before called Sounds, are extensive inlets, leading to another sea in these directions; for the only one of these inlets into which we entered was that which Baffin called Lancaster's Sound; and from what we ascertained of it, I believe that no doubt remained on the minds of most of those who were there, that it was a Strait, or Passage, and not a Sound. This is the rational inference, since we went upwards of eighty miles into it, and yet saw no appearance of land, or any thing else to obstruct our progress.

Various other circumstances might be mentioned that tended to make this spacious inlet an object of interesting inquiry ; but the question respecting it has already been so much agitated, that it is unnecessary to say any thing on the subject, farther than that one of the principal objects of the Expedition was to explore it.

The vessels appointed for this service were His Majesty's ships Hecla and Griper, the former a vessel of nearly four hundred tons, and from her construction, (having been built for a bomb,) well adapted for stowage,—an object of the first importance where we were obliged to carry fuel, provisions, stores, and indeed every article that we were furnished with for the voyage. The Griper was a much smaller vessel than the Hecla, having been formerly a twelve-gun brig. Her accommodations, however, were considerably improved by her having been *rose upon ;* but she was notwithstanding very much inferior to the other ship in every respect, as she neither sailed so well, nor did she carry her own supply of provisions, &c. ; for, although the Expedition was furnished with stores and provisions for two years, yet, in less than half that time, the Griper required to be supplied from the Hecla with different articles. In other respects, however, their equipment was very good, and nothing was neglected to render them fit for the service on which they were to be employed. They were strengthened in every way, as much as wood and iron could strengthen them, having, in the first place, the whole of their outside, from the keel to some distance above the water-line, covered with an extra lining of oak-plank, from three to four inches thick, and, within, a number of additional beams, and other timbers, put into their hold, in order that they might withstand the pressure of the ice, in the event of their being caught between two floes of it. Their bows were also covered with strong plates of iron, to defend them from receiving damage by striking against the floating ice. They were likewise fitted up, inside, so as to make the accommodations of both officers and men as comfortable as the size of the vessels would admit. To guard, as much as possible, against the rigour of the climate, we were also provided with standing bed-places, which were deemed to be warmer than cots, or hammocks; and, in the event of our not effecting the passage, we were provided with planks, tarpaulins, and Russian-mats, for housing the ships during the winter, so as to be able to take exercise on deck in bad weather. The men, as on the former voyage, were furnished by Government with a suit of warm clothes, and a wolf-skin blanket, gratis.

The means of preserving the health of the crews were also well attended to; for besides the salt provisions being of a good quality, and recently cured, there was a large quantity of Messrs. Donkin and Hall's preserved meats and soups supplied. Antiscorbutics, of different kinds, were also provided, such as lemon-juice, sour-crout, essence of spruce, and essence of malt and hops; and, in case of our meeting with Indians or Esquimaux that could supply us with provisions, or any thing else that might be useful, Government sent with us a considerable quantity of toys, and other articles, to barter for whatever they might have to interchange. These articles consisted of jackets and trowsers of coarse cloth, shirts, brass-kettles, knives, forks, and spoons, looking-glasses, glass-beads of various colours, and other matters, either for use or ornament. In fact, every thing had been provided that was deemed likely to be of use in forwarding the object of the Expedition, and in making those who were employed on it as comfortable as the nature of the service would admit.

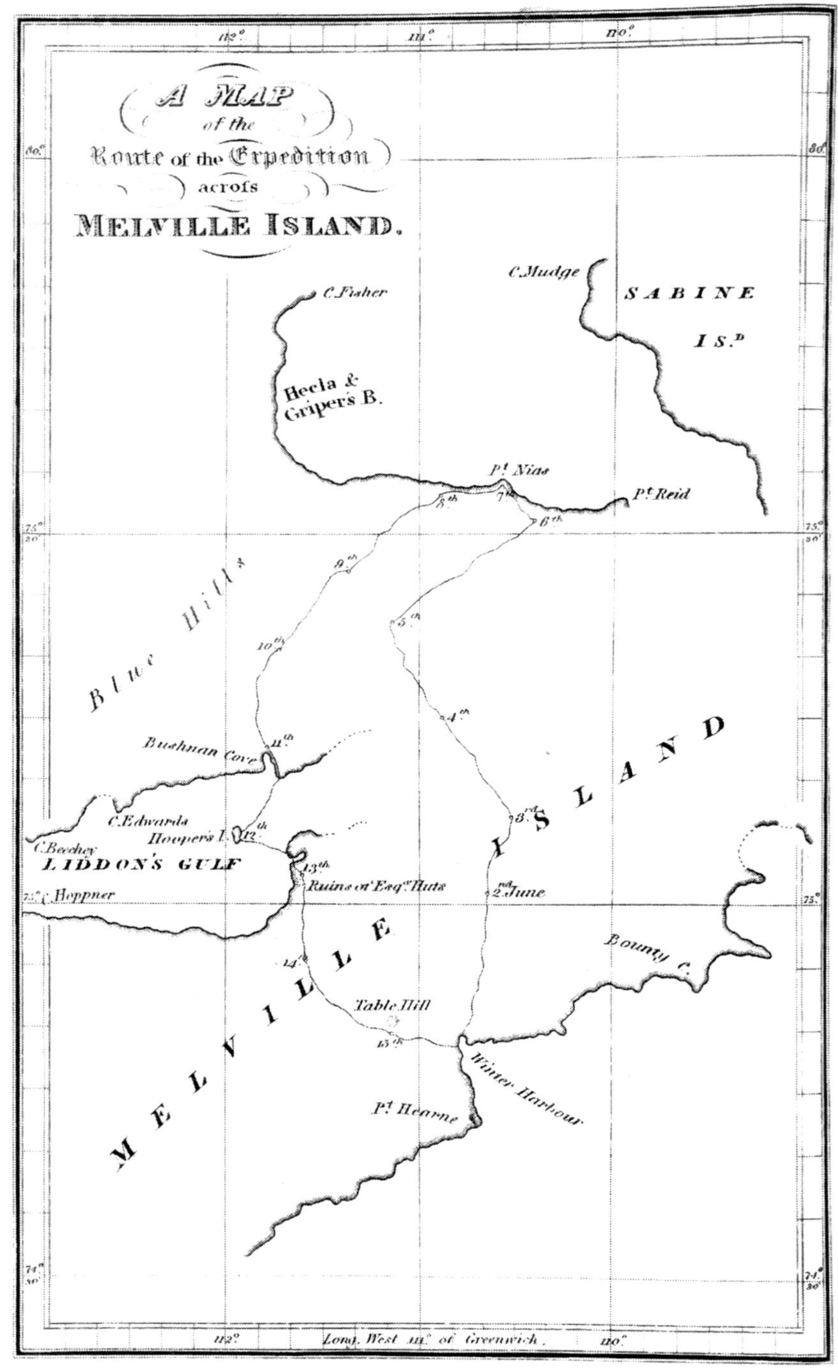

London, Published by Longman, Hurst, Rees, Orme & Brown, Paternoster Row, May 1st. 1821.

A JOURNAL

OF

THE PROCEEDINGS OF HIS MAJESTY'S SHIP

HECLA.

Tuesday, May 4th, 1819. — Many interesting particulars connected with our expedition might be mentioned prior to the details of this day; but as they cannot, strictly speaking, be considered as forming a part of the occurrences of the voyage, I shall begin my narrative only from the time that we started from Deptford. We have been ready for sailing for some days past, but during that time the wind has been from the eastward, which prevented our departure. In order therefore to avoid farther delay, steam vessels were applied for to tow us down yesterday: but, in consequence of the great demand for these vessels for some time past, none could be procured until this morning; the delay occasioned was not, however, much regretted, as it afforded many an opportunity of passing another night amongst their friends whom they were on the point of leaving for some time. The eventful moment of departure at length arrived, for at a quarter before eight o'clock this morning, we cast off from His Majesty's hulk

Dedaingneuse, and were immediately taken in tow by the Eclipse steam-boat, which, notwithstanding the wind, and, for some part of the time, the tide were against us, managed to take us down to Northfleet, a distance, I believe, of eighteen miles, in less than five hours; for we made fast to one of the buoys at the above place at half past twelve o'clock.

The appearance of the country along the banks of the river, as we went down, was at this time extremely beautiful, particularly on the right side, where the villas, &c. that adorn that bank were seen to the greatest advantage, surrounded with groves of fruit and other trees, all in blossom, and the meadows which lay between them and the river abounding with the most luxuriant vegetation, on which were feeding numerous flocks, and herds of sheep and black cattle. In fact, nature and art seemed as if they had combined their efforts, in order to give us a beautiful specimen of the scenery of our native isle, that we might contrast it with the dreary prospects that we soon expected to see in the frozen regions we were about to visit; the comparison might, indeed, at this time be made by most of us, as the greatest part had already seen the snow-clad mountains of the frigid zone.

As there was only one steam-boat procured, that which brought us down returned immediately (we made fast) for the Griper, and arrived with her a little before eleven o'clock at night.

I cannot omit mentioning, in this place, a certain coincidence that has occurred with respect to the day of the month that the expeditions on discovery sailed last year, and this; for it was on the 4th of April we sailed from Deptford last year, and although a month later this year, it appears somewhat remarkable, that, without any preconcerted plan, it should happen to be the same day of the month on which we commence the second voyage.

Thursday, 6th. — We received (from Woolwich) all our ordnance-stores to-day, except the powder, which is expected down to-morrow.

To guard as much as possible against the magnetic influence of iron upon the compasses, a pair of brass guns (six pounders) have been sent for the quarter deck. After the guns and other stores were placed in the respective places where it is intended they are to remain, an experiment was performed for the purpose of ascertaining the effect of local attraction on the compasses; or, to use the term that has been lately adopted, to determine the deviation of the compass, or magnetic needle, with the ship's head brought to the different points of the compass. As the result of this experiment may be better understood by a diagram of the operation than by words only, I have drawn a sketch of the whole process (see Appendix), which exhibits at one view the amount of deviation with the ship's head on every point of the compass except west, W. by S., and W. S. W., the tide being so strong that the ship's head could not be kept steady on these points.

Friday, 7th.—We received our powder this morning, and at two o'clock in the afternoon we cast off and made sail, but the wind being against us, we got no farther than that part of the river called the Lower Hope, where we anchored between four and five in the afternoon.

We were agreeably surprised to-day to find that the Griper behaved so well under canvass; for the general opinion was, from the trial made with her some time ago at Deptford, that she would be very *crank*. The breeze we had to-day was not indeed sufficiently strong to enable us to judge with certainty of her qualities as a sea-boat; I shall therefore avoid saying any thing more respecting her for the present, as we shall have many opportunities hereafter of judging of her under circumstances that will enable us to speak with certainty of her good or bad qualities. All that can be said at present is, that she answers beyond expectation, inasmuch that all those who had any doubts respecting her, and saw her under weigh to-day, are already perfectly satisfied of her safety as far as her construction is concerned in rendering her sea-worthy.

With respect to the Hecla, she appears to answer every expectation, in being one of the fittest vessels that could possibly be chosen for the service we are going upon, for she is easily worked, is very capacious for a vessel of her tonnage, and is remarkably strong, a quality of the first importance in the regions we are bound to explore.

As to the sailing qualities of either vessel, very little can as yet be said; it would be preposterous, however, to suppose that ships bound up with wood and iron, in the way in which they are, can be fast sailers; and even if they were, it would be only a quality of secondary consideration: for our business is not to run, and have only a bird's-eye view of the places we pass, but to examine with patience and perseverance; "for who knows what there is, where man has never been?"

Saturday, 8*th*. — We got under weigh early this morning, and worked down as far as Sea-Reach, where we anchored about seven o'clock, A. M., being unable to proceed any farther, on account of the flood-tide beginning to flow. We weighed again about noon, and worked down to the Nore, where we anchored between four and five o'clock in the afternoon.

Immediately we anchored, the Bee Tender came alongside with the chronometers, and the different nautical, astronomical, and meteorological instruments, &c. supplied for the expedition. With regard to the number and variety of these instruments, we are, as may be seen from the list in the Appendix, as amply supplied as any expedition that ever left this, or, perhaps, any other country before. Besides the instruments provided by government, most of the officers have some of their own, so that altogether it may be presumed we are, as I have just said, as well furnished with the means of fulfilling all the nautical and other scientific objects of the expedition as any of the illustrious navigators who have been employed on similar pursuits before us.

Monday, 10th. — The ship's companies were paid this afternoon the wages due to them since they joined the ships, together with three months' advance, in order to enable them to purchase clothing, and such other articles as they might deem necessary for the voyage; and in case any of them, from carelessness, or due consideration of the climate they are going to, should neglect to provide themselves with the articles of clothing most necessary for their own comforts, a list was made of those things that were deemed indispensably necessary, with which every man was ordered to furnish himself.

In the evening, a lighter came alongside with four bullocks, some casks of beer, and as much fresh water as completed our stock of that necessary article for some months, so that we are now perfectly ready to take our departure.

Tuesday, 11*th*.—The anxious moment of the actual commencement of our voyage has at length arrived; for, at ten o'clock this forenoon we weighed and made sail with a fine breeze from the westward, which enabled us, before dark, to get clear of that intricate passage the Swir, and the different shoals with which this part of the coast abounds.

We commenced our meteorological register to-day at noon, the temperature of the air in the shade was at that time 62°; that of sea-water at the surface 57°, and the height of the barometer 30.19 inches. The specific gravity of the sea-water is intended to be taken also every day at noon; but it would be useless to take it to-day, as it would undoubtedly be affected by the fresh water from the Thames, and the numerous smaller streams that discharge their contents into the sea about this place. The temperature of the air and water, as above stated, is to be taken every two hours, both day and night, and the height of the barometer four times a day; viz. at six o'clock in the morning, noon, six in the afternoon, and midnight. The direction of the wind, and state of the weather, is also to be noted at the time of registering the above observations, together with any other phenomena connected with meteorology that may occur.

Wednesday, 12*th*.—We have been enabled within these two days to judge of the comparative merits, in point of sailing, of the two ships (before the wind), with a degree of certainty that puts the matter completely beyond doubt; the disparity, indeed, is so considerable, that it was deemed necessary to take the Griper in tow this morning. We were obliged to anchor this evening abreast of Winterton Lights, owing to the wind getting so light that it was impossible to stem the flood-tide.

Thursday, 13*th*. — We weighed again last night, and worked to the northward until seven o'clock this morning, when we were again forced to bring to, until the tide came in our favour, which took place about one o'clock. We dropped anchor again in the evening, to preserve the ground we had gained in the course of the afternoon. We had considerable satisfaction to find, to-day, that the Griper answers remarkably well upon a wind, a very essential quality indeed in some situations we may happen to be placed in.

Friday, 14*th*. — We got under weigh again this morning, and were making the best of our way to the northward until a quarter before five o'clock, when we were all on a sudden a little startled by the ship striking on the east end of Sheeringham Shoal. The shock, or rather the shocks, for she touched three times, brought almost every person on deck in a few minutes; but before most of us got there, all was right again. I suspect, indeed, that had it not been for the rough sea that was running, which caused the ship to pitch considerably, that she would have gone over it without touching; but, fortunately, even as it was, there was no damage done.

Thursday, 14*th*.—The wind being still against us, it would again be necessary to anchor when the ebb tide was done; but from the freshness of the breeze, the sea got up so much that this could not be done on an open coast such as we were on, without running the risk of loosing an anchor and cable. In consideration of these circumstances it was deemed the most proper measure to put back to Yarmouth Roads, which was the nearest port, and there to remain until we should be favoured with wind that would enable us to resume our voyage with some prospect of success. Our stay here was agreeably to our wishes of very short duration, for we only arrived there at half past one o'clock, and, about midnight, we were again under weigh. During the time we lay in the Roads, we were visited by Captain Wells and some of the officers of His Majesty's ship Wye, which lay at anchor here.

Saturday, 15*th*. — We have been employed all day working to the northward, and in the evening it fell calm, so that we were as usual obliged to anchor, to prevent our being carried by the tide amongst the sands that lay off this part of the coast.

Sunday, 16*th*. — We got under weigh again early this morning, and made all sail, the wind having at length sprung up right in our favour; this being the Griper's worst point of sailing, she was again taken in tow. In the course of the forenoon, divine service was performed, which almost the whole of the officers and ship's company were able to attend, the weather being so fine that their service was not required on deck. During the day, we passed several flocks of that species of diver called by Linnæus *Colymbus Traile*, and commonly known to seamen, by the name of Loon, or Willock. These birds must be very widely scattered over the northern seas; for we found them last year in great numbers in Davis's Straits, and Baffin's Bay, and occasionally in different parts of the Atlantic during our passage across it.

Monday, 17*th*. — We discharged our pilot this morning into the Swallow revenue cutter. He was charged with a considerable number of letters from the officers and men, this being, in all probability, the last opportunity that we shall have for some time of sending letters to our friends. In the course of the day, we saw several of the divers called in the Linnæan arrangement *Alca Arctica*, and commonly denominated by seamen Puffin.

Tuesday, 18*th*. — Nothing occurred to-day worthy of remark, the weather continues very fine, and the wind still in our favour; in the course of the afternoon we had a distant view of Morven Hill, and several other mountains in Banffshire, that appeared as it were rearing their lofty summits out of the ocean.

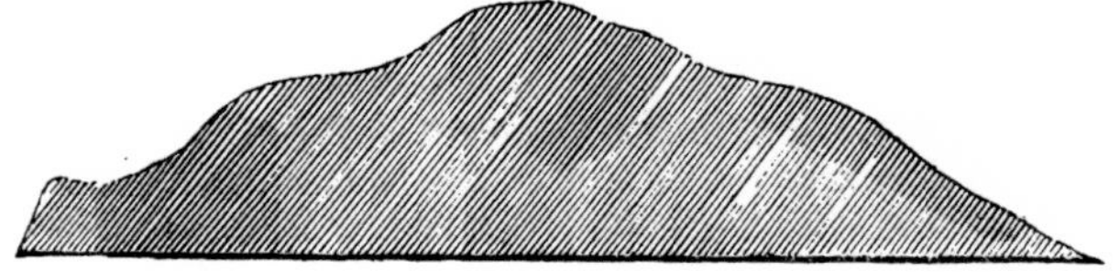

Wednesday, 19*th*. — A similar appearance was presented to-day by Fair Island, on being first seen. It is not indeed of any great height, but it is a fact well known in optics, that, unless a person has something of a correct idea of the distance of an object, he will fancy it great or small, according as he estimates its distance. I do not mean to imply by this, however, that we were ignorant of the distance Fair Island was from us; but merely, that, if we could suppose it to be as far from us as the hills in Banff were when seen yesterday, we should necessarily imagine it to be of considerable height. We continued to approach it until four o'clock in the afternoon, at which time it fell calm, the island at that time bearing north-east of us, and distant about five leagues. In order to profit as much as possible by the delay caused by the weather, the ship's company turned to, to fish, at which they were pretty successful, for a considerable number of cod and coal-fish were caught in course of the afternoon.

On the back and sides of the cod, at least such of them as I examined, I observed several small insects of two different species, one of the shape of a tad-pole with a forked tail, and the other not unlike a small shrimp. During the day, we saw several solan geese (*Anas Bassanus*, Lin.), Mallemuckes or Fulmar Peterel (*Procellaria Glacialis*, Lin.), and a bird some-what resembling a Rail, which kept at such a distance that we were not able to make out with any certainty what species it was.

Thursday, 20*th*.—Our progress was retarded again to-day by calm weather, which continued until six o'clock in the afternoon, when we were again favoured with a fine breeze from the north-east (comp.), which enabled us, in the course of the evening, to get round the north end of the Orkneys, some of which were in sight the whole day. We had a very distinct view of two or three of them, particularly Ronaldsha, and Sandi, on the latter of which there is a light-house. The appearance of these islands were well calculated to prepare our minds to view the regions we are about to visit, with some degree of tolerance; for if, instead of comparing them to the fertile banks of the Thames, we compare them to these bleak islands, the contrast would not differ much wider than if our landscape views to-day were compared to those described on the fourth instant.

Such of the Orkney islands as we had an opportunity of seeing, might, in general, be described as hilly, but neither high nor rugged, and declining gradually, although not with an even surface, from their middle towards the sea, where they in some places terminate in abrupt precipices. The summer did not appear to have hardly commenced here yet; the ground was indeed clear of snow, but vegetation had made but very little progress; for the sides of the hills appeared in the remains of their last year's garb, viz. withered grass, and such hardy herbs as the rigour of the winter had not been able to destroy. We spoke this forenoon a Danish brig from Copenhagen bound to Disco; we asked her name, and several other questions, but owing to the distance she was off, their answers were but very indistinctly heard. She kept in company, or rather in sight, the whole day, but kept edging to the northward more than we did, so that, in the evening, she was a considerable distance from us. We saw several Kittiwakes (*Larus Tridactylus*, Lin.) to-day, for the first time this voyage.

Friday, 21st. — Nothing occurred to-day worthy of remark; in the forenoon we lost sight of the northernmost of the Orkney islands, and in the evening we descried the islands of Barra, and Rona, which are usually reckoned the northernmost land in Europe. It was dusk before we approached near enough to be able to have any thing of a good view of them.

Saturday, 22d.—The breeze happened however to be so light during the night, that we only passed them between seven and eight o'clock this morning, and at such a distance (four or five miles), that we could see them very plainly. Rona appeared to be considerably larger than the other, and is, I understand, inhabited: their distance apart was estimated to be about eight miles. Their appearance in every respect was similar to the Orkney islands, to which groupe indeed they may be considered to belong, although at a considerable distance from it.

Whilst in the neighbourhood of these islands, we saw a great many sea-fowls, particularly of the Peterel tribe, (viz. Fulmar), and Kittiwake gull. These islands, like St. Kilda, and other solitary rocks in this part of the world, are particularly well calculated for being the resort of sea-fowls; because, in the first place, they have around them a wide expanse of that element from which they derive their food; and, in the second place, the inaccessible precipices which here and there overhang the sea, afford them asylums to build their nests in, which the daring inhabitants, with all their intrepidity, cannot always molest.

We threw a quart bottle overboard this afternoon, containing half a sheet of foolscap paper, on which was printed, in six different languages, a request that the person who should happen to pick it up, should send it to the Secretary of the Admiralty, or the Minister of Marine, of the country to which the person belonged, with a note of the time and place where it was found. Besides the request, the lat. and long. of the ship at the time, and the temperature of the air, and sea-water, the force and direction of the wind, and the state of the weather, were also inserted on it. As the whole may be better understood by giving a copy of the paper itself, I shall insert in the Appendix all that it contained. It is intended to throw one of these papers overboard every day in order to increase the probability of some of them being picked up.

The object of them is to afford data for detecting the force and direction of currents in these seas. By knowing the time and place where they were thrown into the sea, and the place and time, where, and when they were found, it is very clear that this object may, in a great measure, be determined, for the elapsed time will give the force, and the relative situation the direction of the current; that is, if the bottle is found immediately, it is driven on shore, or out of the influence of the current.

Some of the bottles that we threw overboard last year for the same purpose, tended very materially to throw some light on this subject. Already one of them was received at the Admiralty some time before we sailed; it was picked up in Killala Bay, in Ireland, about the latter end of March, and it appeared by the date upon it, and the geographical situation of the ship at the time it was dispatched, that it floated about one thousand and eighty miles in the course of ten months, which is upward of three miles a day during the whole time.

There was another of our bottles picked up by a Danish vessel some time before we left England, but

I have not heard the particulars respecting the time, and place where it was found.

It is almost unnecessary to add, that the mouth of the bottle is first secured by a tight cork, which is covered with sealing wax, having the ship's name impressed on it, and over that a piece of white cotton, with a view of making it more conspicuous, and thereby render it more likely to attract notice.

Sunday, 23d.—Divine service was performed this forenoon, at which were present almost the whole of the officers and ship's company, the weather being so fine that very few hands were required on deck.

Monday, 24th.—We had a distant view to-day of that remarkable insulated rock, called Rockal; it looked at the distance we were from it (viz. between four and five leagues) exactly like a ship under sail: it was reported indeed by the person who first saw it to be a strange vessel. Its resemblance not only in form, but also its colour, tended to make the deception more complete, for it appeared to be perfectly white, a hue most probably produced by the excrement of birds. Our distance from it indeed was too great to enable us to speak with certainty on this head; but, from the number of birds we saw in its neighbourhood, and its insular situation, we may fairly conclude that it is well inhabited by the feathered race, for here they are perfectly secure from the attacks of their greatest enemy, man.

If we estimated our distance from it at all correctly, its situation, as determined by His Majesty's ship Endymion, is very accurately laid down, at least inasmuch as it agrees with the mean of the results of the sights taken for our chronometers.* In the course

* Lat. 57° 39′ 30″ N. and longitude 13° 30′ W.

of the afternoon, when at least forty miles from this rock, we found soundings in one hundred and fifty fathoms water; so that it may be regarded as the summit of a very extensive submarine mountain, whose sides, at least the western one, declined very gradually.

Thursday, 27th. — Nothing has occurred for these two days past worthy of remark, the weather has been, generally speaking, very fine; the temperature of the air being most commonly at 50°, and of the sea at the surface about a degree less. This afternoon the weather being almost perfectly calm, we availed ourselves of the opportunity of trying for soundings, on the supposed sunken land of Buss, according to its situation by Lieutenant Pickersgill; who, on his passage to Davis's Straits in the year 1776, struck soundings with a line of three hundred and twenty fathoms in the very place* where we happened to get becalmed this afternoon, but, strange to say, although we had one thousand one hundred and twenty fathoms of line out, we found no bottom. It ought not to be inferred from this, however, that the bank on which that officer sounded does not exist, for it is more reasonable to suppose that he might be mistaken in his longitude of the place, than that the existence of the bank itself should be questioned, more especially as some of our latest charts (by *Steel*) lay the sunken land of Buss down several degrees to the westward of where we sounded to-day. I shall therefore forbear saying any thing more concerning this lost land at present, as we shall most

* The latitude and longitude of the place where Pickersgill struck soundings are 57° N. and 24° 24′ W. which agrees with our situation this afternoon at the time we sounded

probably, in a short time, have an opportunity of determining whether it exists where it is laid down on the charts.

In the mean time, however, it may not be amiss to say a few words respecting the authorities on which the former existence of the land in question rests. The first account we have of it, is derived from fragments of journals, and letters written by Nicolo, and Antonio Zeno, two Venetian navigators, who were employed about the latter end of the fourteenth century by a Scandinavian prince, named Zichmni, in making discoveries in the north seas. And among other places discovered by these navigators, is mentioned a large island which obtained the name of Friesland, situated to the southward of Iceland; but the whole account of this, as well as of most of the other lands that they explored, is so confused and imperfect, that it is impossible to know the situation of the places they speak of; and some writers have gone so far even as to consider their voyages a romance altogether, which I think is rather too harsh a conclusion, for although the imperfect state in which the accounts of their discoveries have been handed down to us, render them of no real utility, we ought not, without some good reasons, to regard them as fabulous.

From the time of the Zenos, two centuries had nearly elapsed before any thing more was heard of their Friesland, when its existence was again revived by one of the ship's belonging to Martin Frobisher's fleet (on his third voyage), having, on her return home in the year 1578, fallen in with a large island covered with wood, in latitude 57°, 30′ N., along which she sailed for three days. The vessel's name was the

Busse, of Bridgewater, from which the island obtained the name of Buss. This then, I believe, is the last account we have of this mysterious island, whose supposed ruins we have this afternoon been trying to find.

Whilst sounding to-day, we availed ourselves of the opportunity thereby afforded, of ascertaining the temperature of the sea, at as great a depth as it had perhaps ever been obtained before. A self-registering thermometer was tied to the sounding line at the distance of ten fathoms from the lead, or rather the clamm*; for it was the instrument used on this occasion. Allowing, then, that there were one hundred fathoms of stray-line or inclination from the perpendicular, which I think is the utmost that could be, the thermometer must have gone upwards of one thousand fathoms below the surface. The temperature indicated by it at this depth was 45½°, the temperature of the water at the surface at the same time being 48½°, and the air 49½°.

Friday, 28*th*. — We found to-day the temperature of water brought from the depth of one hundred and thirty fathoms by Dr. Marcett's Water Bottle † to be 48½°, both the air and sea at the surface being at the time 49°.

Monday, 31*st*. — We tried yesterday and to-day ‡

* This instrument is intended to bring up a greater quantity of sounding, (that is, of the mud, &c. at the bottom) than the usual arming of the lead was capable of bringing up.

† The use of this machine is to bring water up from the bottom, or indeed from any other depth that a person may require; for the shot or weight that shuts the bottle is not let go until it is at the bottom, or at the depth that the water is to be brought from.

‡ Our latitude yesterday at noon was 57° 46′ N. and longitude 29° 09′ W., and to-day latitude 58° 13′ N. and longitude 30° 20′. W.

for soundings, with one hundred and sixty fathoms of line, but found no bottom. The object for sounding, on this occasion, was to ascertain whether a bank exists in the place where the sunken land of Buss is laid down on Steel's chart; but our researches here, as on Pickersgill's bank, have been in vain; so that I think the existence of any remains of Buss's Land (if it ever had any) may now be very justly questioned. At all events, hydrographers may, with perfect safety, henceforth expunge from their charts all traces of it in either of the places hitherto assigned to it; or, in other words, in those two situations where we were induced to look for it.

Tuesday, June 1st. — Notwithstanding the season is advancing, the weather has been for these two days past colder and more disagreeable than we have had it since we left England; the cold indeed has not been sufficient to put us to any inconvenience, but the weather being for the most part of the time foggy and rainy, rendered it somewhat uncomfortable.

Several snow-buntings (*Emberiza Nivalis*, Lin.) were observed in the course of the day flying about the ship, we supposed from the direction of the wind (about N. W. true) that they have been blown off the coast of Greenland, from which we were distant at noon three hundred and seventy-six miles.

Several Arctic gulls (*Larus Parasiticus*, Lin.) were seen to-day for the first time. This bird is commonly called by our Greenland seamen the boatswain, and sometimes dirty Allen, a name somewhat analogous to that by which it is characterized by the Danes, viz. Stroudt-jager, or dung-bird. All these names have had their origin from a mistaken notion that these birds lived on the excrement of the lesser gulls, which, on being pursued, either from fear, or to relieve themselves from the prosecution of fierce enemies, voided something to satiate the voracious appetites of their pursuers, and by that means escape from further molestation at that time. The fallacy of this opinion is now, however, pretty generally known. That the Arctic gulls do pursue those of their own genus which they can master (particularly the kittiwakes) is an incontestable fact; but the object of their pursuit is not the excrement but the prey that the pursued is at that time possessed of, and which at length they are forced to drop, to secure their own safety; which they effect during the time that their enemy is employed picking it up, although that is done in a very short period, for they manage the business with such dexterity, that the object dropped is caught before it reaches the water.

Gulls are not the only birds that disburden themselves of their prey when pursued, for I have often observed last summer that the fulmar peterel or mallemucke, when approached whilst feeding, (which I have seen them always do sitting on the water,) not only abandon their food, but even disgorge what they had swallowed before they would, or, as I imagined, could, take their flight. Several of them that we caught alive at different times, exhibited other proofs of the facility or power which they possess of unloading themselves of the contents of their stomachs; for whenever a person approached them suddenly, they ejected a spout of oil from their nostrils. This is considered by naturalists (which I have no doubt is the case) a means of defence for these birds.

A bird resembling a snipe was also seen to-day, but we had such an imperfect view of him that it was impossible to determine what species he belonged to.

Wednesday, 2d. — The weather has been rather boisterous the whole of this day; in the afternoon in particular it blew a strong gale of wind, which soon rose a heavy sea; and, if we are to put any confidence in an augury, which seamen always regard as a sure indication of bad weather, we may anticipate a heavy gale very soon. The augury I allude to is the appearance this afternoon of a flock of Mother Carey's Chickens, or Stormy Peterels, (*Procellaria Pelagica*, Lin.) under the ship's stern. These birds have always been considered by sailors as the harbingers of storms; and if the reports on record concerning them be true, they certainly deserve the mariner's notice. Although not the bearers of welcome intelligence, yet they warn him of the approaching storm, it is said, sometimes even six hours before it happens. Their appearing so long as this before the coming on of bad weather, may be regarded in some measure as a proof of their possessing some instinct, whereby they know the change that is about to ensue; unless we admit (which I think is not improbable), that their coming to ships is a matter of mere chance, whilst flying from the rage of the tempest that prevails, but at such a distance that it requires hours to reach the vessels. As far, however, as my own observation goes, I cannot bring to my recollection any instance where they were seen before a gale commenced, or at least before such apparent indications of it were seen, as rendered their appearance unnecessary to confirm what might be expected to follow. The reason of their keeping in the vicinity of ships in tempestuous weather, is, very clearly, to get sheltered from the rage of the elements; this indeed was seen very evidently from the manner in which they acted this afternoon, for they always took shelter under the ship's lee-quarter, which position they kept with the utmost perseverance, for they never allowed the ship to go above thirty yards from them before they got up, and came skimming along the surface to the same place (relatively) that they occupied before.

We saw also during the day, several flocks of another species of Peterel, that had not been seen before this voyage, called the Shearwater, (*Procellaria Puffinus*, Lin.) These birds are supposed, from their cry, to be the birds of Diomede, so famous in antiquity from an affecting fable. Linnæus, however, supposed that the Albatross is the bird of Diomede, and has, on that account, named it Diomeda.

Thursday, 3d.—Nothing particular occurred today, except that, in the course of the afternoon the gale moderated, and before the evening the sea subsided very considerably. I remarked that the stormy peterels mentioned yesterday, kept in our vicinity until the violence of the gale was over.

Friday, 4th.—This being the anniversary of our venerable Sovereign's birth-day, his health was drank in our little community with as much respect, and cheerfulness, I may venture to say, as at any table in his extensive dominions; and in order that the men as well as the officers might be able to celebrate the day by an extra bumper, the main-brace was spliced *, and a signal was made to the Griper to do the same; and to finish the festivity of the day, they enjoyed themselves in the evening with the healthy and mirthful amusement of dancing, the weather being at the time both mild and calm, tended very materially to the comfort and conviviality of all on the occasion.

We tried in the afternoon for soundings, with a line of two hundred and fifty fathoms: (no bottom.) At this depth we found, contrary to what has been usually observed, that the temperature of the water was greater than at the surface by a quarter of a degree, the latter being 44¼°, and the former, by the self-registering thermometer, 44½°, the temperature of the air at the time being 43°. This leads me to mention a singular, and to me rather an unaccountable difference in this respect, that occurred to the two expeditions employed last year in the Arctic regions, which is, that we found the temperature of the sea at every depth, and on every occasion where it was tried, to be less than that of the surface at the time; and the expedition to Spitzbergen found it always the reverse; that is to say, the temperature at the surface always less than at the bottom, or at any considerable depth where it was tried.

Can this difference be owing to the greater thickness of the ice at Spitzbergen, which throughout the whole summer prevents the solar rays from warming but a very small portion of the surface of the sea; whilst, on the contrary, the greatest part of

* This nautical phrase signifies any extra allowance of spirits that is given to seamen, in consideration of arduous duties that they have occasionally to perform during bad weather, &c.

the surface of the water in Davis's Straits, and Baffin's Bay, is exposed to the influence of the sun for the most part of the summer?

Saturday, 5th. — Several whales of the species called Finners (*Balæna Physalus*), were seen last evening and this morning. These fish derive the name of finner, from a fin on their back, which is often seen when no other part of their body is above the surface of the water. Some of them are as long as the ordinary-sized Greenland or black whale, that is, from fifty to sixty feet, but never so bulky as that fish. They are much more active, and consequently more difficult to kill than the common whale; for that reason, and their affording but little oil, they are seldom molested by the fishermen; the Esquimaux, however, are said to hold their flesh in higher estimation than that of the black whale, but, from the danger and difficulty that they would have to encounter in killing them, it may be presumed that their palates are but seldom gratified with a dish of this fish. We observed that flocks of Peterels, both of the Shearwater and Fulmar species, kept hovering over the places where these fish came up to blow, no doubt with a view of picking up something in the way of food. Several other of the well-known inhabitants of these northern regions, were seen in the course of the day, for the first time this voyage; such as Terns, or Greenland swallows (*Sterno Hirundo*, Lin.), Porpoises (*bete Phocæna*, Lin.), and the species of Mollusca, called the *Clio Borealis*, and, by the Greenland fishermen, Whale's food. Some Solan geese and seals were also seen to-day, which rather surprised us, for we were at noon four hundred and nine miles from Cape Farewell *, a distance from land much greater than either are usually accustomed to be met with.

Sunday, 13*th*. — Nothing has occurred for this week past worthy of being mentioned, unless the changes in the state of the weather were recorded in the order which happened, and even these were so uninteresting that it would be too tedious a task to notice them; let it suffice, that it has been sometimes fine weather, at other times the reverse, occasionally blowing fresh, and at other times light breezes, but what annoyed us most was, that during the greatest part, indeed I may say the whole of this period, the wind has been directly against us. We had slant of wind in our favour this forenoon, but it soon veered round again to the northward and westward. The weather being favourable this afternoon for making observations, azimuths were taken with the ship's head on different points of the compass, with a view of ascertaining the deviation of the needle from the magnetic meridian. From the result of these observations we find, that the deviation has, as might naturally be expected, increased very considerably since we left England; but its increase appears to have been very regular, for north and south are still found to be the points of change: and the greatest deviation is found to take place when the ship's head is to the westward, which is very easily explained, for the local attraction of the iron in the ship, and the directive power of the earth, are then in some measure co-operating, or perhaps it might be more proper to say, that the latter has less power to counteract the influence of the former, when the ship's head is in that direction.

* Our latitude at noon being 55° 03′ N. and long. 36° 00′ W. by chronometer.

Monday, 14*th.*—We passed a considerable quantity of sea-weed to-day, some of which was picked up, and found to be the common kind of sea-wrack (*Fucus vesiculasus*) so abundant on our own coasts; we passed also in the afternoon a piece of pine-wood about six feet long, which appeared to have been for a considerable time in the water.

Tuesday, 15*th.* — We were favoured this forenoon with a fine breeze from the southward and eastward, and, in order to take advantage of it as much as possible, the Griper was taken in tow. About noon we saw land at a very great distance, bearing N. E. by E. by compass, or about north true: Cape Farewell being the nearest land to us in this direction, there could be no doubt of this being it. If we take then the situation in which that Cape is laid down in the Requisite Tables, which I think is one of the best authorities we can refer to, and compare it with our situation to-day at noon, it will appear that the land seen to-day must have been one hundred and thirty-three miles from us, even of difference of latitude alone; for according to these Tables (third edition) Cape Farewell is in lat. 59° 38′ N. and longitude 42° 42′ W., and we were at noon by account in lat. 57° 25′ 44″ N. * and longitude by mean of the chronometer 42° 43′ 42″ W. As an additional proof that the land seen to-day must have been very distant, we crossed the meridian we were on at noon to-day, on our way home last year, in latitude 58° 50′ N., and saw no land at that time to the northward of us.

* It may be presumed that although our latitude to-day is only by account it cannot be much out, for we were by meridian altitude (of the sun) yesterday, in latitude 57° 36′ 43″ N.

Thursday, 17*th*. — We found to-day that there is a considerable current settling to the southward here, for the latitude observed *, and that by account differed, since yesterday, eight miles, which will of course be the daily rate of the current.

Friday, 18*th*. — We made the ice, for the first time, at an early hour this morning; it was in the form which they called "loose streams," that is, a collection of broken pieces of ice so detached from one another that a ship may sail through them. In the course of the day, several icebergs were seen, some of them of a size sufficiently large to attract the attention of those who had never seen any thing of the kind before; but as most of us had seen last year those stupendous masses that were met with in Baffin's Bay, and the upper part of the Straits, those seen to-day were ill calculated to attract much notice. I understand that the fishermen consider it as a sign of a good season to meet the ice in the early part of the year well to the southward, for in that case they reckon that it must have broke up to the northward early in the spring. I do not perceive however that any inference can be drawn from our having met with it in so low a latitude †, for the season is now so far advanced, that it has had sufficient time to drift this far without any necessity for an early breaking up: for my own part, indeed, I think that the "Fiords," or inlets about Cape Desolation and its neighbourhood, are quite sufficient to produce all the ice that is usually met with off Cape

* The latitude by meridian altitude to day was 58° 29′ 56″ N. and by account 58° 58′ 55″ N., and that observed yesterday was 58° 12′ 43″ N. and by the dead reckoning 58° 33′ 56″ N.

† Our latitude to day at noon was 59° 38′ 41″ N.

Farewell, and the mouth of the Strait on the Greenland side.

We no sooner fell in with the ice this morning, than flocks of the little divers, called Rotges (*Alca Alle*, Lin.), were seen flying, swimming, and diving about in its vicinity. It would appear, that the neighbourhood of ice is the favourite haunt of these birds, for I do not remember having seen any of them last year, except when we were amongst it, or at least at no great distance from it, and I believe none were seen this voyage until we made the ice. In fact, they might, with propriety, be called, the Ice-bird, and, if I mistake not, they have been so denominated. Another species of diver was seen to-day for the first time this voyage, which, like the preceding, is seldom seen except in the vicinity of ice; it is called by seamen, Dovekey, (*Colymbus Grylle*, Lin.)

Saturday, 19*th*. — It has been observed, that the colour of the water has changed since we got amongst the ice, for, instead of the clear blue colour of the ocean, it has been within these two days of a dirty brownish tinge, not unlike the colour of the sea at the estuary of large rivers. The temperature of the water is also very sensibly affected by the ice, for since we came amongst it, we find that the mercury seldom rises more than 4° above the freezing point; the temperature of the air is likewise proportionably low, the extremes of the range of the thermometer, in the shade, for these two days, being between 33° and 43°. The true variation of the compass was obtained to-day, by taking azimuths on a floe of ice, at such a distance from the ship as to be clear of all local attraction. The result of these observations gave 48° 40′ westerly variation. It may be said that this is the only instance in which the true variation was ascertained since we left England; for magnetic observations taken on board of a ship in these high latitudes, especially in this part of the world, are not to be much relied upon, on account of the compasses being so much affected by local attraction, which is, at the same time, continually changing, according as the ship changes her position; or, in other words, in proportion as she approaches, or recedes from the magnetic pole, so will the effects of the local attraction be increased or diminished.

About eight o'clock in the evening, the weather having cleared up, we had a distant view of the land about Cape Desolation *, it was estimated to be from twelve to fourteen leagues from us, a distance by far too great to enable us to say any thing respecting it, any farther than that it appeared to be high and rugged, and seemed as if it consisted of a number of islands, being seen in detached pieces.

I understand that we sailed this forenoon over the place where His Majesty's ship Sybille laid down Cape Farewell †; how far that promontory was from us at that time it is impossible to say, but it may be presumed to have been some distance off, for no land was in sight at the time. I ought to observe, indeed, that the state of the weather for the greatest part of the day was not very favourable for seeing any great distance. We found a current to-day setting S. 50° W. at the rate of six miles per day.

* The northern extreme of the land bore by compass E. 41° N. and the southern extreme E. 24° S. the ship's head at the time being N. N. W.

† We were at noon in latitude 59° 48′ 26″ N. (by meridian altitude) and longitude 47° 47′ 36″ W. by the chronometers.

Sunday, 20th. — We had a distant view again this morning of the land seen yesterday, but although we were rather nearer to it to-day than we were last evening, our view of it was less distinct, or properly speaking, more deceiving than before, for the shape of it was altered so much by refraction, that a hill could scarcely be distinguished from a valley. In fact it appeared to be all of one uniform height, or like what is commonly called "Table land;" and at one time, in addition to this uniformity in height, it presented the most fantastic appearance that can well be imagined, being distorted in such a manner that the tops of the hills appeared broader than their basis. In the afternoon, a strong breeze sprang up from the southward and eastward, of which we availed ourselves in making our passage across the Straits, our object being to get over to the west land. We passed in the course of the afternoon through a considerable quantity of heavy ice, being evidently fragments of icebergs, or the outskirts of the glaciers that form along the shore. The parts that were above the surface of the water, presented in some of them the most grotesque shapes, such as arches, caves, arcades, and dilapidated columns, with immense capitals; which a fanciful imagination might be able to find to have some resemblance to the different architectural orders. Among other things with which these masses of ice were compared, one of them that we passed about noon was said by somebody to resemble that part of a pulpit which overhangs the clergyman when in that sacred rostrum. It is probable that this simile originated from an association of ideas produced by the recent occurrence of circumstances, for we had at the time just come on deck after attending divine service.

Wednesday, 23d.—Nothing of any interest occurred for these two days past, the weather has been for most part of the time foggy, with occasional showers of rain; but we suffered but little inconvenience from either, because we have scarcely met with a piece of ice to retard our progress since we left the coast of Greenland, so that fewer hands were required to be exposed to the inclemency of the weather in working the ship. During these two days, several seals, porpoises, and birds of different kinds, whose names have been already mentioned, were seen, besides two species of birds whose names have not been noticed before this voyage. The one is commonly called by seamen Burgomaster (*Larus Glaucus*, Lin.), a name very clearly of Dutch origin, and said to have been suggested to the fishermen of that country, from observing that this bird exercised as much power over all the other aquatic birds of this country, as the magistrate of that name used to exercise over his fellow-citizens.

The other bird alluded to is the Red Phalarope (*Phalaropus Hyperboreus, seu Tringia Fulicaria*, Lin.), of which we saw several large flocks, close to an iceberg, to which a boat went for the purpose of making (magnetic) observations. *

In returning from this berg, we saw indeed another bird that had not been seen before this voyage, and which I do not remember having seen last year either, although mentioned by ornithologists as one of the visitants of these regions; it has various names,

* It was found to be so steep however all round, that it was impossible to get upon it.

such as puffin, caulterneb, and Greenland parrot, (*Alca Arctica*, Lin.) Of these names, however, I believe the first is that by which it is most generally known. Whilst close to the iceberg above mentioned, we sounded in two hundred fathoms, white sand. The object for sounding was to determine whether the berg was aground, and the conclusion was that it was not, for its height was estimated to be only about fifty feet above the surface of the water.

Thursday, 24th. — I have omitted to mention another species of the feathered tribe that was seen yesterday, for the first time this summer; it is called, from the whiteness of its plumage, the ivory gull, (*Larus Eburneus*, Lin.) Although this name is very appropriate, inasmuch as it characterizes the colour of the plumage of those specimens that are to be seen in ornithological collections, yet it is far from being descriptive of the whiteness of their garb when alive, which certainly equals, in the purity of its colour, new-fallen snow.

Friday, 25th. — We have made very little progress to-day, having fallen in again with the ice, which is so closely packed to the westward, that it is impossible to force through it; a great number of icebergs have also been in sight the whole day, one of which appeared to be very large, both with respect to its height and extent. Two Greenland, or black whales (*Balæna Mysticetus*, Lin.) were seen this morning for the first time; and I understand that two white bears (*Ursus Maritimus*, Lin.) were seen on a piece of ice this afternoon, by the Griper's people.

Saturday, 26th. — We have been since four o'clock yesterday afternoon closely beset with the ice in every direction; the open sea may be seen indeed to the eastward, but between us and it there are several miles of close-packed ice, and to the northward and westward, there is nothing to be seen as far as the eye can penetrate, but one continued body of ice. The average thickness of that around us, is from four to five feet, and the extent of the pieces seldom exceed forty or fifty feet; and, generally speaking, they are smaller than that. We find on many of them pieces of quartz and granite, and occasionally heaps of sand and gravel, which I think renders it probable that this ice has been formed amongst the archipelago of islands that lie to the northward and westward of us. There are several icebergs situated here and there amongst this pack, but they are in general of a small szie. The delay occasioned by the ice, for these two days, has afforded us an opportunity of making a considerable number of observations*; some of which could not be done had the ship been at sea; and others were performed with greater certainty on the ice than they could be done on board: I allude, in the first instance, to the magnetic observations, and, in the second place, to the facility with which we were enabled to take lunar distances. As both these objects then are deemed of considerable importance (the latter in particular being so, on account of its affording us an opportunity of judging of the going of the chronometers), we have

* Our latitude to-day by meridian altitude was 63° 59′ 29″ N. and longitude by mean of several lunar distances 61° 12′ 15″ W. and by chronometers 61° 26′ 10″ W. The variation was found to be 61° 15′ westerly, and the dip, or inclination of the magnetic needle, 84.

very little reason to regret the delay occasioned, as yet.

In the course of the afternoon a large whale came up to breathe, in a small opening between two pieces of ice, within a few yards of the ship, and remained there for a considerable time, and would probably have stopped much longer had not the curiosity of some of the seamen induced them to go to the edge of the hole where she lay, in order to have a better view of her. My object in being so particular about this whale, is, because she went down in a manner, which I understand from the fishermen on board, is very unusual for these fish to do; that is, tail foremost. It may be remarked, then, that this deviation from the usual method of diving, evinces a considerable share of sagacity in these animals; at least it shews, that they have sense enough to depart from their usual habits to accommodate themselves to circumstances; for had this fish gone down in the way which they are accustomed to do, it is more than probable that her tail would have entangled her in the ice.

Sunday, 27th. — We are still closely beset by the ice. We find by our observations to-day, that we have drifted twelve miles to the southward since yesterday at noon, for our latitude to-day by meridian altitude was only 63° 46′ 50″ N.; and yesterday it was 63° 59′ 29″ N. The actual distance indeed that we have been carried to the southward since yesterday, is more than twelve miles; for the direction that we have been drifting is S.W. by S. by compass, which by taking the variation, as found yesterday, will be about S. S. E. ½ E. true. It will be seen from this circumstance, that what I suggested yesterday respecting the place where the ice with which we are surrounded came from, is, in some measure, confirmed from our observation to-day of the direction of the current by which it is carried along.

Our change of position during these four and twenty hours has altered our soundings in a contrary way to what might be expected; for, although we have been drifting away from the land, we find that the water gets shallower, for we sounded yesterday in one hundred and twenty-five fathoms, fine sand; this morning in one hundred and twenty fathoms, and in the afternoon it decreased to one hundred and fifteen fathoms, the same sort of bottom as before. A fresh breeze sprang up this forenoon from the eastward, which, before the evening, rose such a swell that we were obliged to put fenders of junk over the ship's side to prevent her from being damaged by the ice, which was all in motion.

We added another Gull to-day to our list of birds; its common name is the Black-backed, or Black-mantled Gull, (*Larus Marinus*, Lin.)

Monday, 28th. — Shortly after day-light this morning, a white bear was observed on the ice close to the ships. He came indeed so close to the Griper, that they fired at him from the ship, and wounded him, but not so bad as to disable him much at first. On being pursued, however, and again struck, he either voluntarily or accidentally fell into the water between two pieces of ice, and in a short time disappeared. He was supposed to have been attracted to the ships by the smell of some herrings that were roasted in the Griper the evening before. The keen scent of these animals is well known to our Greenland fishermen, and I am told that they very frequently take advantage of it to decoy them off from the land, by burning crang, or some other oleaginous refuse, which brings them so close to their ships that they very often kill them without much trouble.

Tuesday, 29th. — Although the first day or two that we have been detained here, might be in some measure considered as usefully spent in making observations; yet such a continuation of delay as we have now had in this place, tends at length to try our patience, more especially as the prospect of getting released from our present situation, appears to-day less flattering than we have had it yet; for the motion amongst the ice, caused by the swell, yesterday, and last night, has jammed it together much closer than it was before, and a fall of snow that we had this morning has given it the appearance of being consolidated into one immense field. About seven o'clock in the evening, the weather being very clear, we saw land bearing by compass, from W.N.W. to W., distant, as near as we could judge, from twelve to fourteen leagues. From our situation *, and the direction in which this land was seen, it is probable that what we saw was the islands at the entrance of Frobisher's Straits, or that which Davis called Lumley's Inlet; it appeared indeed to us like three islands, one of which seemed to be considerably larger than the other two. We sounded to-day both in the fore and afternoon in one hundred and thirty-five fathoms, fine sand and small black stones.

* Our latitude to-day at noon (by account) was 63° 32′ N. and longitude 62° 17′ W. and the entrance of Frobisher's Straits, or Lumley's Inlet, is said to be in latitude 63° 08′ N. from which it is very evident that the land seen this evening must be about the entrance of these straits.

Just after the sun went down this evening, the sky to the northward and westward presented the most beautiful appearance I ever remember having seen; it is impossible for me indeed to describe it, and I have no doubt but the painter would find it a difficult matter to represent it. I shall therefore only observe, that the prevailing colour was red, of all the different shades, decreasing gradually from the deepest, near the horizon, until in the zenith it vanished in a clear blue sky. And the clouds which were illumined by these brilliant rays, presented as great a diversity of shapes as there were variety of tints.

Wednesday, 30th. — The ice having been observed to open a little this morning, we availed ourselves of this favourable opportunity to get into clear water, which, by dint of perseverance in towing and warping for about seven hours, we at length finally succeeded in getting again into the open sea.

I formed a piece of ice from the floe alongside of us this morning into a cube, whose sides measured four inches and eight-tenths; and when it was put into a bucket of sea-water at the temperature of 31°, and of the specific gravity 1.023, only six-tenths or one-eighth of it remained above the surface of the water.

Thursday, July 1st. — We have been running to the northward all day along the edge of the western ice, which extends to the westward as far as we could see; and as we had a view in the afternoon of a considerable portion of that coast, it is probable that the ledge of ice we have been sailing along for these two days reaches the land, or at least within a short distance of it. To the eastward of us the sea is perfectly clear, with the exception of some loose streams of ice in our immediate vicinity; but these are evidently nothing more than a few fragments that separate occasionally from the main body of the ice to the westward; for we can plainly see the clear water beyond them.

We have passed a considerable number of icebergs in the course of the day, some of them of a very large size.

Friday, 2d. — Nothing occurred to-day worthy of remark, except that in the evening a large bear was seen walking about on the edge of the ice, as we went along; but as we had a fine breeze in our favour at the time, we passed by without molesting him.

Saturday, 3d. — This has been another day barren in events, but very important to us in another way. I allude to the progress that we have made to the northward during these four and twenty hours past, for we have this afternoon crossed the Arctic circle, and consequently are now in the region of perpetual day, for some time to come.

Although we have not had the sun, indeed, actually above the horizon during the whole day, or, properly speaking, for four and twenty hours together, yet for some days past there has been scarcely any darkness, even at midnight; for the twilight, ever since we crossed the parallel of 62° north latitude, has been so great, that we have been enabled to see the direction, or, as it is called, the lead, most proper to be taken to get through the ice.

Monday, 5th. — We passed a piece of ice this forenoon on which was lying a large Walrus, or, as it is commonly called, a Sea-horse, (*Trichecus*, Lin.) We fired at him as the ship passed him; but if he was wounded it must have been very slightly, for he rolled himself off the ice into the water, with as much, if not greater ease, than a person could expect from his unwieldy form and size. His back appeared to be of a dark bay colour, and what we saw of the under part of his body seemed to be of the same colour, but of a lighter hue, and mottled with white spots. His tusks, I think, were between eight and nine inches long.

Tuesday, 6th. — We were more successful to-day in an attack we made on one of the same kind of animals before mentioned. About noon, we observed five of them lying on a piece of ice about a mile and a half from the ship. A boat was immediately equipped for attacking them, and on our way towards them it was agreed, that, instead of firing at the whole indiscriminately, we should all aim at one; and for the sake of convenience, and likewise to avoid having occasion to speak when we came near them, it was settled that the one which happened to be nearest to us should be our object.

Having every thing thus properly arranged, we pulled slowly and quietly towards them unobserved, until we were within forty yards of the piece of ice on which they lay. The one that lay in the middle, and apparently the largest, now lifted his monstrous head; and the moment he perceived us, he roused the rest of his drowsy companions that were huddled around him. We had by this time got within a few yards of them, and, according to our preconcerted plan, just as they were in the act of rolling themselves into the water, we all fired at the one which was nearest to us. He was wounded so badly that he came up again instantly close to the boat, and apparently with a view of attacking it; but the rencounter, if it may be so called, was of very short duration; for the moment he appeared above water, he was pierced to the heart with a small harpoon. Notwithstanding he was thus mortally wounded, we had very nigh lost him; for in his violent struggles he broke the harpoon, (part of it remaining in his body,) but before he had time to sink, he was again struck, and secured. His weight and dimensions, &c. are noted below.* In the mean time I

* Weight, including 16lbs. for the blood lost before he was weighed	1400	
Weight of the heart	8	
Do. liver	24	
Do. kidneys	5	
Do. spleen	4	
	Feet.	In.
Length from the snout to the end of the hind flippers	10	3
Circumference behind the fore flippers	6	10

ought to mention that the other four escaped, without attempting, as is customary with these animals,

---

	Feet.	In.
Circumference of the neck - - -	4	5½
Do. of the head (round the eyes) - -	2	7
Extent of the fore flippers when extended - -	5	10
Breadth of the fore flippers at their extremities - -	1	0
Extent of the hind flippers when extended - -	4	10
Breadth of the hind flippers at their extremities - -	2	0
Circumference of the fore flippers - - -	2	0½
Do. hind flippers - - -	1	9½
Both the fore and hind flippers had each five toes joined by membranes, and each toe consisted of three bones or phalanges; near the extremity of each toe of the fore flippers there was a small nail, and a small depression in the same place on each of the hind ones.		
Length of the middle toe of the fore flipper 6 inches, and of the hind - - - -	0	7
Do. from the end of the fore flippers to the shoulder joint - - - - -	2	0
Do. do. hind flippers to their insertion in the body - - -	1	9
From the anus to the organs of generation - -	2	4
From the organs of generation to navel - -	0	7
Length of tusks - - - -	0	5
Breadth between the extreme points of the tusks -	0	7
Do. at their roots or insertion into the jaw - -	0	4
Teeth on each side of the upper jaw 5 inches, and in the same place in the lower jaw 4 inches; they were situated at some distance from one another, and scarcely protruded beyond the gum.		
Distance between the eyes - - -	0	9
From the eyes to the tip of the snout - -	0	7
Do. to the orifice of the ears - -	0	3
No external ears, orifice large enough to admit a goose quill, nostrils of a lunated form, one inch in diameter, and about ¾ of an inch apart; bristle in the upper lip two inches long, and about the thickness of pack-thread.		
Length of the bone of the penis - - -	1	1

The

to rescue their wounded companion. We followed them for some time, but they appeared to be so much frightened that it was impossible to get near them again. Their vigilance and terror, indeed, was so great, that at one time, when upwards of half a mile from us, attempting to get on another piece of ice, they perceived us going towards them, when they immediately abandoned the ice and dived again into the deep. I observed that one of them had lost one of his tusks, a thing indeed that I am not much surprised at; for it is chiefly by means of them that they manage to get upon the ice; so that, when we take into consideration the enormous weight of their bodies, which must on such occasions be chiefly, if not entirely, suspended by their tusks, it will appear rather a matter of surprise that accidents do not befal them oftener than they seem to do. It is said also that they occasionally lose their tusks, and sometimes their lives, in their conflicts with the Polar bears. But to return to those facts that came under our own observations, I shall briefly state such anatomical remarks as I have made on the construction and appearance of the abdominal viscera of the Walrus that we killed to-day. After being weighed, and the dimensions of the principal parts of his body taken, he was opened in a longitudinal direction, from the neck to the after part of the body, by which means all the internal parts were exposed to view at once in their respective situations.

The hair on the body was thin, and rather coarse, and its colour was the same as that described on the Walrus seen yesterday, that is, a dark bay on the back, becoming gradually of a lighter colour on the sides, and the under part of the body mottled, not unlike the common seal.

The thorax was, as in terrestrial quadrupeds, &c. separated from the abdomen by a diaphragm. The heart was the only viscus in this cavity that I was desirous of examining ; and, unfortunately, the harpoon with which the animal was killed, as I have already mentioned, entered it, and lacerated the greatest part of it in such a manner that very little can be said respecting its peculiarities, if it had any. What I was more particularly desirous of seeing was, whether the *foramen ovale* was open or not ; and, from what I saw, I feel satisfied that it was not open, for a cicatrice was very plainly to be seen in the septum between the auricles, with a sort of sinus leading from one side of it to the left auricle ; these, I have no doubt, then, were the remains of the passage in question. The stomach appeared small, considering the size of the animal. It lay transversely, immediately behind the diaphragm, in a sort of sigmoid flixure. The contents of it was examined very minutely ; but it was found to contain nothing but a greenish, oleaginous matter, of a slimy consistence. My object in being particular in the examination of the stomach, was to ascertain whether it contained any stones, because we have well authenticated accounts of their being found in the bowels of these animals. Le Sieur de Villefort, Enseigne de Vaisseau, who sailed under M. de Beauchesne Gavin (a French navigator that went on a voyage to the South Seas many years ago), mentions their having killed a sea lion* in Port Desire, in whose stomach they found

* It is perhaps necessary to mention, that the animal called the Sea Lion by the old navigators, is the same that is now generally known by the name of Walrus, or Sea Horse, in the Arctic Seas ; but I understand that in the Straits of Magellan, and on the islands in its neighbourhood, they are still called Sea Lions.

several stones; and I am informed that a number of stones were found in the stomach of a Walrus that was killed last summer by the expedition that went to Spitzbergen.

All that I have now to say of this animal is a few words respecting him as an article of food. The flesh of the sea-horse has been represented by different navigators as very good eating; but, with due deference to their opinion, I must own that as far as I am able to judge, nothing but absolute want could ever induce a person not accustomed to such food to eat it. In the first place, immediately under the skin, there was a layer two inches and a half thick of fat, that differed not materially in appearance, and not at all in its nature from whale's blubber; and the flesh, or muscular substance underneath this oleaginous coating, was as black as the crang† of a whale, and smelt so intolerably, that even the dogs we have on board would not touch it. It is but just, however, to mention that we cooked the heart, which was found to be tolerably good eating; but the disgust occasioned by the offensive odour from the carcase of the animal was so great, that we could hardly rid ourselves of the idea that the heart did not partake in some degree of the disgusting qualities of the body. The fat, or blubber, however, has been turned to some advantage, for it was stripped off, and put into a cask, until an opportunity occurs for boiling it, when it is expected to produce from thirty to forty gallons of oil.

We had to-night, for the first time this season, a

* This is a term used by the Greenland, or whale-fishermen, which signifies the fleshy, or muscular part of the whale, that is left after the blubber is flinched or taken off.

meridian altitude of the sun at midnight, or, properly speaking, below the pole, for we have now of course no night; but, as the terms day, and night, are convenient when speaking of the time when any event occurs that is necessary to be mentioned, I shall always make use of them for the sake of perspicuity, although no natural distinction of the kind now takes place.

Friday, 9th. — Nothing has occurred for these three days past deserving of particular notice. The weather has been variable, sometimes fine, at other times the reverse; but our greatest annoyance has been, and still is, the ice, with which we are constantly hampered. There is one thing we find, which is, that, by standing to the eastward, we get clear of it; but our object is to get to the westward, if possible.

Sunday, 11th. — As we were sailing along amongst the ice this forenoon, a large white bear was observed on a piece of it close to the ships. A boat was immediately lowered to go after him. The weather happened to be foggy, so that he did not see us until we were within about a hundred yards of him; he was walking about at the time, but immediately he perceived us he crouched down on the edge of the ice, and watched our approach very attentively, as if in expectation that we should in a short time become his prey. We were, on the other hand, no less sanguine that he should very soon be our captive, and in order to make sure of our mark, we continued to pull towards him until the boat was within about forty yards of him, when we all fired. One shot brake his right hind leg, and the rest (viz. three) struck him in different parts of the body. On being wounded he made a hideous roar, and grasped with his teeth at the places where he was struck. He then plunged into the water, and tried to escape in that way; but, on finding that we were gaining ground upon him, he attempted to get again on the ice; but he was by this time so much exhausted by loss of blood that before he could get out of the water we secured him by throwing the bight of a rope round his neck. His weight and dimensions are noted below.*

*Weight - - - -	895 lbs.	
	Feet.	In.
Length from the snout to the tail - - -	8	2
Circumference round the middle - - -	6	0
Length from the snout to the shoulder joint - -	3	0
Height from the heel of the fore-paw to the top of the back between the shoulders - - - -	3	7
Do. from the heel of the hind-leg to the top of the rump - - - - -	3	4
Circumference of the fore-paw - - - -	1	11
Breadth of do. - - -	0	8½
Length from the fore-toes to the knee-joint - -	2	5½

It will be seen that his weight is not at all in proportion to his dimensions; for he was a very large animal, as far as length and height went; but, although six inches longer than the bear we killed in this country last summer, he was upwards of two hundred pounds lighter.

On opening him, we discovered the cause of this disparity; for the whole of the alimentary canal was in a high state of gangrene, the liver and lungs were very much inflamed, and the spleen apparently shrunk considerably below its natural size, the stomach was empty and collapsed: in fact, the whole of the abdominal viscera bore evident marks of disease.

	Feet.	In.
Circumference of the fore-leg below the knee - -	2	5
Do. of the hind-paw - - - -	1	10
Do. of the hind-leg - - -	2	4
Breadth of the hind-paw - - - -	0	8
Length from the hind-toes to the knee-joint - -	2	3
Length of the tail - - - - -	0	6
Circumference of the head before the ears - -	3	1
Do. of the neck - - - -	3	9
Distance from the snout to the eye - - -	0	8¼
Do. between the eye - - -	0	6
Longest axis of the eyes - - - -	0	1
Depth of the snout - - - - -	0	3½
Do. from nose to under part of the lower jaw - -	0	5½
Breadth of septum narium - - -	0	0½
Nare, elliptical		
Length of the ears - - - -	0	3
Breadth of do. - - - - - -	0	2½

Front teeth in each jaw 6 inches; canine 2 inches; molares or grinders 5 inches; length of the upper tusks $1\frac{8}{10}$ inch; breadth between their tips 3¼ inches; length of the lower tusks 1¾ inch; (the tip of the right side tusk was broken) breadth between their tips 3 inches.

The liver weighed 16 lbs.; the lungs 14 lbs.; the heart 6 lbs.; the kidneys 3 lbs.; and the spleen 1½lbs.

The weather has been colder to-day than we have had yet, being half a degree less, indeed, than we had it during the whole of last voyage, our lowest temperature, last year, being 26½°, and to-day it was as low as 26°. We suffer, however, no inconvenience from the cold, but the moisture that freezes on the rigging renders it disagreeable to handle.

Thursday, 15*th.*—Nothing has occurred for these three days past deserving of remark; the weather has been, I may almost say, invariably foggy, which, together with the quantity of ice that we have been constantly hampered with, has rendered our progress to the northward very slow; for our latitude to-day, at noon, was only 70° 27′ N., which is only a little more than one degree farther than we were four days ago. We have reason to suppose, however, that the three or four last degrees of latitude that we have come through, are the most difficult to navigate of any part of these seas, for they are the narrowest part of the Straits, and at this season of the year will, I have no doubt, be always found choked with the ice that drifts down from Baffin's Bay. Two boats were sent this forenoon to an iceberg, to bring some of it on board for dissolving into water. As this ice appeared to be more compact than what I have usually observed the berg-ice to be, I formed a piece of it into a cube *, for the purpose of determining its specific gravity, which was found however not to differ materially from what we have been accustomed to find it by similar experi-

* The sides of this cube measured six inches and $\frac{8}{10}$, and when put into a tub of sea-water at the temperature of 33° and of the specific gravity 1.0256, nine-tenths of an inch remained above the surface of the water.

ments last year; that is, about one-seventh remaining above the surface of the water.

Friday, 16*th*. — A small piece of ice was picked up to-day, however, whose specific gravity differed very much indeed from any that I have ever seen in these seas before. Its size would not admit well of being made into a cube, it was therefore formed into a rectangular parallelogram, two inches seven-tenths in breadth, and one inch seven-tenths in thickness; and when put into a bason of salt water, at the temperature of 35°, and of the specific gravity of 1.0262, only one-tenth of an inch remained above the surface of the water, or, in other words, one-seventeenth of the whole.

We passed the Brunswick, of Hull, to-day, on her way home: they *broomed* * to us, that they had taken nineteen whales; and, as she passed the Griper, they told them that there were about fifty whalers to the northward (close to the coast of Greenland), between the 74 and 75 degrees of latitude. This was all the communication we had with her; or, properly speaking, that the Griper had, for she passed too far from us to speak her.

I have omitted to mention before, that, during these two or three days past, we saw several large

* This is a term used by the whale fishermen to express the manner in which they communicate to one another the number of whales they have taken. The way in which the intelligence is conveyed is this; on board the ship that is asking for the information in question, some person holds up a broom in a conspicuous place where it may be seen by the other ship, where some person with a similar instrument gives the required information by lifting a broom up over his head as many times as the number of fish they have taken; hence the origin and meaning of the term *brooming a ship*.

flocks of eider ducks (*Anas Malissima*, Lin.) flying to the eastward.

Saturday, 17*th.* — We made fast this afternoon to a floe of ice, where we remained for some time, which afforded us an opportunity of making some magnetic and other observations. In order to make sure of being clear of the influence of the ships upon the compasses, the observations were made at least a quarter of a mile from either of them. The variation at this place was found by the mean of several azimuths, to be 81° westerly, and the dip, or vertical inclination of the needle, 84° 6′. The latitude of the place of observation (reckoning from noon) was 72° N., and longitude, by sights taken for the chronometers at the time, 60° 5′ W. We found, on different parts of the ice that we walked over this afternoon, large quantities of earth and gravel; this is, however, such a common thing, that it hardly deserves to be mentioned, for scarcely a day ever passes without our seeing either stones or earth on some of the floes that we are amongst.

Monday, 19*th.* — The weather for some days past has been very foggy, which, I think, is in some measure owing to our being so far from the land; for I observed last year, when we were detained for some days at Waygat Island, that there was very often a thick fog over the surface of the sea at some distance from the land; whilst over the land itself, and along the coast, for a space of two or three leagues from it, there was commonly a fine clear sky. Paradoxical as it may appear, yet we find, that although the weather is in general so cold that the fog freezes on the rigging, that the ice is undergoing dissolution very rapidly, for on most of the floes we find large pools of water, from one of which we supplied the ships (with water) two days ago.

Although it must certainly be admitted (from the circumstance that I have just mentioned), that the sun contributes very materially to the destruction of the ice, yet I concur in opinion with the intrepid navigator, Davis, and the illustrious Cook, that the sea is the great destroyer of the ice in these regions.

We find that there is a constant current setting to the southward, which has been observed, indeed, more or less, ever since we entered the Straits. Its daily rate, and the exact course it takes, is not, indeed, very easily ascertained with great precision; for the various courses we are obliged to make amongst the ice, are such as to baffle all attempts at comparing the latitude observed with that deduced from the dead reckoning; and I have no doubt but the ice affects, in some measure, the direction of the current near the surface.

Tuesday, 20th.—On account of the fogginess of the weather, we got so close to a large iceberg, to-day, before it was seen, that we were obliged to lower our boats in great haste to tow the ship off from it; and, notwithstanding the smartness with which every thing was done, she went over a tongue of it that projected some distance from the body of the berg. This tongue happened, fortunately, however, to be about twenty feet below the surface of the water, so that we went over it without touching, and, in a few minutes more, got clear, altogether, of this threatening mass of ice, for such I must certainly call it, for the side of it that we ran along was considerably higher than our mast-head, and some parts of it projected beyond: a perpendicular line rose from its base, or at right angles with the surface of the water. And in addition to these circumstances, it was full of vertical fissures, or rents, which showed, in a very unequivocal manner, the danger of approaching too near it. The depth of water alongside of it was found to be one hundred and twenty fathoms; and, as it appeared from the tide-mark on it, to be aground, its height above the surface of the water might be estimated at one hundred and twenty feet; for the proportion of the ice, above, to that below the surface of the water, will generally be found to be nearly as one is to seven. We shot a seal this evening, of the common species. (*Phoca Vitulina*, Lin.) He was lying on a piece of ice at the time. It is unnecessary to give any description of him, as he differed in no respect from the seals that are seen on our own coast: his length, from the snout to the tail, was five feet one inch, and the circumference round the thickest part of the body three feet six inches.

Wednesday, 21*st.*—The weather cleared up to-day for the first time for some days past; and about eight o'clock A. M. we had a very good, although a distant view, of the coast of Greenland, bearing by compass from south to east of us. The mountain called by Davis, "Hope Sanderson," was readily recognised by such of us as had seen it last year; although its distance from us was estimated to be about forty miles, it bore, by compass, 8° S. 30′ E. Some of the Women Islands were also in sight. It appeared to me that there was more snow on this part of the coast, than was on it last year when we passed it; but our distance from it was too great to enable us to say any thing with certainty on this head.

We found an immense number of icebergs off this coast; no less than eighty-eight were seen this morning at one time from deck, and most of them so large that I have no doubt of their being a ground, for we sounded at the time in one hundred and six fathoms—sand and pieces of broken shells. Between us and the land there was also a considerable quantity of loose ice, sufficiently open, however, to navigate amongst it, to the northward; but as I have said some time ago, our object is not to get to the northward along this coast, but if possible to penetrate to the westward. What time it will take to accomplish this desirable object in this high latitude, is a question that must certainly remain in doubt until the thing is done, for last year's experience does not afford us any ground to draw a conclusion from on this subject; we found then (as we do now) a barrier of ice to the westward, from the time that we first made it until we got nearly to the top of Baffin's Bay; and although we never succeeded in getting through it, it was certainly not from want of attempting to do so. Whether these attempts might not have been successful if persevered in, is a thing that does not become me to give an opinion on.

We are possessed however of some knowledge this year, that we knew nothing of last summer, with regard to the extent of this ledge or barrier of ice; for then it was doubtful how far it might extend to the westward, but now we know perfectly well how far it can extend in that direction. But, to be brief on the subject, I believe the intention is, to make every effort to force our way to the westward from this place, so as to make the entrance of our hopeful inlet, Lancaster's Sound; we are not indeed quite in the parallel of latitude * of it yet, but as the land tends a little to the eastward on the south side of that opening, a passage across at this place will be shorter than farther to the eastward.

This day, in addition to its being fine and clear, was, I think, the warmest day that we have had since we left England, for at two o'clock in the afternoon the thermometer in the sun rose to 82.

In the evening, as we were making the best of our way to the westward, a large bear was observed on a piece of ice close to us, but time was deemed too precious to lose any of it to go after him.

Saturday, 24th. — Nothing has occurred during these two days past deserving of remark; we got beset amongst the ice on the evening of the 22d, and have been so situated ever since; we have at different times during that period endeavoured to force the ships through by warping, but we have made but very little progress, the ice being so close and heavy, that our utmost efforts avail but little; there are prospects, however, of clear water to the westward, for the sky in that direction has a watery appearance, and the ice is dissolving very fast, its surface being full of pools of water, in one of which was caught, two days ago, a small fish answering to the description of the *Gadus Virens* of Lin.

As there was nothing particularly doing, a series of experiments were again performed this afternoon,

* The entrance of Lancaster's Sound may be said to be in latitude 74° N., and ours to-day at noon was 72° 58′ 12″ N.

for determining the deviation of the compass; the mode of operation was similar to that described some time ago, when an experiment of the same kind was made: that is, a set of azimuths were taken with the ship's head on every second point of the compass, and the difference of these azimuths from the true variation found on the ice, will, of course, be the deviation on these respective points. In this experiment a newly invented needle by Mr. Jennings was used, and as far as we could judge from this trial it appeared to answer remarkably well. It differs in its construction from the common needle, for instead of one bar, or needle, it consists of two placed at right angles to one another, so that the magnetic north and south falls in a line between the two opposite arms of it. As the result of this experiment may be more easily comprehended by a diagram than by words, I have drawn one *, which exhibits at one view the whole operation, or rather, as I have just said, the results thereof.

It will be seen from this experiment that the deviation has increased very considerably since it was tried before; this is, however, nothing more than what might be expected, or, in fact, it is only what we knew, from other circumstances, must happen; for it is very clear, that as the directive power of the magnetism of the earth upon the compass decreases as we approach the magnetic pole; so will the power or rather the effect of the iron in the ship increase.

Sunday, 25th. — The ice having slackened a little during the night, all hands were employed the whole day tracking and warping the ships to the

* See Appendix.

westward; and in the evening, in consideration of the great exertions made, and the length of time they were employed, each man had half a pound of Donkin's preserved meat, and a gill of rum served out to them, as an extra allowance.

Monday, 26th. — We were employed again to-day in a similar way as above mentioned, but with less success, for the ice closed so much to-day that our utmost endeavours to force through it were of little avail.

Tuesday, 27th. — Although yesterday's exertions were not of much use, we were not discouraged on that account from recommencing the same labour again to-day, and I have much pleasure in being able to say, that the unwearied efforts displayed not only to-day, but for some days past, were this afternoon crowned (as good causes generally are, when persevered in with zeal and proper management) with success, for we got into what may be called clear water, that is to say navigable, although not altogether free from ice. From similar motives to those mentioned on the 25th inst. the men had again this evening an extra allowance of fresh meat served out to them.

Wednesday, 28th. — I have remarked that since we lost sight of the coast of Greenland very few icebergs have been seen; to-day especially there has not been above five or six seen altogether, and these were of an inferior size. This is no doubt owing to the water increasing in depth as we proceed to the westward, so that they cannot ground. We sounded to-day in two hundred and ninety-six fathoms, a depth evidently too great for icebergs to ground in, unless they were of an extraordinary magnitude. The floe ice is also much thinner than it was a few days ago; some of it indeed that we passed to-day was so honey-combed, or as it is commonly called, so rotten, that some parts of it would not bear a man's weight. I think that this rapid dissolution may in some measure be attributed to the greater depth of the water here than to the eastward; for it is well known that shoal water freezes more readily than deep water, consequently when ice happens to drift into deep water, it will be destroyed quicker than in shoal water.

Thursday, 29th.—We got yesterday evening into a clear sea, and there is to-day every appearance of its continuing so; the sky looks watery to the westward, and we have had all the forenoon a considerable swell from that direction, so that we may, I think, with safety presume, that the sea is open at least as far as Lancaster's Sound, and as we know that there is a greater depth of water in that inlet than where we are now, it is not likely that we shall find much obstruction from ice there.

We were at noon only one hundred and sixty miles from the entrance of it, having, in the course of the last twenty-four hours, ran upwards of one hundred miles; a distance, certainly, that in temperate climates would be performed by a ship under the most ordinary circumstances; but in these regions, and after such tardy movements as we have for some time past been accustomed to, appears to us a great run, and, taking every thing into consideration, is so in reality.

We saw several whales to-day for the first time since we entered Baffin's Bay, or at least since we passed the latitude of 70° N., for I believe the line of division between it and Davis's Straits is not yet well defined; it may, therefore, in speaking of it, be better perhaps to refer to some parallel of latitude.

Friday, 30th. — The sea still continues open, and there is every prospect of its being so to the westward, for the sky in that direction promises well, and we have, as I mentioned yesterday, a considerable swell. The weather being fine and clear this forenoon, we had very excellent sights for the chronometers, from which, and our latitude at noon, we found that we were no great distance from the entrance of Lancaster's Sound; it was indeed computed at the time, that if the breeze continued as we then had it, that the west land would be seen in the course of the afternoon, and to our great joy these expectations were fulfilled about five o'clock, for at that time land was descried from the mast-head, which we knew from our latitude to be the mountains on the south side of the inlet just mentioned. The welcome news was immediately telegraphed to the Griper, then both ships set all sail they could possibly carry, having, as it were, received fresh vigour from the prospect now before them.

As we drew in with the land every eye appeared to be directed towards that spacious inlet so often the theme of conversation for these eleven months past.

So much indeed has been said about it, that were we quite ignorant of the place, we must have felt some pleasure in seeing it; but to us it is peculiarly interesting, for most of us have seen it before, or, more properly speaking, we were witnesses of the promising appearances it afforded of being the place, that not only we, but many other navigators, for upwards of two centuries, were in search of.

At the same time that we are thus delighted with having the object of our hopes in sight, a sort of secret anxiety hovers occasionally over the mind, on recollecting that it has been affirmed, from *ocular demonstration*, that the magnificent opening now before us is *only a bay*. It would be needless, if not improper, however, to enter into a lengthened detail of the reasons that might be adduced against that opinion, for such only can I call it; let it suffice then, that there is at present every prospect of our being soon able to decide the subject in question, in a manner that will henceforth leave no doubt about the matter; for the sea is quite clear to the westward as far as we can see, and we have a fine breeze of wind; it is not indeed directly in our favour, being from the N. W., but it is sufficiently so, if it continues, to enable us to get to the entrance of the Sound, as it is gratuitously called, before to-morrow morning.

It is astonishing the number of whales that have been seen to-day; no less than fifty are said to have been seen in the course of one watch, (viz. four hours,) this afternoon. May this circumstance not be considered as an indication of the opening before us being a passage from Baffin's Bay to another sea, into which these fish are now going, in consequence of their being pursued and harassed by the fishermen in these seas?

The mountains appear to have more snow on them than they had last year when we were here; this may, however, in a great measure, be accounted for, from our seeing them a month earlier this year, for it was on the 30th of August that we were at this place last voyage. Along the coast, however, and for about three hundred feet up the side of the mountains, the land is, with very few exceptions, perfectly clear of snow. We estimate the height of the mountains to be from sixteen hundred, to two thousand feet above the level of the sea.

Saturday, 31st. — We got this morning off the place that was called, last year, Possession Bay, from our having landed there and taken possession of the country. As we had it in a different point of view from that in which it was seen last year, it was not recognised until the pole erected on the top of one of the hills was seen. As soon as we got abreast of it the ships were hove to, and a boat went ashore with Mr. Parry and Capt. Sabine to make magnetic and other observations *, and during the time they were employed in making these observations, two men and myself were directed to proceed up the stream which flows through the valley, with instructions to observe if any pieces of wood or bark were to be seen in the bed of it, and to make such remarks on the nature and productions of the place as might be deemed useful. We commenced our excursion from the mouth of the stream, at which place it is, as near as I could judge, from thirty-five to forty yards broad; and at low water, as was the case when we landed, not above knee deep: there is at this place however a bar across it, within which it both deepens and widens. The depth of it, for about one hundred and fifty or two hundred yards within the bar I was not able to determine, being

* The latitude at the mouth of the stream was found to be 73° 31′ 16″ N., and longitude 77° 44′ 42″ W. (by chronometer); the variation of the compass by the mean of several azimuths 108° 50′ westerly, and the dip, or vertical inclination of the dipping-needle, 86° 9′.

too considerable to wade across it: its breadth at that place was, I think, from forty-five to fifty feet. The tide went up it to the distance of two hundred and fifty or three hundred yards, as was evident by the tide-mark left on its banks, and the bones of whales that were lying on the left side of it at the above distance from its mouth. The bed of the stream above the bar as far as the tide went consisted of soft vicid mud; beyond this it became rough and hard, consisting of loose stones and sand, which was indeed the nature of the bottom all the rest of the way as far as we went: it continued likewise nearly of an uniform breadth, that is, from forty to fifty yards, and every part of it beyond where the tide flowed, was fordable.

The first thing that attracted our notice in going along the bank of the stream, was to meet human tracks in so perfect a state, that, had the place been known to be frequented by man, we should have supposed that people had been here only a few days before; but one of the men who was with me, as well as myself, remembered that we had been on the very same spot, where the tracks were observed, last year gathering plants, so that we had not the smallest doubt of their being the remains of our own footsteps made last year, for had any Esquimaux been at this place since we were here before, it is more than probable that they would have taken away the pole on the hill; for, from what we saw of them last year, nothing could be a greater prize for them than a piece of wood of the size of that in question. Besides, we observed that the impression of the heel of the shoe was deeper than that of any other part of it, which would not be the case were they the tracks of Esquimaux, for they never have heels to their shoes or boots; and, in fact, the size and shape of the footmarks were such as to satisfy us perfectly as to their origin. From this circumstance we may conclude that there is no great fall of snow in this country in the winter, for doubtless the melting of it would have effaced these tracks. After tracing them for some distance we resumed our course up the stream until we came to the foot of a mountain, which from the sea appeared to terminate the valley through which it flowed: but instead of finding the source of our stream here, as we imagined, we found that it issued from another valley to the right, or southward and westward. Our time being limited, we could not follow it any farther; at this time we were, as near as I could judge, about three miles and a half, or four miles, at the farthest, from the sea. At this distance from the coast there were only two or three small patches of snow in the whole valley, and there was very little of it indeed for a considerable way beyond this up the sides of the mountains. The only animals we saw during our excursion were a Fox, (*Canis Vulpes*, Lin.); a Raven, (*Corvus Corax*, Lin.); several Ring-Plovers, (*Charadrius Hiaticula*, Lin.); and Snow-Buntings, (*Emberiza Nivalis*, Lin.); a bee was also seen, from which we may infer that there is honey even in these wild regions. We saw several tracks of bears, and some cloven-footed animal, from their size apparently those of a reindeer, neither of them however appeared to be very recent. Considering the high latitude in which this place is situated, vegetation flourishes remarkably well, for wherever there was moisture tufts of grass and various plants grew in considerable abundance; creeping, or ground willow, was the only ligneous production we met with, the diameter of the thickest of them that I saw did not exceed that of a person's finger, and, generally speaking, they were not so large.

The fixed rocks consisted chiefly of basalt and granite, and in the valley there was a vast quantity of limestone, in loose fragments; but I do not recollect having seen any rocks of it: granite, quartz, sandstone, trap, felspar, and various other minerals, were to be met with in considerable abundance in the bed, and about the banks of the stream before-mentioned. On our way back to the boat I picked up a piece of whalebone, two feet ten inches in length, and two inches broad: it had forty two holes in it, placed nearly in a straight line, and at regular distances from one another along one of its edges: these holes were perfectly round, and of a size sufficient to admit a goose-quill. Besides the holes just mentioned, there were also fine oval holes along the middle of it, at the distance of eight inches apart. We supposed it had been part of an Esquimaux sledge; and from the situation in which it was found, it is probable that it had been carried there by some of these people; for it was between three and four hundred yards from the sea, and about the same distance from the stream we went up; so that it could not be brought by either to the place where it was found.

On returning from our excursion, we found that the tide had risen so much that we could not wade across the bar at the mouth of the stream. The tide appeared to flow from the northward, or most probably out of Lancaster's Sound; for this place is situated to the southward and eastward of it. It was just low water at the time we landed, and during the three hours we were ashore, it rose between three and four feet; but from the distance up the beach that the bones of whales, sea-weed, and other things that must have been washed up by the sea, was found, it would appear that the tide rises considerably higher than what might be expected from the result of our observation on it to-day. I ought to observe, however, that in all probability, a very heavy sea sets into this bay occasionally, for when we landed, although the wind was very moderate, there was a very considerable surf breaking on the beach; so that when it blows hard from the eastward, it may be presumed that the sea runs so high as to have washed the bones above-mentioned up to the place where they were lying; that is, some distance beyond the regular tide-mark. The water deepens very suddenly in this bay, for we sounded as we were coming ashore, and found fourteen fathoms' water within a cable's length of the beach; and even closer than that its depth must be considerable; for just as we were landing, two whales were observed so near the shore, that I expected at one time that they would run themselves aground. Whilst we were ashore they tried for soundings on board, with a line of two hundred and ninety fathoms, and found no bottom; but on recollection, I ought not to mention this as a remarkable circumstance, for they sounded in a thousand fathoms last year, in the Isabella, in the very same place, or at least pretty near it. As the staff planted at that time on the hill, already mentioned, is still standing, it would be unnecessary to erect another this year; but, in order to leave some memorial of this our second visit, a sort of obelisk, or rather a pile of loose stones, was erected on the right bank of the stream, and about two hundred yards from the beach; and under the pile was buried a quart bottle, containing a slip of paper, on which were written the names of ships, and commanders, and the time when we were here. Having now given an account of every thing that I saw during this excursion, that appeared to me to be deserving of notice, I shall again resume the narrative of our transactions on board. Immediately the boats returned (one being on shore from the Griper), we made sail towards Lancaster's Sound; but the wind being at the time rather against us (N. E. by compass) we made but little progress during the remainder of this day.

Sunday, August 1*st.* — The wind still continuing to blow out of the Sound, we have as yet got but a very little way into it; every thing else, however, appears favourable, the sea is perfectly clear to the westward, as far as we can see, and a heavy swell is setting from that direction, from which we may conclude that there is neither land nor ice very close to us on that side. We passed several streams of ice to-day, indeed on the north side of the Sound, but they lay so close in with the land, that they offered no obstruction to our progress; and, with regard to icebergs, it may be almost said, that they have totally disappeared, for there has been only one seen to-day. It has been observed that since we got within the capes that form the entrance of this magnificent Sound, that the colour of the water changed from its usual light green colour, to a dirty brownish hue.

Monday, 2d.—There being but very little wind this forenoon, we availed ourselves of the opportunity thereby occasioned for sounding, which occupied a considerable portion of time, for we had no less than one thousand and forty-eight fathoms of line out before we found bottom; it was estimated, however, that the actual depth was not above eight hundred and fifty, or nine hundred fathoms, as there was a very considerable portion of stray line. The deep-sea-clamm was used on this occasion, the soundings brought up, consisted chiefly of mud, intermixed with small stones, and pieces of broken shells of a very delicate texture. At eight o'clock in the evening a breeze sprang up from the southward and eastward, accompanied by fine clear weather, which enabled us to have an excellent view of the land on both sides this spacious opening, and although we had not as yet got so far into the Sound as we were last year, frequent visits were nevertheless made to the Crow's Nest*, to look for Croker's Mountain, for such was our anxiety, that we began to look for what we had good reasons to suppose did not exist, and that too before we got far enough to see them if they

* This is the name given by the Greenland fishermen to a look-out place they have at the mast-head. It is frequently made of a cask, by taking one end out, and cutting a scuttle in the other for a person to get through; the use of it is to shelter the person looking out for whales, or the best lead amongst the ice, from the inclemency of the weather. We have two crows' nests up, one at the main, and the other at the fore-mast head, and whenever we are amongst the ice, one or other of them is always occupied by some person looking out for the best way to get through, and to-day they have, as I have mentioned above, been frequently visited by persons looking out for what I hope we shall never see.

did exist. There is every appearance, at present, however, of our being able before long of satisfying ourselves on this point; I shall therefore forbear to say any thing more on the subject until that period comes. We saw an immense number of whales to-day again, between thirty and forty being seen in every watch; it has been remarked, that a great many of them were of a small size. I observed that they went in shoals in the same way that porpoises usually do, generally coming to the surface nearly about the same time, and diving in the same manner. We passed in the course of the day a great number of what is commonly called sea-blubber, (*Medusa*), on which I think it is very probable the whales feed; for it is a sort of food well adapted to the formation of their mouth, requiring little or no mastication, an operation which the whale is by no means calculated to perform.

As we came along to-day, we observed that the stream, or ledge of ice mentioned yesterday, still stretches to the westward, but so close in with the north land as to be no impediment in our way. Amongst it were seen this evening, three icebergs, but of so small a size that we would have hardly noticed them, had it not that so few have been seen of late.

Tuesday, 3d. — We made considerable progress to the westward to-day, for we were at noon (by chronometer) in longitude 80° 30′ W., and since that time we have had an excellent run, for at eight o'clock in the evening, we were by account in 82° W., and if the breeze continues but a few hours as it is now, we shall decide whether land exists where it is said to have been seen last year; at present the weather is perfectly clear, and there is nothing to be seen to the westward but a clear sea!

The south land, after passing Cape Castlereagh, trends to southward and westward, forming a large bay, the bottom of which was so distant from us, that it is presuming too much indeed to call it a bay, as it might, for aught we know, be a passage to the southward. The land to the westward of this bay, or opening, appeared to be lower than that on the opposite side of it, and the formation, or contour of it, differed also from that of the land to the eastward; for it appeared somewhat like that which is called Table Land, whilst the land that we have passed is full of acuminated hills, rising one above another from the sea-side, to the top of the mountains. On the north side, and a little to the westward of the bay or opening that I have just been describing, there is a similar gulf, or passage, and of greater extent than the above; our distance from the northernmost part of it was likewise too considerable to enable us to speak with certainty of the continuity of the land; it appeared to us indeed as if it consisted of a number of islands. The land to the westward of this opening differed also in its features from that on the north side of the entrance of Lancaster's Sound, for its outline appeared to be more regular, and less elevated than the latter, and it has much less snow on it. As we were sailing along this forenoon, we happened to pass close by an iceberg, to which a boat was sent to take some azimuths, and, to our surprise, the result of them gave less variation, nearly by two degrees, than we found in Possession Bay, notwithstanding we have every reason to think that we are approaching the Magnetic Pole; but these observations were taken rather too near noon, so that they are not so much to be depended on as those taken the other day.

Whilst the boat was at the berg, they were employed on board sounding; they struck bottom in three hundred and seventy-three fathoms, soft mud, and at the same time a tide, or current, was found setting N. 65° E. true, at the rate of seven fathoms per hour.

Wednesday, 4th. — The momentous question so often alluded to in the course of this narrative, (and indeed a subject of conversation for nearly a twelvemonth past,) has this day been decided in the manner in which I always thought it would be, that is, that no land exists on the west side of Lancaster's Sound, where it was said to have been seen last year; for we were to-day at noon in longitude 86° 56′ W., which is nearly three degrees to the westward of where it was laid down. It would perhaps be unbecoming to take a retrospective view of the opinions and arguments advanced by those who maintained that Lancaster's Sound was of all others the place that appeared most likely to be the opening or inlet through which the passage so long sought after would ultimately be found; because a review of that kind might be considered as a triumph over those who have the misfortune of being this day proved to be wrong. Although people may refrain, however, from making an ostentatious parade about their own merit or judgment, yet they cannot avoid feeling a secret satisfaction that their opinions have turned out to be true; nor is it indeed necessary to stifle these inward pleasures. But, to abandon the subject, I shall resume my diary by relating the rest of the events of the day, leaving to others the task of contrasting and judging of the respective merits of the deeds and opinions of the parties or individuals concerned, for upwards of two centuries, in projecting or performing voyages to this country, similar to that on which we are employed.

We tried for soundings several times during the day with different lengths of line, from fifty to one hundred and seventy fathoms, but never struck bottom; and, as we had a fine breeze in our favour, it was not deemed proper to lose time in sounding to any greater depth; and probably had the Griper been able to keep up with us, we should not have sounded so often, or to such depth as we did.

We lost sight of the south land since eight o'clock this morning, (the weather being perfectly clear,) and we have been at an average about twenty miles from the north land during the whole day, (but sometimes much nearer,) so that these straits, if they may be so called, are certainly of the first magnitude, both with regard to their breadth, and depth.

The land on the north side that we passed to-day is of a different description from any that I have seen in this country before; the whole of the coast appeared somewhat like an immense wall (in ruins) rising almost perpendicular from the sea, to the height, as near as I could judge, of about five hundred feet. The surface of this precipice consisted of horizontal strata of different thicknesses, and the debris that fell from them formed a kind of buttresses at the foot of the rock. On some of the strata also that projected out farther than the rest along the face of the precipice, there were collections of the mouldering remains of the superincumbent rocks; so that from the variety of shapes and sizes that these heaps of rubbish assumed, the regularity of the strata, and the uniformity that prevailed in the height of the rock, this bold coast presented altogether a very interesting appearance. Notwithstanding its general character was such as I have just been describing, yet in some parts of it there appeared to be inlets or chasms in which were apparently very secure harbours; but our distance from it was too great to enable us to speak with any degree of certainty on this point.

The surface of the country inland, as far as we could see, had very little snow on it, which I thought might possibly be owing to its being so plain that no part of it afforded shelter for the drift-snow to lodge in; its height was also very inconsiderable, for it appeared to rise but very little beyond the cliffs along the coast. We found the sea quite clear of ice as we came along during the day, with the exception of a few small bergs; but, in the evening, we came to what appears to be an island, with a ledge of ice extending from the north and south ends of it as far as we can see. That which runs from the north end appears to reach as far as the land; but as it happened to become hazy just as we made the ice, it is possible that we might have been deceived as to its extent. At all events, as long as we are not interrupted by land, a little stoppage by ice is a matter of very little consequence; for I have no doubt but we shall manage to get through it. Between the island just mentioned and the north land, or that along which we have been sailing all day, there appears to be a large open bay, or, it might perhaps be more properly said, that the land opposite this island trends to the northward and westward, instead of due west as before. As we approached the ice this afternoon we saw from twenty to thirty whales.

Thursday, 5th.—The weather had been foggy since yesterday evening until five o'clock this afternoon, so that we had been during that time little better than stationary, standing alternately off and on along the edge of the ice, in readiness to take advantage of the first opening that would be discovered when the weather cleared up; but to our disappointment, when this happened (between five and six o'clock in the evening), we found that the ice extended from the island mentioned last night to the north land, a distance of about thirty miles. This body of ice appeared so compact that it would be folly to attempt to force through it, more especially as it extended to the westward farther than we could see; we had the satisfaction, however, of not seeing any land beyond it in that direction. We had no other choice then but to remain inactive, looking at the slow dissolution of this immense barrier of ice, or proceed to the southward in hopes of finding a passage to the westward in that direction. As the latter route (although not leading so directly to the westward) afforded more immediate employment, and, at the same time, prospect of success, it was determined to try what could be done by shaping our course to the southward and westward. As we were sailing along the edge of the ice, we discovered another island, about six or seven miles to the southward and westward of that seen last night, and about the same distance, farther on in that direction, more land appeared. The whole of the space between these islands and the land just mentioned was full of ice, which extended indeed for several miles to the eastward of them, so that we could not approach within some distance of either the one or the other. These islands, as well as the land beyond them, have very much the appearance of that which I have been describing yesterday; the islands in particular appeared to rise almost perpendicular from the sea to the height of between two and three hundred feet; they had very little snow on them, their top or surface being, like the land alluded to, almost level. In this respect, however, the land to the southward and westward of them differed from them very materially, for the interior of it, at least that part of it that bounded our view, rose to a considerable height, and the hills that composed it were well covered with snow; its surface was, however, generally speaking, smooth, that is, free from rocks or abrupt precipices. The depth of water off these islands corresponds (as I have generally observed to be the case) with the boldness of the coast, for we sounded in the forenoon in one hundred and thirty-five fathoms (soft mud), and in the afternoon it increased to one hundred and seventy-five fathoms, the same sort of bottom. Although we are at present checked a little by the ice, our hopes of success had reason to be increased by a certain circumstance that was observed to-day. The circumstance I allude to is the vast number of white whales (*Beluga*, Lin.) that were seen in the course of the day, from which it is not unreasonable to conclude that there is a passage from where we are, as far at least as M'Kenzie's river, for that traveller mentions his having seen them there. People inclined to be sceptical, however, would probably consider this circumstance as of little or no importance, and perhaps not at all deserving of being noticed in the light in which I have mentioned it; but as I am not a cold speculator, disregarding every thing except facts that amount almost to a positive proof, I hope to be excused for mentioning such circumstances as these, as they may be attributed to my confidence of success. As there was nothing particular doing in the forenoon, a couple of boats were sent to try if they could kill one of the fish above mentioned; but we found that they were too wary for us, notwithstanding every art was practised for the purpose of getting near them, by pulling and sculling after them, and, at other times, lying still when they happened to be coming towards us. The latter method appeared to promise most success; and had we a gun harpoon, I have no doubt but we might have succeeded, for they generally came within thirty or forty yards of us before they dived. On coming under the boat, they used to remain for some time apparently viewing our motions; but they took care to keep always at such a depth that it was impossible to reach them. The average length of these fish was, as near as I could judge, from eighteen to twenty feet; their tail was horizontal, like the rest of the order (*Cete*) to which they belong, and they had a spiracle in the crown of their head, through which they respired in the same manner as the common whales do: their colour was, with few exceptions, perfectly white; these exceptions were two or three that I saw of a dusky hue.

Whilst we were pursuing them to-day, I noticed a circumstance that appeared to me rather extraordinary at the time, and which I have not indeed been able to account for yet to my satisfaction. The thing alluded to, is a sort of whistling noise that these fish made when under the surface of the water; it was very audible, and the only sound which I could compare it to, is that produced by passing a wet finger round the edge, or rim of a glass tumbler. It was most distinctly heard when they were coming towards the surface of the water, that is, about half a minute before they appeared, and immediately they got their head above the water the noise ceased. The men were so highly amused by it, that they repeatedly urged one another to pull smartly, in order to get near the place where the fish were supposed to be, for the purpose of hearing what they called a "whale-song:" it certainly had very little resemblance to a song, but sailors are not generally the most happy in their comparisons.

Several fish of another genus of the cetaceous tribe were seen this forenoon for the first time this voyage, viz. the Sea Unicorn, or Narwhal, (*Monodon Monoceros*, Lin.) They were seen together in a shoal, in the same manner that the White-Whales went.

Friday, 6th.—The weather having cleared up about noon, land was seen very distinctly to the southward and eastward of us, which forms, with the land to the southward and westward of the two islands before mentioned, a large inlet or opening leading about S. S. W. true. The west side of this inlet is full of ice, so that in getting on we shall be obliged to sail along pretty near the south-east land. I shall therefore not say any thing respecting its appearance at present, as we are likely to see more of it hereafter. We sounded to-day in one hundred and eighty fathoms, soft mud. A great number of white-whales were seen again to-day, and a few also of the common, or black-whale; seals were also seen in great numbers, both on the ice and in the water. The compasses have become within these two days so sluggish in their motions, that they are almost useless, for all bearings of land are obliged to be taken by astronomical observation, that is, by the bearing of the sun, and the ships are indeed conducted more by the same means than by the compass, so that, when that luminary is obscured by foggy weather, it is a difficult matter to know which way we are going.

Saturday, 7th.—As we happened to be at no great distance from the south-east land to-day, it was deemed an object of importance to draw close in towards it, for the purpose of sending a boat ashore to make (magnetic) observations, the compasses being as I have already mentioned, in such a state *, that we have reason to suppose that we are at no great distance from the magnetic Pole. † It will be seen from the result of the observations made on this occasion, that our supposition cannot be far wrong; for the dip, or vertical inclination of the dipping-needle, was 86° 28′, and the variation 118° westerly; and Captain Kater's azimuth compasses, notwithstanding their delicate construction, were so sluggish in their motions, that they required to be very nicely levelled, and frequently tapped before the card traversed. From these circumstances it may be very easily seen what little dependence there is to be placed in our compasses on board, which, in addition to the disadvantages they labour under from their construction, are at the same time so much affected by local attraction, that they can no longer be trusted to as guides; but if successful, the more difficulty the greater merit. Besides the Egyptians are said to have circumnavigated Africa long before the use of the compass was known, and why should not we circumnavigate America two thousand years after,

* I need only mention one circumstance to shew the state in which the compasses were in on board, which is, that when the ship's head was west, the variation was 180°, or, in other words, the north point of the compass pointed south.

† The latitude of the place where these observations were made, was 72° 45′ N., and longitude 90° 10′ W.

without the help of that useful instrument? I wish only that no greater obstacle than the want of compasses may impede us, and then I am sure that we shall accomplish our object; but to leave the subject for time to prove, I shall briefly notice such circumstances as came under my observation to-day during my excursion on shore.

The part of the coast where we landed, and, indeed, every part of this land that we have yet seen, is, generally speaking, low near the sea-coast, and rising gradually inland; but no part of it, as far as our view extended, rose to a sufficient height to be called mountainous. It had very little snow on it, its appearance at a distance was very barren, and on getting to it we found that its distant prospect had not deceived us; for it was one of the most sterile spots that I have yet seen, even in the Arctic regions. Of vegetation, it could hardly be said that any existed; a few small tufts of grass along the banks of the streams, and, here and there, some stunted poppies, composed the chief part of the Flora of this place. Lichens might also be enumerated amongst the vegetable productions of this land, but as these are to be met with in every place where rocks exist, it can hardly be necessary to mention them. It appeared to be also very thinly inhabited by animals of any description; all that we saw were a couple of Ptarmigans (*Tetrao Lagopus*, Lin.), and a few Snow-buntings. We have reason to suppose, however, that some quadrupeds live on it, although we did not see any, for we found in a sort of cave, or excavation in one of the rocks, a quantity of white hair, or fur, which we supposed to be that of a fox; and, in the same place, there were several seals' bones, from which it may be concluded, that the visitant of that retired spot must have been, at all events, a carnivorous animal. No traces were seen of any human beings being here before ourselves, but if any should ever happen to visit the same place hereafter, it is probable that they will not have the same thing to say, for, on the top of a hill, about half a mile from where we landed, we planted a pole that might be seen at some distance, having a piece of board nailed across the top of it, on which were painted these words: "His Britannic Majesty's ships, Hecla and Griper, August 7. 1819," and at a short distance from the staff was buried a quart bottle, in which was a slip of paper, containing the following short, but very explicit, piece of information: "His Britannic Majesty's ships, Hecla and Griper, were off this coast on the 7th of August, 1819, in search of a north-west passage." With respect to the mineralogy of this place, I have only to remark, that the fixed rocks consisted chiefly of limestone, which was in a very disintegrated state, being somewhat like lime in the act of slaking. The surface of all the loose pieces of stone in the neighbourhood of these rocks was incrusted with lime, which had, apparently, been in a fluid state, for it looked more like the top of a cauliflower than any thing else I could compare it to. This incrustation was not confined to limestone alone, for I observed that quartz, granite, hornblende, or whatever other minerals happened to lie on these rocks, were coated in the same manner.

The limestone appeared to compose only the surface of this land, for the bed of a stream * that ran between two rocks of limestone, was

* The temperature of the water of this stream was 42½°, that of the air in the shade 51½°, and of the earth near the surface 34½°.

composed entirely of clay slate, and the rocks along shore, wherever they appeared, were also of this kind. The beach did not appear to be much beaten by the sea, for the rocks and loose stones that composed it did not bear the marks of much attrition. This may, in a great measure, be attributed to the manner in which it is guarded by ice, for all along shore there was a chain of large pieces of it from eight to ten feet thick, which of course shielded all within it from the violence of the sea, that is to say, if such ever exist.

The most part of this ice was floating when we landed, but when we came off the greatest part of it was aground, having been left on the beach by the ebbing of the tide, which during the three hours we were ashore had fallen six feet. It had ebbed before we landed about eighteen inches, so that the rise and fall of the tide at this place may be estimated at twelve, or fourteen feet. We observed that the ebb set to the southward and westward, consequently the flood must come from that direction, a circumstance which I think must be evident to every person as very much in our favour; for if the flood came from the Atlantic, why not come through the extensive passage formerly called Lancaster's Sound? To this it may be answered, indeed, that the opening or inlet which we are in, may communicate with the Atlantic through Cumberland's Straits, or any of those passages between this and Hudson's Bay, and that the flood may come from that direction. That such may be the case is certainly true, but when a question admits of two solutions, it is not unreasonable to put that construction on it, that is most congenial to a person's views. But to abandon this field of conjecture, I shall briefly state the few remaining occurrences that came under my observation in the course of the day. When speaking of the beach, I omitted to mention, that, in the little pools of water left when the tide ebbed, we found myriads of small shrimps, or what are vulgarly called sea-lice; on the beach there were also a great number of shells of different kinds, the greatest part of those that I saw consisted of the Venus and Mya genera.

Sunday, 8th. — We came this morning to a compact barrier of ice, that extended in an oblique direction from the west land, to the south-east land, or that which we were on yesterday. We were by this means reduced again to two alternatives, viz. to wait here* until an opening might happen to take place in the ice, that would enable us to proceed on, or to return again to the northward, to see if any favourable change had taken place there of which we might take advantage. As the distance we have to go back is not very considerable, it was deemed most proper to retrace our course again to the northward, than to remain inactive at this place. Other considerations might also be mentioned, tending to favour this resolution; in the first place the northern passage, if I may so call the opening described on the 5th instant, appeared to lead directly to the westward, or in fact it seemed to be a continuation of the spacious passage, through which we came from Baffin's Bay; and, in the second place, we have had experience enough of the ice to know that extraordinary changes take place in it, without any apparent cause, for we have often seen the most compact bodies of it opening, without either wind or tide

* Our latitude at noon was 72° 13′ N. and longitude 90° 29′ W., which must have been very nearly the farthest that we went in this inlet.

affecting it in any way that we could perceive. Under these circumstances, we are not without hopes that, by the time we have reached the place alluded to, some favourable change may have taken place in the state of the ice. Although I have thus endeavoured to shew, that the northern passage appears to lead more directly in the way in which we want to go, yet I am far from thinking that the inlet which we are in, does not also communicate with the sea seen by Messrs. Hearne and M'Kenzie. Its extent, indeed, and the depth of water that we have found in it, are too considerable to lead us to suppose that it terminates near where we were when stopped by the ice; for at that place, it must have been at least from forty to fifty miles broad, and the depth of the water, although we were only a few miles from the land, was from thirty to forty fathoms; and yesterday, when we were more amid channel, we tried for soundings with a line of two hundred fathoms up and down, and yet we did not strike bottom.

From these considerations then, in addition to the fact mentioned yesterday respecting the tide, it, I think, appears very obvious, that this inlet communicates with the ocean, through another channel besides that through which we went.

Monday, 9th.—We have been working to the northward all day, along the eastern edge of the ice, that is, between it and the south-east land. In this channel we have, during these few days past, seen such a number of the common, or black whales, that our (Greenland) masters seem to think that an establishment, or factory, situated here for the purpose of killing whales, would be very likely to turn out a lucrative speculation; for, in addition to the oil that might be collected, a vast quantity of ivory might also be procured; for we have seen, during the time that we have been in this inlet, hundreds of narwhals, or sea unicorns, and I understand that their horns are very good ivory. I have of late spoke so often of magnetism, that introducing that subject again, will, I have no doubt, appear little better than a recapitulation of what has already been said. I cannot help mentioning, however, that we observed to-day the compasses to be so much affected by local attraction, that, in whatever direction the ship's head happened to be placed in, the north point of compass pointed towards it. This was more particularly obvious in Captain Kater's suspended needle, which, from the delicacy of its construction, went round regularly as the ship's head moved, when she went about: the other compasses, indeed, traversed so badly, that they frequently remained almost stationary for some time after the ship changed her course; but by being tapped a little by the hand they generally traversed round, until, as I have already said, their north point coincided with the direction of the ship's head. The cause of this directive power of the ship on the compasses may easily be accounted for, at least, it appears to me to be simply thus: that, as the greatest part of the iron in the ship is situated before the binnacles, that is, between them and the ship's head, the north point of the needle will of course be attracted in that direction. It is unnecessary to observe, from what has been said, that the compasses are now become totally useless. An instrument was got up to-day, however, that promises to be a very good substitute for them whenever the sun shines; but when that luminary is not visible, it will be of no manner of use, for it is in fact a sun-dial, divided like the mariner's compass-card into thirty-two points, or rhumbs; and for the sake of greater accuracy these points are again sub-divided into degrees. In the centre of it there is an index, gnomon, or nave, that revolves on a pivot, so that by knowing the time of the day, the course the ship is steering is easily ascertained by turning this index towards the sun; for it is obvious that when the azimuth or bearing of the sun coincides with that point of the dial that is of the same denomination, all the other points of the horizon will correspond with the respective points of the same name on the dial-plate. For instance, at noon, or when the sun is due south, if the point of the dial marked south be turned towards the sun, all the other points of it will be directed to those of the same name in the horizon; and that which points towards the ship's head, if the dial is a midship's, will of course be the direction she is going in at that time. I ought to observe at the same time, that the dial should be adjusted at least every three quarters of an hour, to correspond with the motion of the sun in azimuth, and whenever the ship alters her course it will necessarily require to be adjusted afresh. From these different corrections or adjustments being so often required, it would seem at first to be rather a troublesome guide, and, when compared with that invaluable instrument, the compass, it certainly is so; but under the present circumstances, it is, as I have already remarked, an useful instrument. The makers, and if I mistake not the inventors of this instrument, are Messrs. Atkins and Harris.

Tuesday, 10th. — The weather has been foggy during the greatest part of the day, so that the compass-dial above described has been of very little use to us; our course was so bounded however by the land on one side, and the ice on the other, that a compass was very little required, for it was impossible for us to go much out of our way.

The land that we have passed during these two days, appeared to be as barren as that on which we landed to the southward (on the 7th inst.); it differed from it however in some respects, being in the first place considerably higher, and along the coast much more rugged, not unlike the land on the north side of the passage.

Wednesday, 11*th*.—The weather being foggy the greatest part of the day, it was impossible withou compasses to know which way we were going; we therefore made fast to a floe of ice, and watered the ship from the pools on the surface of it. In the course of the afternoon several Narwhals were seen about the ship; and, as we had nothing particular to do at the time, a boat was lowered and sent after them, to try to kill one if possible; in this they succeeded without much difficulty, for one was secured by the first harpoon, and I have no doubt, had fishing been our object, but many more might have been got. Notwithstanding his size, we managed to hoist him on board without being cut up; we could not conveniently weigh him; but I should imagine from his bulk, when compared with the sea-horse, or Walrus, that we killed some time ago, that he would have weighed upwards of two tons. The different measurements taken of him are inserted in the following page: I have therefore to add only the few remarks that appeared to me worthy of being noticed. In the first place, then, as the horn is the most prominent

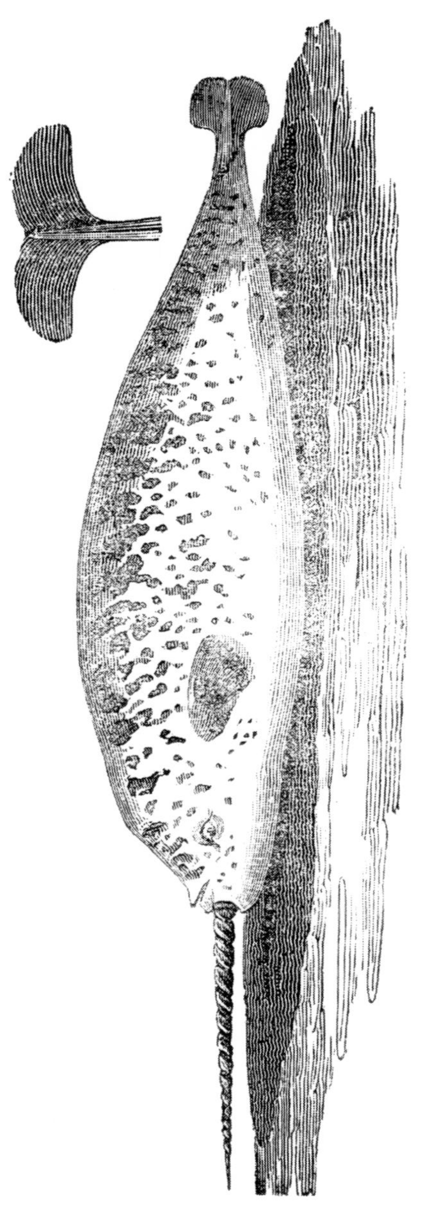

object about this fish, it may not be improper to say a few words respecting it, in addition to the dimensions given below. It protruded from the left side of the upper snout, in a line parallel with the

Dimensions of the Narwhal.	Feet.	In.
Length of the horn * beyond the head - -	4	2
Circumference of the horn at its root - -	0	$5\frac{7}{10}$
Do. at the tip - - -	0	$2\frac{6}{10}$
Length of the body from the root of the horn to the fork of the tail - - - -	13	5½
Estimated circumference of the thickest part of the body	9	0
From the root of the horn to the eye - -	1	0
From the angle of the mouth to the end of the lip -	0	6½
Breadth across the mouth at the broadest part - -	0	9
Depth of the snout across the mouth - -	0	9
From the root of the horn to the fore part of the fin -	2	4½
Breadth of the fins at the root - - -	0	6½
Do. at the broadest part - - -	0	7½
Length of the fins - - - -	1	3
Expansion of the tail - - -	3	4
Depth of do. - - - -	1	2
Circumference of the smallest part of the body; that is, at the place where the tail began to expand -	1	8½
From anus to the fork of the tail - - -	4	6
From the fork of the tail to the teats (two in number) -	4	8
Do. to penis - - -	6	4
Do. to umbilicus - - -	8	0
From the eye to the orifice † of the organ of hearing -	0	5½
Diameter of the spiracle (which was situated in the crown of the head, and 1 foot 2½ inches from the snout) - - - - -	0	2¾
Thickness of the skin - - - -	0	0½
Do. of the blubber, at an average - -	0	3½

* The end of the horn was hollow in consequence of a piece having been broken off. It is probable that at least six inches of it had been broken.

† It was so small that it was some time before we discovered it. It being of a size sufficient only to admit a small probe.

body of the fish taken lengthwise; on the opposite side of the snout there was not the least appearance of a horn, or protuberance of any kind, as is said to be frequently observed in these fish: but much greater anomalies than this have occasionally been met with, for instances are known where the two horns grew to the usual size, and, if I am rightly informed, many instances have occurred where the horn on the right side has protruded through the skin. The female of this fish is said never to have any horns, and, owing to this circumstance, I have been told that it frequently happens at the custom-houses, where our whalers give an account of the fish that they kill during the season, that all the unicorns they have taken are said to be "she ones," in order to evade the duty on the horns. The narwhal has no teeth, nor the appearance of any other substance that can answer as a substitute for them, so that their food, like that of the common whale, must be of a very soft nature; their tongue is also like that of the latter fish, not at all calculated to assist in mastication, being nothing but a mass of soft fat adhering nearly throughout to the under part of the mouth. The eyes were small, considering the size of the fish; they were deep-seated, but not so far in as to be situated in the socket of bone that was underneath them. The form of the eye, or rather of the eyelids, was that of a triangle, whose sides measured about three-fourths of an inch. The tail of the narwhal is like the rest of the cetaceous order, horizontal, and consists, like that of the common whale, of gristly fat, covered with skin, like the rest of the body. The fins are also formed of the same materials, so that it may be said that these fish differ in every respect from the rest of the finny race, except in form, and the element in which they live: they have been indeed very properly named by Dr. Shaw, the fish-formed mammalia. The skin on the back and sides was mottled, of a black and white marble colour, and that on the under part of the body was nearly all white; it was very soft, and was formed, like that of the black whale, of vertical fibres, somewhat like a transverse section of a piece of wood.

Immediately under the skin there was a layer of blubber, from three to four inches thick, which enveloped the whole body; this coating was stripped off and put into casks, and it is expected when boiled to yield from sixty to seventy gallons of oil. The muscular part of the body was exceedingly black, and so soft as to be torn very easily by the hand. The lungs were large and of a light fleshy colour: the heart was also of a very considerable size, but its parietis was not strong in proportion to its bulk The liver was of a dark brown, or chocolate colour, and very oily. The stomach contained nothing but a small quantity of a greenish oily liquid; and the rest of the alimentary canal, although of considerable size, had nothing in it at this time but a small quantity of the same sort of fluid. The kidnies were large, and were composed of a congeries of small round masses like those of an ox. The urinary bladder was not larger than that of the animal just mentioned; the testes were, however, much larger than those of any of our domestic quadrupeds.

I have now only to observe, that the relative situation of all these viscera, was the same as in terrestrial animals of the mammalia kind.

In concluding the diary, or events of the day, I ought to mention that we sounded in the afternoon, whilst fast to the floe, in one hundred and seventy fathoms water, soft clay-coloured mud. Our distance from the east land at the time was from eight to ten miles.

Thursday, 12th. — We observed to-day that the compasses traversed with greater facility than they have done for some time past; Mr. Jennings' insulating compass was found to agree within five degrees with the plane of the magnetic meridian *, so that we may infer, that by going to the northward we recede from the magnetic pole. It must not be understood, however, from this, that the compasses have improved so much as to be of any use yet to navigate, or steer the ships by them; on the contrary, we were obliged to remain fast until six o'clock this morning to the floe that the ships were secured to yesterday forenoon, on account of the weather, during that period, being so foggy that it was impossible to know which way to steer. The distance that we have gone, indeed, from the place where I spoke of the compasses last, is not sufficient to make any great difference in this respect: for our latitude to-day at noon was only 73° N. and longitude 90° 34′ W. We sounded this evening, in one hundred and ninety fathoms water, (soft mud).

* As it is possible that this expression may appear equivocal, it may perhaps be necessary to observe, that by saying that the compass agreed within five degrees with the plane of the magnetic meridian, I meant that the north point of the compass, or rather the needle itself, coincided within five degrees with the plane of the M. meridian, as determined by an azimuth compass on the ice.

Friday, 13*th*. — A boat went ashore this forenoon, to examine an inlet or creek that appeared in the east land, where they found a very good harbour, having an island at the entrance of it, that sheltered it from the violencé of the sea: there was depth enough of water in it for a ship of any size, so that if this place should ever happen to be frequented by shipping, we can assure them of finding at least one secure harbour on this coast. It is situated in latitude 73° 12′ N., and longitude 89° 41′ W.

The land here is much higher, and the coast bolder than to the southward; it is composed however of the same materials, viz. limestone. We find also, as I have frequently observed before, that the depth of the water increases according as the coast becomes bolder; this forenoon when we were only about two miles from the shore, we had no less than one hundred and thirty fathoms water, (soft mud).

Since we got into deeper water, I observed also that the whales have been seen in greater numbers, and as for the narwhals they are seen swimming about at all hours of the day in shoals: it would appear from what we see that this is their time for copulating.

Sunday, 15*th*. — We are still retarded by the ice, which extends, as I have mentioned some time ago, from the north land to the two islands that lie between it, and the south-west land. The distance between these islands and the nearest part of the south-east land (off which we are at present) is found to be considerably less than was expected, when we went down the inlet in which we have been for some days past; from the result of the different angles taken for the purpose of determining the width of this opening, it is found that the distance between the easternmost island, or that first seen, and the S. E. land, is only twenty-eight miles, and between it and the other island still less, being no more than twenty-six miles and a half.

A boat landed to-day again on the east coast, which they found to be more barren, if possible, than where we landed on the 7th inst. From the mineralogical specimens brought off, it appeared to consist, like that to the southward, of limestone, in some pieces of which were found fossil shells, flint, and agate; several pieces of madrepore were also brought on board. A pile of loose stones was erected on the top of a hill, near where the boat landed, under which was buried a quart bottle, containing a slip of paper intimating our being off this coast on such a date. The dip and variation of the magnetic needle was, as might naturally be expected from recent observations, found to be less here than to the southward; the latter was only 115° W. Whilst the boat was on shore, we sounded in one hundred and seventy fathoms water (soft mud), being at the time not more than two miles and a half, or three miles at most, from the land. It is, perhaps, hardly necessary to remark, that the soundings and the formation of the coast corresponded, as I have always observed to be the case before, in the latter being bold, and in some places precipitous.

Monday, 16*th*. — Whilst we were sounding this afternoon, a boat was made fast to the deep-sea-line, in order to try the force and direction of a tide or current that seemed to exist; the result of the trial indicated its direction to be N. N. W. (true), and going at the rate of a quarter of a mile per hour.

The ice forms still a compact barrier to the westward, so that it would be vain to attempt to force through it; we are, as usual, constantly surrounded by whales, unicorns, and, within these two or three days past, seals of the kind called by seamen saddleback, from a dark-coloured stripe across their back.

Thursday, 19th. — Nothing occurred during these two days past deserving of particular notice, the ice forming still a compact body to the westward, all that could be done was to sail about along its edge, watching the first favourable change that might occur, to push through. Although that wished-for change has not yet taken place, there is every prospect to-day that it will soon happen; for a strong breeze of wind sprang up last night from east by north (true), which already seems to have had some effect on the ice, for we found several loose streams, and detached pieces of it, scattered about to-day in all directions. It is probable then, that if the wind veers round to the northward and westward, that we shall soon have a clear passage; for there is plenty of clear water between this and Baffin's Bay to receive an immense quantity of ice. As we have some reason to hope, then, that this will soon take place, we got close in with the north land to-day, in order to be in readiness to get on immediately an opening occurs, which is presumed, from the direction of the wind, will take place between that coast and the ice.

Friday, 20th. — We found to-day, that our anticipations respecting the ice has turned out just as we wished and expected; for a narrow channel was discovered between it and the land, which we entered, as might be expected, with great pleasure; but the wind having become very light after we got close in with the land, we made but little progress; we have the satisfaction, however, of finding, that there is an open channel along the coast as far as we can see to the westward. We got in the afternoon abreast of a deep bay in the north land, where we sounded in one hundred and thirty-two fathoms water, (soft mud).

Sunday, 22d. — The weather was calm the greatest part of yesterday, so that nothing was done worthy of being mentioned. A light breeze sprung up, however, this forenoon, which enabled us to get on a little way. The part of the coast that we passed to-day was very much intersected with bays and inlets, some of which were of considerable extent. The appearance of the land itself was somewhat similar to the same line of coast to the eastward, only it was more broken, and consequently it presented a greater variety of shapes. In some parts of it there were perpendicular cliffs of very great height, but still retaining, like the other parts of this coast already described, a stratified appearance.

As the ships were making but little progress, on account of the lightness of the wind, a couple of boats were sent ashore in the afternoon to a sort of headland off which the ships happened to be at the time; but a breeze of wind having sprung up shortly after we landed, our stay on shore was but very short. A few observations were made, however, by which it was determined that the variation of the compass was 129° W.; the longitude of the place. by sights taken for the chronometers, 91° 55′ W.; and the latitude, by Cole's method, 74° 40′ N. What little we saw of this coast was as barren as any place that we have yet landed on; for, with the exception of stunted poppies, there was scarcely any other vegetable production to be seen on it. It appeared to be also but thinly inhabited by the animal kingdom; for all those that we saw were some mallemucks that were hovering about the face of the rocks, where they apparently had nests; a couple of glaucous gulls, with their young: the old birds were shot, and the two young ones, being unable to fly, were brought on board alive. There was also another gull shot, which was about the size of the glaucouses, and resembled them almost in every other respect, except in having the primary feathers of the wings tipped with black, from which it was concluded to be that species of gull called the *Larus Argentatus*, which forms the connecting link between the glaucous and the herring-gull. Although the land seemed to be but thinly inhabited, the sea appeared to be as well stocked as usual; for, during the short time we were on shore, six large whales were seen close in with the land, and a number of seals and sea-horses were also seen in the course of the day. The land appeared also to be indebted for a considerable portion of its constituent ingredients to the sea; for the rocks, which were of limestone, contained an immense quantity of marine fossil shells, and madrepores. The former, in particular, composed such a large proportion of the fixed rocks, that it would be difficult to find a single fragment of them of any size that did not contain many shells; and if pieces in which they were most abundant were to be selected, hand-specimens might have been got in which there were dozens of them. They were all, or at least all those that I remembered having seen, of the bivalve kind, and appeared to consist chiefly of varieties of the Venus genus.

In that part of the rock that was washed by the sea, I observed some horizontal strata of beautiful white marble; and I saw several loose pieces of it amongst the debris of the rocks that overhang the shore. These rocks, at the place where we landed, rose to the height, I should imagine, of between three and four hundred feet above the level of the sea; but, from the quantity of rubbish that fell from them, the only part of their surface that could be seen, was about twenty feet of their base, where these mouldering remains were washed away by the sea, and from sixty to eighty feet of the top of them, from which the fragments in question fell. Their surface, both at their top and base, was stratified. The strata at the base appeared to be horizontal; but those at the top seemed to dip a little to the westward, — a thing that I observed, indeed, in all the rocks that form this coast to the eastward. And, from other similarities of appearance between the part of the coast that we landed on this afternoon, and that to the eastward, I have little doubt but all of it is composed of limestone. Now, to conclude the remarks that I have been enabled to make during our visit on shore to-day, I have only to add one circumstance, which, I must confess, I feel less pleasure in relating, than any other of the occurrences of the day: it is, that we found the ebb-tide come from the westward. This circumstance may, however, be attributed to localities, so that we have no reason to draw any unfavourable inference from it. The tide ebbed during the time we were on shore, which was about fifty minutes, between ten and eleven inches.

As soon as the boat returned on board, we made all sail to the westward; but the breeze subsided before we got more than a few miles on, and it continued almost a calm during the rest of the afternoon. The weather being fine and clear, we had a very extensive view in the evening, when the sun got low, so that if any thing was wanting to increase our hopes, the prospects before us to-night are certainly quite adequate to satisfy every person; for there are two large openings or passages in sight to the westward, the one leading about north-west, and the other west-south-west (true); the former is perfectly clear of ice, and what ice there is in the latter does not appear to be sufficiently close to obstruct our passage. Before concluding my account of the events of this day, I ought to mention that two icebergs were seen this evening, because they have, for some time past, become rare objects.

Monday, 23d.—Our success to-day has been greater than the most sanguine could have expected, for we were to-day at noon in the ninety-fifth degree of west longitude, having, in the short space of the last twelve hours, got no less than three degrees to the westward; and if it were not for a ledge of ice that we fell in with this afternoon, it is probable that we should have added three degrees more to this day's run. We have no reason to complain, as yet, however, of the delay occasioned by it, for although it has indeed prevented us from making a straight course to the westward, it is not so compact as to obstruct us entirely, or indeed to prevent us from making very considerable progress through the lanes or channels that intersect it. But before I enter any farther into a detail of the occurrences of this day, I must observe, that we are in the southernmost of the two passages mentioned yesterday afternoon; the land between them, indeed, appears to be only an island, for we found after getting round the S. E. end of it, that it trended away to the northward and westward. On the east end of this island, if I may venture to call it so, there are two remarkable hills, resembling at a distance two boats, bottom up: from this circumstance, the headland on which they are situated, obtained the name of Boat Cape. Three or four leagues to the westward of this island, there is another smaller island, which differs from the former in its general features; in the first place it is lower, and in the next place its surface is more regular, and its coast is not bounded by rocks like that on which we landed yesterday; in this last respect, indeed, both these islands differ from the north land, for neither of them, as far as we have yet seen, have what is usually termed, a bold coast. The whole of the space between these two islands is full of ice, the most part of which appeared to be one floe, whose surface differed from what we have generally seen before, for it was full of round hummocks, that rose between two and three feet above the surface of the floe: it was remarked also, that this ice was much heavier than any we have seen before this season, being estimated to be at an average between eight and nine feet thick. It was observed to-day, that, as we came to the southward and westward, the compasses became more sluggish again in their motion, so that it may be presumed we are again approaching the magnetic Pole.

Tuesday, 24th. — I omitted to mention, that when we were abreast of the two islands described yesterday, that there was a long piece of land to the southward of us, which ran in a direction nearly east and west. The distance between this land and the islands above-mentioned, is, as near as we could estimate, about thirty miles. We never came close enough to it to be able to say any thing respecting it, any farther than that it resembled the land on the west side of the inlet that runs to the southward in the ninetieth degree of west longitude, which has already been described; and, from the trending of the north side of that land, as far as we saw it, it is probable that what we saw yesterday is a continuation of it; but as this is a matter of very little consequence to us, it is quite unnecessary to say any more on the subject.

To commence then with an account of the occurrences of the day, I have to observe that we have had another fine run to the westward; for we were at noon in longitude 98° W., and we have every prospect of getting on, indeed, more so, if possible, than we ever had before; for, with the exception of some streams of ice to the southward and westward of us, there is an open sea, as far as our view extends. In addition to that, another circumstance occurred to-day, from which, I think, a favourable conclusion may be drawn. The circumstance in question is, that we have had a fresh and steady breeze all day from the northward, a thing that has not happened before to the same extent since we entered these Straits, if the passage that we have come through may be so denominated; for the wind, whenever it blew steadily for any length of time, has always been from the eastward or westward, or, in other words, in the direction of the passage; and, as far as my own experience goes, and, indeed, by what I can learn from others, it appears to be almost a general rule, in straits, or narrow channels, for the wind to blow either out or into them, particularly when it blows fresh, as was the case to-day. It may be presumed then, upon these grounds, that we have now got an extensive sea to the northward of us. We passed three or four low islands to-day again; but as it would be somewhat difficult, and at the same time of little importance to give their relative situations, with respect to one another, I shall merely observe, that their features are entirely of a different cast from the land to the eastward, their surface being smooth, low, and apparently sandy; the depth of the water corresponds also with the nature of the land, for we sounded at one time in thirty-four fathoms, and the greatest depth of water we sounded in was seventy-eight fathoms.

Wednesday, 25th. — The wind being from the westward to-day, we have not been able to make much progress. The islands mentioned yesterday were in sight all day, and a range of higher land, apparently islands also, were seen to the northward. The sea still continues to be shallower than we usually had it, for we sounded several times to-day in from thirty to forty fathoms water, when at least seven or eight miles from the land.

Thursday, 26th. — The wind still continues to blow from the northward and westward, so that all the ground we have gained for these two days has been by beating to windward between the land and the ice, which we find extends in a compact body to the westward, at the distance of between four and five leagues from the islands to the northward. In some places indeed this channel of clear water is much narrower, but the ice does not in any place, as far as we have yet seen, join the land, and I think it is probable that as long as we find land to the northward to stop the polar ice from drifting down upon us, that we shall always find a passage to the westward along the land. I do not mean, however, to say that a passage will without any interruption be constantly found to exist between the land and the ice; on the contrary, I am aware that a southerly wind may give us occasional checks, by forcing the ice in with the coast, but immediately the wind changes to the opposite direction it will necessarily have the contrary effect. This is not indeed a matter of speculation, nor do I intend it to be considered as such, for both this and last year's experience have afforded us so many instances of the truth of what I have said, that I have no hesitation in giving it as my opinion that the vicinity of land to the northward will always be in our favour. My object in being so particular on this point is, because there are some amongst us quite of a different opinion.

Friday, 27th. — We had a slant of wind in our

favour to-day, which enabled us to make considerable progress, for we were at noon in longitude 102° 30′ W., latitude 75° 03′ N.; and, as far as present appearances go, we have every reason to suppose that, if the wind continues, we shall add a few more degrees to the number before this time tomorrow. No land has been seen to the southward for these three days past, but the ice extends in that direction as far as we can see, and is about the same distance from the islands to the northward as I mentioned yesterday. I ought to observe, that as we came along, more islands have been seen to the northward; they are of the same character as those I described four days ago, that is, low near the coast and rising gradually towards their centre.

Saturday, 28th. — A boat was sent this forenoon to an island to make observations for determining the variation of the compass, which, somewhat to our surprise, was found to have changed from west to east, or, in other words, it exceeded 180°, if the usual term of westerly variation was to be continued. In consequence of the sluggish manner in which the compasses traversed, and the observations being made very near noon, when the sun moved slow in azimuth, the result of these observations were, as might be expected, rather wide of one another, for the first set of azimuths I took gave the variation 167° E.; the next set 168° E.; and the third and last set 169° E.: the magnetic dip, or vertical inclination of the dipping-needle at this place, was 88° 27′.* The place where these observations were

* For the magnetic dips given in different parts of this journal, I am indebted to Mr. Griffiths (of the Griper), who has been good enough to furnish me with these observations.

made we found to be in latitude 75° 9′ N., and longitude, by chronometer, 103° 50′ W. The tide was flowing when we landed, and, during the four hours we were on shore, it only rose sixteen inches; the flood came from the northward and westward. This island was, as near as I could judge, about ten miles in length, that is, if it is taken for granted that its greatest diameter is from north to south or in the direction that we viewed it; but it is possible that I may be premature in thus attempting to give its dimensions before we have seen all round it, for it may extend to the westward farther than we have any idea of yet. It resembled exactly, as to appearance, the islands that we have been passing for several days past, that is, low near the coast, and rising gradually towards the interior. The sea-coast, and a considerable part of the surface of it, indeed, as far as we went inland, was composed of fine sand; and the fixed rocks, wherever they were seen above the surface, was found to consist of white sandstone of a very soft and fine texture; and I have no doubt but the islands that we have passed lately are composed of the same kind of stone, for ever since we got amongst them the soundings have been found to consist of fine sand; whilst that brought up by the lead, when we were passing the high land to the eastward, consisted of soft mud that effervesced when touched with acid. The vegetation on this island was, when compared with what we have lately seen, rather luxuriant; moss in particular grew in considerable abundance in the moist valleys, and along the banks of the streams that flowed from the hills. These streams were, indeed, at this time almost dried up their source, viz. the snow, being entirely dissolved; along the beach, however, there were numerous fragments of heavy floe-ice aground, and in one place there was an extensive ledge of it firmly attached to the beach, with its surface covered with sand, in such a manner, that a cursory observer might take it to be a part of the land.

We saw no animals of any kind on this island; but we found evident proofs of its having been frequented, not only by different species of the brute creation, but that it had also, at some period or other, been inhabited by man; for, at the distance of about a quarter of a mile from the shore, we found the ruins of six huts close together on the side of a hill. From the dilapidated state of these ruins, it was impossible to draw any certain conclusions as to what time they had been inhabited, but it must have certainly been a long time ago, for nothing remained of them but the stones that marked their size and site; and, from the small number of stones that the ruins were composed of, it is probable that they were only temporary residences. They had been all nearly about the same size, that is, about twelve feet long and from eight to ten feet broad, besides a space about three feet square formed by four flags set up on their edge, at the end of each hut. I understand from those that have been often amongst the Esquimaux huts in Greenland, that they have always a small apartment of this sort at one end of their hut, in which they keep all their provisions; so that we may infer from this circumstance that the ruins we have seen to-day belonged to a small tribe or party of Esquimaux that were here probably on a summer excursion. Those inclined to give these ruins greater antiquity, may consider them as one of the resting-places of the Esquimaux in their emigration from Asia to Greenland; for, according to the tradition of the Greenlanders themselves, their forefathers came originally from the westward. But be this as it may, it does not at all appear to me that the ruins we have seen to-day are likely to be one of the stations occupied at that remote period, more especially as a more probable way of accounting for them may be assigned to a party of Esquimaux having visited these islands during some of their excursions from the coast of America; for we know, from Hearne's Account, that that continent is inhabited by these people nearly opposite to where we are.

Although we are left in doubt as to what time this island was visited by man, we have very unequivocal proofs of its being recently inhabited by different animals, for we found numerous tracks of what we supposed to be reindeer, some of them apparently very lately made; and several of their horns, and small portions of their hair, were found in different places where they had been lying. We had an equally good proof of this place being frequented by Musk-oxen (*Bos Moschatus*, Lin.), for we found the skeleton of one in a perfect state, except that the bones of the legs were separated from the rest, most probably by some carnivorous animal. The skull and horns were perfectly entire; but from the appearance of the horns, and indeed of the bones in general, they must have been exposed to the weather at least one winter. Whether the cloven tracks we saw were chiefly those of the musk-oxen, or reindeer, it is impossible to say; but if we were to judge from the number of deer's horns we saw, we should be inclined to consider them as being principally those of the latter animal. It would appear that bears also frequent this land occasionally; for we found two or three of their skulls, and their tracks were pretty numerous along the beach. On the sand-hillocks along the shore, there were immense numbers of small sea-shells of the Venus kind, which had unquestionably been carried there by some animals, for they were considerably beyond the tide-mark.

From all these circumstances, then, it is very evident that this island is frequented occasionally by different kinds of animals, although we had not the good fortune of seeing any of them, which indeed is not to be much surprised at, for the weather became hazy very soon after we landed, and continued so during the whole time we were on shore, so that it would be more a matter of chance than any thing else if we saw any animal.

On the top of a hill, or rather a rising piece of ground, about two miles from where we landed, a pile of loose stones was erected, close by which a quart bottle was left, containing a slip of paper mentioning as usual the ship's name, and our being off this coast on such a day, &c. Whilst the boat was ashore they sounded on board in forty fathoms (mud); and, by making a boat fast to the deep sea-line at the time they were sounding, it was found that a current or tide set to the southward (true) at the rate of half a mile per hour.

Monday, 30th. — The weather being foggy the whole of yesterday, and during the greatest part of this day, it was impossible to know which way to steer amongst the ice, which, during these two days, has, as far as we could see, surrounded us in every direction. Our chief occupation, therefore, during this period, was sounding ; and by means of a small net, and a dredge that were occasionally fastened to the deep-sea-line, a great variety of small shells and star-fish were brought up from the bottom. About five o'clock this afternoon, however, we found employment more congenial to our wishes, for the weather having at that time cleared up, we cast off from a floe to which we had been fast, and made sail to the westward, round the south end of the island on which we landed two days ago.

Tuesday, 31st.—We made fast to a floe of ice again last night and remained there until nine o'clock this forenoon, when we cast off and made sail as near as we could judge to the westward. I have said as near as we could judge, for it was impossible to say with certainty which way we went, for the weather was so hazy the whole day that the sun was never seen distinctly ; but we were able, for most part of the time, to distinguish the direction he was in from the brightness of that part of the heavens, and directed our course by it accordingly, for the compasses have for some days past been again quite useless, their north point being invariably directed towards the ship's head in whatever direction it may happen to be in. At night, then, when the sun went down (for he sets now for a short time) and left us as it were without any means of knowing our way, necessity suggested a plan to steer by, which deserves to be remembered, inasmuch as it is one of the best proofs of the truth of the old proverb, "that necessity is the mother of invention," and at the same time shews under what circumstances we were occasionally obliged to prosecute our voyage. The instance in question, then, that occurred as the only means left for us to direct our course by, was to keep the Griper right astern of us; which was her position when we shaped our course by the last faint view we had of the sun. We sounded frequently during the night, and indeed throughout the whole day, as a necessary precaution under the circumstances we were placed in. The greatest depth of water we found during the whole day was fifty-two fathoms, and the least twenty-three fathoms (mud and sand). We had ice around us in every direction the whole day, but we never found it so close at any time as to obstruct our passage; and, had it not been for the state of the weather, it is probable that we should have found openings clear of it altogether. We had, in the course of the day, a very good view of the manner in which the floe-ice is formed; for the surface of the water being smooth, the snow that fell upon it formed what is called sludge, which, no doubt, had the weather been a few degrees colder, would have become ice. In those places where there was a considerable portion of open space between the larger pieces of ice, the undulations of the surface of the water gave this sludge a curious variegated appearance, not unlike the painted imitations of blue and white marble, the sludge forming the white, and the surface of the water the blue part of it.

Ever since we got amongst these low islands, it has been remarked that very few birds, or indeed animals of any kind, have been seen. A few Mallemucks and Seals, I believe, would comprise the whole list.

Wednesday, September 1*st.*—When the weather cleared up this morning, we found ourselves within three or four miles of what appeared to be another flat island, apparently of greater extent than any of those we have passed to the eastward. The eastern extreme of it bore at this time N. by W. (true), and the western extreme due W. (true). We happened to be sounding at the time it was seen, and, notwithstanding the nature of the land, we found ourselves in forty-five fathoms' water, soft mud.

Melville Island.

We have been running along this land (for it is presuming too much to call it an island), the whole day, and we find that it presents, as far as we have yet seen, the same appearance as that part of it that we first saw in the morning; that is, low near the coast, and rising gradually towards the interior, but the height of any part of it we have yet seen is very inconsiderable. Its surface is, generally speaking, even, and is, I may almost say, entirely clear of snow, for I saw only one or two small patches of it the whole day; the sea to the southward, however, is covered with ice as far as we can see, and along the shore there are pieces of it aground all the way that we have come to day, but the channel between the land and the ice is sufficiently wide for our purpose, being at an average from two to three leagues in breadth, and the least depth of water that we sounded in to-day was seventeen fathoms, and it was supposed that we were on a bank, for we were at the time about five miles from the land. I believe that I have omitted to mention that no land has been seen to the southward since the 24th of last month, all the islands that we have passed since, being to the northward of us.

The same paucity of animals, as I observed yesterday, still exists; a solitary Phalarope was the only bird seen to-day, and one or two seals were all that we saw of the watery inhabitants.

Thursday, 2d.—The wind having died away about noon, two boats were sent ashore to make observations, and to afford a party of the officers an opportunity of having an excursion on the land that we have been coasting along during these two days. We found it to be inhabited, like the island that we landed on, on Saturday last, with musk-oxen and reindeer: of the latter we saw a couple, but they were so frightened by the sight of a dog that we had with us, that we could not get near them.

From the immense number of cloven tracks, and the great number of deer and musk-oxen's horns that we met with, it is very clear that this land must be well stocked with these animals; a great part indeed of the body and skin of one of the latter animals was found in such a perfect state, that there was no doubt of its having been killed this summer. The hair was exceedingly long, and as fine as any wool; its prevailing colour was black, mixed with a little white hair of the finest texture, and shorter than the other. Several of the skulls and tracks of bears were also found here, so that we may presume that they are likewise inhabitants of this land; and on the top of many of the dry hillocks that we passed, we found numerous burrows, some about the size of rabbit holes, and others much smaller; the former we supposed to be fox-holes, and the latter of field-mice. That mice are inhabitants of this land is beyond a doubt, for we saw a great many of their skeletons lying about the holes above mentioned. Of the feathered tribe I believe only one species was seen, namely, the Ptarmigan, and of these several were shot by some of the officers of the Griper; but whilst we were ashore, several large flocks of snow-buntings passed the ships, a flock of geese, and another of ducks, were also seen coming off from the land, most probably commencing their migration to a milder climate.

Along the beach, there were an immense number of small shrimps, and various kinds of shells, the latter indeed we found abundantly scattered about every where as far inland as we went, being, no doubt, as I have already observed, carried there by birds, or some quadruped that feeds on the animals they contain. The soil of this land is much superior to any that we have yet seen in these regions; along the shore indeed, and for a little distance inland, it consists only of fine sand, but, beyond this, the surface is covered with black mould, which, in a temperate climate, I have no doubt would be very productive, for even here, in the valleys and places where there was any moisture, it produced grass of considerable length, and the finest moss in abundance. At this time, however, the soil was so much dried up, that the greatest part of the vegetation was in a state of decay.

My description of this land to the eastward, renders it unnecessary to say any more about it, for the formation of it where we landed to-day, agrees exactly with that described yesterday. Of its minerals, little, or, I may say, nothing, can be said, for rocks, or even loose stones, of any size, were rarely to be seen. On the tops of the hills and places where nothing grew, the surface was covered with small pieces of a greenish friable stone, that crumbled easily by the pressure of the hand. A few small pieces of quartz, clay, slate, and limestone, were also occasionally met with; but, as I have already said, not in sufficient abundance to be considered as forming a constituent part of the country.

Several sets of azimuths were taken on shore, but we found that their results taken separately differed in the same manner as those taken at the last place where we landed; collectively, their mean result gave the variation 149° easterly. The dip, or vertical inclination of the magnetic needle, was found to be greater at this place, than at any other, where it has been tried before, being 88° 45′. The latitude of the place where these observations were made, was 74° 58′ N. and longitude by chronometer 107° W. We had much pleasure to-day again, in finding that the flood-tide comes from the westward; it was ebbing when we landed, and it was found that during the five hours we were on shore, it only fell about four feet, so that we may conclude that the rise and fall of the tides at this place are very inconsiderable. If we were to judge, however, of their rise and fall from another circumstance that was observed, we should be apt to draw a very different conclusion: the circumstance I allude to, is the skeleton of a whale, and some pieces of fir-wood, that were found at the distance of between two and three hundred yards from the beach, and which were supposed to have been washed up there by the sea. That the wood had been carried hither by the sea, is I think beyond a doubt* ; and as to the bones of the whale, it is very obvious from whence they came. The only way then in which I can reconcile this fact, with the rise and fall of the tide, is by supposing that, in the spring, when the ice breaks up, pieces of it may be driven up considerably beyond the tide-mark, by the violent shock, or pressure of one floe being driven upon another by the wind, &c., consequently, whatever happens to be lying on the beach will, of course, be forced inland by the ice. That floes do force smaller pieces of ice on shore in this manner, when they happen to come with velocity against the land, is a fact that I have no hesitation in affirming to be true, from the many instances that I have seen of ice aground where we knew it could not have been floated by the tide. I am not disposed, however, to assert that this is the way in which the bones and pieces of wood in question, were carried to the place where they were found; I have only suggested that they might possibly be driven there by the above means.

* The pieces of wood in question bore indeed evident marks of their having been brought here by the sea, for they were bruised into thin laminæ, and fibres, by the pressure of the ice.

Friday, 3d. — We were coasting along the land again to-day, but the wind being very light we made but little progress; our longitude in the afternoon by chronometer was only 108°. We have the satisfaction however of finding that want of wind is our only obstacle, for the sea is quite clear along the land.

Saturday, 4th. — At seven o'clock this afternoon, we accomplished the first portion of the discovery of the north-west passage, deemed by the British government worthy of reward! for at that hour we crossed the meridian of 110° of longitude, west of Greenwich. The exact time of our crossing it was well ascertained, for we had good sights for the chronometers at six o'clock P.M., the mean of which gave longitude 109° 50′ W., and the patent log shewed when the other ten miles had been accomplished. The only land in sight at this time was that on which we landed two days ago, and it is somewhat remarkable, that, at this very place, there should be a bold cape, which is indeed the first and only high land that we have seen since we made this coast. The ridge of high land, or mountains, that terminated in this promontory, extended inland as far as we could see. A little to the westward of the above cape, a low projecting point of land juts out to the southward, so as to form between them a sort of open bay. The land to the westward of this assumes again its usual form, namely, low, smooth, or even surfaced, and rising gradually from the coast towards the interior. The sea to the southward is still covered with ice, but there is as usual an open channel between it and the land, as far as we can see to the westward, so that nothing appears to be wanting but a brisk breeze of wind to enable us to get on. I observed this afternoon a notable instance of the restless, or ambitious disposition of the human mind, for I remarked, that for some time past, mostly every person expressed it as the consummation of their wishes, if we could only reach the longitude of 110° W. this season; but no sooner was this completed, than it was begun to be computed, what time it would take us to reach the longitude of 130° W., or the second place specified by the late Order in Council respecting the north-west passage; and some are even so sanguine as to consider it very probable, that we shall get that far before the winter sets in. It is not my intention to make any animadversions on the subject, nor did I indeed mention the above circumstance with any other view, than merely, as I have said, to show that, when man is possessed of any object that he may have been in pursuit of, so far from being satisfied therewith, he immediately sees another object, the possession of which would, in his opinion, add more to his happiness than that which he has obtained. In the instance in question, however, I think our ambition is a very laudable one; and however improbable its accomplishment may appear, we certainly ought to live in hopes.

Sunday, 5th. — I omitted to mention in my diary of yesterday's occurrences, that we passed, early in the morning, a part of the coast where there was an opening in the land which some were disposed to consider as an inlet, or division between the part of the land that we are abreast of at present, and that on which we landed on the 2d instant, or, in other words, that they are two distinct islands. I am inclined, however, to think, that this is not the case, for in the first place we passed the opening in question at night, so that it was impossible to say, with any degree of certainty, how far it extended; and, from the great length of this land, it is but natural to suppose that it has considerable breadth also, and that the opening above mentioned is only a deep bay or inlet that runs into it. After prayers to-day, all hands we called on deck, when Mr. Parry told the ship's company, in an official manner, that we had last night passed the meridian of 110° west of Greenwich, and by that means became entitled to the reward of 5000*l.* promised by parliament to the first ship that reached that longitude beyond the Arctic circle. He took also this opportunity of informing them, how highly satisfied he was with their past conduct, and that he had no doubt, by their continuing the same zeal and perseverance they have hitherto shown, but that we shall ultimately accomplish the object of the expedition, and by that means become entitled, not only to the whole of the pecuniary reward, but to the much more lasting honour of being the first discoverers of the north-west passage; an honour, indeed, which our most illustrious navigators for centuries back sought for in vain. The enthusiasm excited by this short, but pathetic speech, was truly astonishing, for the ardour that it inspired might be seen in every countenance; and I have no doubt whenever an opportunity occurs of showing the impression it made, its good effects will be very evident; but, to do every officer and man on the expedition justice, I firmly believe they require no stimulus to urge them to their duty. In the afternoon we came to a low projecting point of land, from which a ledge of compact ice extended to the southward until it joined the main body of it. As it would be in vain to attempt to pass through this barrier, we prepared to anchor, and at three o'clock P. M. we came to with the small bower, in eight and a half fathoms' water, at the distance of about three quarters of a mile from the shore. I think it may be considered a remarkable instance in our voyage, that the first anchor we let go since we left England was in the 110° of west longitude.*

Monday, 6th. — A boat went on shore last evening after we anchored with two or three of the officers, who, as usual, erected a pile of loose stones in a conspicuous place; close by which they buried a quart bottle, containing a slip of paper, on which was written the ships' names, and the rest of the information usually given on these memorials. We landed again this forenoon at the same place, for the double purpose of making observations†, and bringing on board a quantity of turf, which was reported by some of those who went ashore last evening to be found here in considerable abundance, and of a quality that promised that it would be found useful as an article of fuel. That which was brought on board, however, does not appear to answer the favourable report made of it; but from what I can

* The place where we anchored this afternoon, is, I believe, to be called Coppermine Roads, in consequence of its being in the same longitude as the mouth of the river of that name, which Mr. Hearne travelled to.

† The latitude of the place where we landed to-day was found to be 74° 46′ 46″ N., and longitude, by the chronometers, 110° 50′ W., the variation, by the mean of several azimuths, 127° E., and the dip 88° 30′.

learn, those who went for it, had not the good fortune of falling in with the spot where the best kind of it was seen yesterday. Another article of fuel was found to-day, however, which, if we should have the good luck of finding in a considerable quantity, will be of the most essential benefit to us. The article I allude to is coal, several small pieces of which was found by different persons scattered about on the surface of the ground; but not in sufficient quantity to be of any other use than as specimens of mineralogy. All the pieces of it that I saw were of a slatey texture, light, and burnt quickly with a clear white flame, and its colour had something of a brownish tinge. The basis of this part of the coast is composed of white sandstone, and the greatest part of the surface of the little peninsula * on which we landed, was also covered with loose fragments of the same material. The vegetable productions at this place were less abundant than where we landed on the 2d instant to the eastward, but our stay on shore was so short, that we saw but little of the country; but, if we were to judge from the general appearance of the land, we should suppose it to be equally as productive as any other part that we have yet seen of this coast. No quadruped of any kind was seen, but we found traces of the place being frequented by rein-deer, and musk-oxen, for besides their tracks being very numerous, several of their horns and bones were found scattered about. Of the feathered tribe

* This peninsula was formed by a sort of open bay on one side, and a little inlet or harbour on the other; one of the boats sounded the mouth of this harbour, and found the greatest depth of water to be only fourteen feet.

a considerable number were seen, particularly ducks, which were observed in small flocks along the shore, but they were so shy that we could not get within gun-shot of them; several glaucous gulls, and tern were also seen, and they seemed likewise to keep at a greater distance than usual. A solitary seal, I believe, was the only inhabitant of the sea seen to-day.

Tuesday, 7th. — We weighed between four and five o'clock yesterday afternoon, but we had not been above four hours under sail when we were obliged to make fast to a floe, the ice being so close in with the land that it was impossible to force through it. We remained in this place until two o'clock this afternoon, at which time the ice being observed to slacken, we cast off from the floe and made sail; but we had not got on above a few miles, when we found ourselves stopped again by the ice. Our only alternative was, therefore, to secure the ships again to a floe close in with the land, to prevent our drifting to the eastward; for we found the ice, at a little distance from the coast, to be moving in that direction with considerable velocity: most probably by the action of the tide. As we were coasting along this afternoon, two herds of musk-oxen were seen grazing at the distance of about three-quarters of a mile from the beach. One herd consisted of nine, and the other of five of these cattle. Our distance from them was too considerable to enable us to have any thing of a good view of them. I shall, therefore, merely observe, that their prevailing colour was black, and as far as we could judge, their size was about equal to that of a Shetland cow. We had also a distant view of two rein-deer this afternoon, so that

I am in hopes that we shall be able, before long, to give a better account of some of them, than the bare statement of a distant sight.

Wednesday, 8*th*. — The ice still forms a compact body to the westward, so that it would be vain to attempt to force through it. We found that, during the flood-tide, it drifts, as I mentioned yesterday, to the eastward: we, therefore, in the afternoon, cast off from the floe to which we had been fast, and towed the ships to a hummock of ice that was aground in twelve fathoms' water, at about a quarter of a mile from the shore, where they were secured, to prevent their being carried to the eastward along with the drifting ice. A party of the officers that went on shore to-day killed several grous, and a white hare (*Lepus Variabilis*, Lin.): a fox, some field-mice, several snow-buntings, were seen, and a large white bird, supposed to be an owl, probably the snowy owl of Pennant and Letham, (*Strix Nyctea*, Lin.) Four musk-oxen were also seen to-day before the boats landed, but those who went on shore had not the good fortune of falling in, or even seeing them after they landed. Several pieces of coal were picked up again to-day, and it was found that the same soil, mineral, and vegetable productions, prevail here as at the last place we landed.

Friday, 10*th*. — The wind being these two days past chiefly from the southward and westward, has consequently kept the ice closely packed in with the land, so that we are still obliged to remain in the same place that we have come to on Wednesday last. As nothing particular has been doing during this period, parties have been away for most part of the time shooting.* Their success hitherto, however, has not been very considerable, for two or three hares and a few grous are all that have been killed. All the hares are perfectly white, and of a large size; one of the first of them that was killed weighed eight pounds, which, I believe, is about the average weight of all of them that we have seen since. The plumage of a few of the grous are also entirely white, but generally the backs and coverts of the wings are speckled with rusty yellow and dark spots, but the colour of the under part of the body of all of them is white. They are rather larger than the common partridge, but not quite so heavy as the red grous, or *Tetrao Scoticus* of Letham. A musk-ox was seen by some of the men who were on shore yesterday, one of whom fired at him, and, according to his own account, wounded him, but not mortally, for, after spurring or tossing up the ground for a little time, he took to the hills with greater speed than an animal of his shape was supposed capable of going. Although we have not yet seen many of these animals, it is very evident that this land must be frequented, if not constantly inhabited, by them in great numbers: for their bones and horns are found scattered about in all directions, and the greatest part of the carcase of one of them was seen to-day by one of the

* A party went also to gather coals yesterday, and although it may be said that they were pretty successful when the quantity they collected is compared with what we have usually seen of it, yet I am not inclined to believe that we shall replenish our stock of fuel much in this country, unless we have the good fortune of discovering a bed of coal, for, after some hours' search in the place where it appeared to be most abundant, they only brought on board about half a bushel.

parties that were on shore. The skulls of two carnivorous animals have also been picked up here ; one of them is evidently that of a wolf, and the other, which is considerably smaller *, appears to be the skull of some animal of the feline tribe, most probably the amorock of the Greenlander, which is supposed to be an animal of the lynx species. For the description that John Sackhouse (the Greenlander that accompanied us last year) gave of it, appeared to make it an animal of this kind, for, if I am well informed, he described it as being very clear-sighted, and that it bounced with great rapidity on its prey. Notwithstanding the tide has such influence in driving the ice about, we find that its rise and fall is very inconsiderable, for, by a staff planted in the tide-mark on the beach, it appears to be no more than three feet ; its effects on the ice, however, is the same as I have already mentioned, that is, carrying it to the eastward during the flood-tide, and the ebb-tide in the contrary direction. It has been remarked that the ice we have seen of late appears to swim lighter than that in Baffin's Bay. In order, therefore, to determine whether there is any real difference in its specific gravity or not, I made a cube † from a piece of the hummock, to which the ships were fast these two days ; and from

* It is much broader, however, in proportion to its size than the wolf's skull ; in its shape it resembled very much the skull of the wild cat, but was considerably larger.

† The sides of this cube measured one foot three inches and a half, and when floating in the sea alongside the hummock of ice from which it was made, two inches and three quarters of it remained above the surface of the water. The temperature of the water at the time was 31°.

the result of the experiment it appears, that it is specifically lighter than any ice that we have ever submitted to a similar trial before; there being about one-fifth of it above the surface of the water ; whereas, in the former experiments of the same kind that were made at different times, we generally found that one-seventh was about the proportion of the ice above, to that below the surface of the water.

Saturday, 11*th*. — One of the parties that were on shore to-day shot a musk-ox, but he was so far from the ships that they could not bring him on board. I shall therefore forbear saying any thing respecting him in this place, as we shall most probably have him on board to-morrow, and then a particular description will be given of him. I may observe, however, in the meantime, that a stake of him brought on board, was found to be much more palatable than we had reason to expect, from the accounts given of the rankness, or musky taste of their flesh. The specimen that we have had of it to-day, however, is perhaps not sufficient to enable us to say much for or against the matter; but I am in hopes that we shall soon be able to speak with certainty on the subject, for a herd of seven or eight of them were seen by another party that were on shore to-day, but the weather becoming rather thick, they were deterred from following them. I may remark, indeed, in this place, that the weather has within these two or three days past assumed a very wintery aspect, for the sky is almost constantly cloudy, the wind is much sharper than usual; and whenever we have a calm, as has been the case for most part of this day, there is always a little snow falling. In fact, every thing tends to indicate the approach of winter; at night, in particular, when the sun goes down, it is impossible to avoid reflecting on the nearness of that period that will inevitably arrest our progress for this season. It is possible, indeed, and I hope probable too, that if we once got through the ice with which we have of late been hampered, that we may get on a few degrees yet before the winter sets in; but certainly the advanced period of the season, and our experience of these seas, does not encourage us to be too sanguine of doing much more this year.

Sunday, 12th. — A good deal of anxiety prevailed to-day for the safety of a party of six men and an officer (the master) belonging to the Griper, who went away about four o'clock on Friday morning, with a view of travelling fifteen or twenty miles inland, for the purpose of ascertaining the nature of the country, and to see whether reindeer, or musk-oxen were more numerous towards the interior than along the sea-coast. It was desirable also to know how far this land extended to the northward; but, as it was not intended that they should be away more than a day, they took only provisions enough with them to last that period. They have now, however, been away upwards of double that time, which begins to cause some uneasiness respecting them, more especially as the weather since yesterday afternoon, has been very unfavourable for them, being hazy, and snowing almost constantly during the whole time. In order to direct them, poles, with flags on them, have been set up on the top of the highest hills in the neighbourhood to-day, and to each of these poles a bottle was fastened, containing directions how to find their way to the next post, and ultimately, to the ships. At two of the larger poles (on one of which an ensign, and on the other an union-jack were hoisted) provisions were also left for them; and, after dusk, a large fire was lighted on the top of one of the most conspicuous hills near the coast; and, on the top of a pole erected at the same place, was fastened a lanthorn, which, from its elevated situation, must be seen at a considerable distance. Lights are also hoisted at the ship's mast-heads, guns are fired, and rockets set off at regular intervals; in fact, every thing has been done, and still is doing, that can be deemed likely to be of any service in directing the party in question to the ships.

Monday, 13*th*. — Arrangements having been made last night, four parties started at day-light this morning in different directions, in hopes of falling in with the unfortunate people above-mentioned, for such we had to-day every reason to consider them; for the length of time they had been absent, the inclement state of the weather during these two days past, and the inadequate manner in which they were provided to withstand it and hunger together, were certainly sufficient reasons to put every person in a state of anxiety, if not apprehension, for their safety. In the afternoon, however, we were relieved from this state of inquietude by the appearance of one of our parties returning with four of them. From them we learned that the other three could not be far distant, because they only parted with them yesterday; moreover, the officer who went with the party is one of the three that are now missing, and from knowing him to be an intelligent man, every person felt satisfied that they would soon make their appearance also ; and before dark we had the satisfaction to find our expectations fulfilled. The feet of most of them are very much frost-bitten, and they are all very much fatigued, but I have no doubt, from the proper manner in which they were managed on first coming on board, but that they will all in a short time get perfectly well. With regard to food, it appears that they were by no means badly off, for they managed to kill as many grous as they could eat. It appears that they lost their way the second day, or rather the night of the first day, they went away ; consequently, very little information can be gathered from them as to where they had been during the rest of the time. They seem to think that they were never above twenty, or at most five-and-twenty, miles inland. They found the country, after travelling fifteen or twenty miles from the coast, to be much more fertile than in the neighbourhood of the sea; the vallies and level plains in particular they describe as abounding with grass and moss. On these plains they saw several herds of reindeer, and two animals of the deer kind, but much larger than the reindeer ; they supposed them to be the elk, and their description of them seems to answer to that which we have of these animals. They saw also a number of hares inland, but no musk-oxen. Some of those, however, who have been in search of the stray party during these two days past, saw some herds of these cattle. In the course of their wandering, they fell in with a small lake of fresh water, in which they found fish, two of which they brought on board were found to be a species of trout. As it was after they lost their way they fell in with this lake, they of course cannot say what direction it is in, or how far it is off: they describe it to be about two miles in length and one in breadth. Before I conclude my account of the mixed feelings and occurrences of this day, I cannot help mentioning an event that took place, which, although of no great moment in itself, yet, owing to the time that it happened, we could not avoid feeling it as an additional misfortune at the time. The event in question is an accident that happened to one of the seamen (named William Lancaster), who was inadvertently coming up the ship's side with a pot of water off the ice, when one of the guns was fired to direct the parties on shore, by which he got his face, breast, and right arm very severely scorched with the powder.

Tuesday, 14*th*. — It may be considered a very fortunate circumstance that the stray party returned yesterday, for had they been out last night, it is more than probable that they would not have outlived it; for it came on to blow very fresh after sunset, and the thermometer at three o'clock in the morning fell as low as 9°, and the average temperature ever since has been no more than 15°, so that we may very reasonably conclude that people exhausted in the way in which they were would have very little chance of withstanding the rigour of such weather for any length of time.

Wednesday, 15*th*. — The weather being clear today gave us an opportunity of ascertaining the geographical situation of this place. The latitude was found to be 74° 27′ N., and longitude, by chronometer, 112° 11′ W. It is, perhaps, proper to remark, that these observations may be a little out, as the altitudes were taken with the natural horizon, which was covered with ice. The error thereby occasioned cannot amount, however, to any thing very considerable in the latitude, but I conceive it best to mention under what circumstances observations are taken, when there is any chance of their being doubtful.

Thursday, 16*th*. — We had the pleasure of finding this morning that the strong north-west wind that we have had during these two days past has forced the ice off from the land for a little distance; no time was lost, therefore, in availing ourselves of this opportunity of getting on; but our success was not of long duration, for, after getting between eighteen and twenty miles to the westward, we were stopped again by the ice, which extended in a compact body from the land to the southward and westward as far as we could see. It was very heavy ice, but it was broken up so much that we could not get a piece large enough to make the ships fast to; and the water was found to be so deep, that it was not deemed prudent to anchor so close in with the shore as it would be necessary to do; we, therefore, stood back to the eastward again, and at half past eight o'clock we made fast to a hummock of ice aground in fifteen fathoms' water, about seven or eight miles to the westward of the place which we started from in the morning. After passing a headland four or five miles to the westward of where we made fast this evening, we found that the land trended to the northward and westward, and that its formation beyond this cape is also quite different from any part of this coast to the eastward, being more like the land on the north side of the passage between the 86° and 92° of west longitude, that is, bold, and in some places precipitous, and the debris that fell from it forming buttresses in the same manner as on the coast alluded to.

Friday, 17*th*. — We cast off again this morning, and stood to the westward until we came to the ice which we found to be nearly in the same situation where we were stopped by it yesterday. It was observed to be much heavier than what we have generally met with before, being somewhat like that which they describe the Greenland ice to be; so that I think it is most probable, that it is not formed here, but drifts down from higher latitudes, or what may be termed the Polar Sea.

It was packed equally as close in with the land as we found it to be yesterday, so that it would be vain to attempt to force through it; besides, the land, as I have already said, trends to the northward, a circumstance which may be regarded as rather against us; for were it possible even to get on between the land and the ice, as we have usually done, it would in the present instance only take us out of our way.

We know so little, however, of what is before us, that it is perhaps hazarding too much, to say that a change in the direction of the coast is to be considered at once as an unfavourable circumstance. I shall therefore not dwell any longer on the subject, as we shall most probably have an opportunity very soon of determining the point in question in a more satisfactory manner than by conjectures. After tacking about for some time along the edge of the ice, we stood again to the eastward, and at six o'clock in the afternoon made fast to a hummock of ice aground about a cable's length from the shore, and nearly in the same place that we started from in the morning. We had not been fast above two hours when it was observed that the ice was closing in upon us; to avoid therefore getting jammed between it and the land, we cast off again, and kept sailing about during the remainder of the night, wherever we could find clear water.

Saturday, 18*th*. — It froze so hard during the night, that at six o'clock this morning the ships were regularly beset in the bay-ice: we tried to send the boats to a piece of ice aground near the shore, with a hawser to make the ship fast to it, but it was found that the young ice was already too strong for them to get through it. We were therefore obliged to let go an anchor in thirty-nine fathoms' water, to prevent our being carried to the westward (amongst the heavy ice) by a strong tide or current that was setting in that direction. It now appeared, from the effects of last night, and indeed from the state of the weather for this week past, that the winter has at length fairly set in, and that, unless some strenuous exertions are made, we are likely to get beset here for the winter, and as far as appearances go, we could not be caught in a less desirable place, for it is a completely exposed coast, without a bay, or even a projection of any kind in the land to afford the least shelter.

After duly considering all these circumstances, then, it will be seen that further attempts to prosecute the voyage any further this season, would be endangering the safety of the ships, and that too without the prospect of any benefit. We therefore got under weigh between nine and ten o'clock in the forenoon; and very much against our inclination, although to all clearly necessary, we stood to the eastward, in hopes of being able to reach the harbour that we passed on the sixth instant, before the ice got too strong to force through it. From noon until six o'clock in the evening, we were favoured with a fine breeze from the southward and westward, so that we got back a considerable distance; but no sooner had the wind become light than our progress was stopped by the bay-ice, notwithstanding every effort was made to force through by breaking it up with capstan bars, blocks of wood, and by rolling a boat amongst it under the ship's bows. At the very time that our progress was thus arrested, the necessity of getting on became more evident than ever, for a large floe was observed to be moving to the westward with considerable velocity, and at the same time closing in with the land, from which we were not distant above a quarter of a mile. Our situation was therefore a very precarious one indeed, but as it was impossible to avoid the danger that threatened us, we let go an anchor in ten fathoms of water, after being driven within less than a cable's length of the shore. Here we awaited with great anxiety the approach of the floe, for although we were driven towards the shore by it, we were not actually in contact with the floe itself, but were carried along with the bay-ice that it impelled towards the land. Close to where we anchored there happened, very fortunately for us, to be a large hummock, or rather a pile of heavy pieces of ice aground, so that when the floe arrived, this pile received the shock of it, and the collision was certainly tremendous; for immense masses of the floe were broken off, and piled up on the top of what was already aground, from which most of them fell, or slided back again on the floe, and this operation continued for some time, until at length the force of the floe, which was at first going at the rate of two miles per hour, was almost entirely spent. It is unnecessary to observe, that had the ships been caught between the floe and the hummock just mentioned, that their destruction would have been inevitable.

Sunday, 19*th*. — Although we escaped last night without sustaining any damage, the Griper was not quite so fortunate, for she lost an anchor and the best part of a chain cable, by the edge of the floe touching it * as it passed. The boat that they had under the bows breaking the bay-ice was also carried away by the floe. But these are trifling losses when we consider what mischief might have happened had not the pile of ice before mentioned fended off the violent pressure of the floe; for had the ships received the shock, I have little doubt but it would have forced them up on the beach; and had we indeed been only but a few yards nearer the outer extremity of the heap of ice in question, the consequences might have been equally destructive. Nothing occurred to-day worthy of notice, the ice being closely packed all around us, we had no other choice but to remain still in the same place where we brought up last night.

Monday, 20*th*. — Between four and five o'clock in

* I have understood since that the cable was not carried away, but unshackled in order to get clear of the ice.

the morning, the ice was again observed to be moving to the westward; every necessary precaution was immediately taken, to secure the ships in such a manner as to be protected as much as possible, by the hummock or pile of ice so often mentioned, the measures adopted had the desired effect with us; but the Griper was again less fortunate, for about half past eight o'clock the edge of one of the floes that were passing at the time having come against her, she was forced in a few minutes aground on the beach; fortunately, however, it happened to be low water at the time, so that when the tide flowed, she got off without sustaining any damage. But her situation for some time was certainly critical, for when she heeled over, there were only six feet water on that side next the shore, but the beach happened very luckily to consist of sand, so that no injury was occasioned by it.

The wind being from the northward and eastward, and blowing pretty fresh all day, has cleared the immediate neighbourhood of the coast of ice, so that I am in hopes that the first slant of fair wind that we have will enable us to get on. Every day, indeed, tends to show the necessity of getting on as quickly as possible to some place of security, for the weather of late has been, I may almost say, constantly cold, and boisterous; and the drift snow that comes off from the land, gives the whole scene a dreary aspect. A musk ox was seen last night going along the beach, and two or three covies of grous have been seen at different times from the ships; but at present something of greater moment than going after them, employs every one's attention.

Wednesday, 22d. — It blew very strong from the northward all yesterday, so that it was not deemed prudent to get under weigh, more especially as the ice was observed to be moving about with greater velocity than usual, owing no doubt to the force of the wind. Early this morning, however, the wind moderated a little, and at the same time veered round to the northward and westward. Of this favourable change we took immediate advantage, and at five o'clock was under weigh, in order to make the best of our way to the eastward. We suffered very little interruption from the heavy ice, but our progress was so much obstructed by the young, or bay-ice, that had we not been favoured with a strong breeze of wind, it would have been impossible to force through it. We had a good opportunity to-day of seeing the effects of the frost, in forming ice on the surface of the sea, at a time even when there was a strong wind, and consequently a considerable ripple on the water, circumstances which by some men have been considered capable of preventing the formation of ice. But I think from what we have seen to-day, that we may very reasonably conclude, that when the cold is very intense, ice may be formed on the surface of the sea, even in a gale of wind; for the thermometer to-day was never below 17°, and yet ice was, as I have already said, forming very rapidly. It may be said indeed, that there was so small a portion of the surface of the water clear of old ice, that there could not be much of a sea running, and such was certainly the case; but I observed that the young ice, or sludge as it is first called, smoothed the surface of the water immediately it began to form, in the same manner as oil does when poured on a turbulent sea. It appears to me then, that ice may by formed in an open sea, even in the most boisterous weather, provided the temperature is as low, as we have reason to expect it to be, in these regions in the winter; there may be also another requisite, which is, that the water should be, as in these seas, not very deep.

But as future experience may enable us to speak with more certainty on this subject, I shall avoid saying any thing more about it at present. And to finish my account of the occurrences of the day, I have only to add, that between seven and eight o'clock in the evening we brought to, about two miles to the eastward of the place, where we let go the first anchor, on the 5th instant.

Thursday, 23d. — We got under weigh this morning, and ran in within three-quarters of a mile of the entrance of Coppermine Harbour, where we anchored again about noon, in hopes that when the boat which was then away sounding, would return, that we should immediately prepare to get into the harbour. But when they came on board, we learnt that the greatest depth of water at the entrance of it is fourteen feet, which is less than either of the ships draw. Between two and three miles to the westward of it, however, they found another harbour, or rather a small bay, which is in some measure secured to seaward, by a reef of rocks that runs in a slanting direction, across part of the entrance of it, in such a manner as to prevent any large floes of ice from being driven into it. It is not, perhaps, a place that we should choose * for our winter-quarters, had we time to look about for a better; but under present circumstances we may consider ourselves fortunate, in finding that there is such a good harbour within our power to reach, for the winter is making rapid strides. There is, indeed, very little of the surface of the sea now that is not covered with ice, and close in to the land it is already from four to six inches thick, all along the coast, so that we shall have to saw our way into the harbour. The people who were away sounding to-day, saw several seals, which are the only animals of any kind that have been seen during these two days past.

Friday, 24th.—We got under weigh early this morning, and ran to the westward to the mouth of the harbour intended for our winter residence, where we anchored about eight o'clock. Immediately after breakfast the crews of both ships commenced sawing a channel into the harbour, in which operation they were pretty successful, having before six o'clock P.M., sawed a canal thirty-five feet in breadth, and upwards of half a mile long, into which the ships were tracked in the evening. The thickness of the ice through which they sawed to-day, was from seven to eight inches. It is intended to resume the same operation to-morrow, for the harbour is at least three miles in length; and I understand that the intention is to get within about half a mile of the top of it; for it has been sounded that far to-day, and it has

* After getting into this harbour, and after having had time to examine it more minutely, we found it to be as secure a place to winter in as we could wish for, as will be seen hereafter.

been found that there is plenty of water for us even within a cable's length of the shore.

We found on the ice, close to where they were cutting the canal to-day, a dead swan (*Anas Cygnus*, Lin.), which is the first and only bird of the kind that we have seen in these regions. It was in a very perfect state, and must have necessarily lain here but a short time, for there was no ice here less than three weeks ago, when we passed this place going to the westward.

Saturday, 25th. — All hands were employed again to-day cutting the canal through the ice, and instead of hauling the pieces that they cut out, into the open sea, as they did yesterday, they forced them under the floe, which was found to be a much more expeditious way of getting rid of them, than floating them out of the canal. But in speaking of an open sea, I must observe, that according to the strict meaning of the word, there is no such thing now existing within our view; for the place where the ships lay yesterday morning, and, indeed, the whole of the sheet of clear water that lay outside of them, is now covered with ice of last night's formation; and that on the canal was so strong this evening as to bear the weight of a person. In consideration of the hard labour that the men have had for these two days past, an extra-allowance of Donkin's preserved meat has been served out to them each day.

Sunday, 26th. — From seeing the rapid increase in the thickness of the ice, and consequently the additional labour that must be incurred by any delay, it has been deemed proper to employ all hands again to-day, in cutting the canal, in which work they have now become so expert, by these two or three days' experience, that notwithstanding the increased thickness of the ice, they have cut through more * of it to-day than either of the preceding days, and that too in less time. For at a quarter past three o'clock in the afternoon, the ships were warped to the top of the canal, when the men, in the usual way in which British seamen express their joy, gave three hearty cheers, as a proof of the pleasure they felt at having in safety reached their winter-quarters, after having performed, on every occasion, all that was possible for men to do; and, what is more, after having accomplished infinitely more than any numerous adventurous seamen who have been employed (at different times for upwards of two centuries past), in search of the same object. In concluding my account of the operations of this season, it is certainly a tribute due to every officer and man on the Expedition, to say, that they always evinced the utmost zeal for the service on which we are employed; and I do not think that it can be considered that we hold what we have done in too high an estimation, if we say that our zeal and perseverance have been rewarded with ample success; nor can it be said that our hopes are too sanguine, if

* After they had done cutting the canal to-day, its length was measured, when it was found that they had cut the

1st day	1200 yards,	
2d —	1284	do.
3d —	1598	do.
Total	4082	do.

making the whole length of the canal equal to $2\frac{1}{3}$ miles nearly.

we flatter ourselves with the expectation of being equally successful next season.

However, as we are likely to have time enough to speculate on this subject, before we leave this place, it is unnecessary to say any more about the matter at present; I shall therefore conclude my narrative of the operations of this season, by briefly stating the few remaining occurrences of this day. In the first place then, I have to remark, that in speaking of this place in future, it will be always called *Winter Harbour*, which is the name that it is henceforth to be known by. I may say of this harbour, as I have just said about our future prospects, that as we are to be here for a considerable time, it is unnecessary to enter into a lengthened detail respecting it at present, as we shall be able to give a better account of it, and its neighbourhood, before we leave it, than we can give at this time. It may not be improper, however, to observe, that as far as we are able to judge, it appears to be a place as well adapted in every way, for wintering in, as any that we could find in these regions, allowing that we had a whole arctic summer to do nothing else but look for a harbour; for its mouth, or entrance, is, as I have already remarked, partly guarded from the violence of the sea by a reef of rocks, over which there is, in some places, not above one fathom of water; and between this reef and the land, there is for most part of the way, a bar, or bank, over which we found, in some places, only 3½ fathoms water; and where the ships are, although nearly at the top of the harbour, and within eighty-one fathoms of the beach, we have five fathoms water, which is the more remarkable, since the shore, and, indeed, the whole of the land around the harbour, and its vicinity, is low. This country has now a very bleak appearance, for the whole of the surface of the land is covered with a thin layer of snow; and in the vallies, and those places where vegetation was most abundant, it is in some parts of considerable depth. Notwithstanding the best pasture is in this manner already covered over, we have the satisfaction of finding that the reindeer have not yet left this neighbourhood, for two very large ones were seen this forenoon at a short distance from the ships. The nature of the land is certainly not favourable for approaching these timid animals unperceived; but still I am in hopes that we shall succeed in killing some of them. Two covies of grous were also seen to-day, so that it is to be expected that we shall be able to procure some of them also.

Thursday, 30*th*.— The people have been employed for these four days past unrigging the ships, and taking the boats, yards, masts, and rigging* ashore, where they are to remain all winter, under a shade that is to be erected for them. The lower masts and rigging are not to be touched, and I believe that our main-top-mast is not to be removed, in order that parties that may be away shooting, may see the direction the ships are in, at a greater distance than they would otherwise do. Of this indeed, I have already seen the advantage, for I could see the masthead to-day when several miles into the country, and

* Our anvil was lost the other day by breaking through the ice whilst they were taking it on shore.

as the sun gets lower, its utility as a distinguishing mark will be more perceptible. The weather, for these three or four days past, has, considering the time of the year, been tolerably fine, and the mean temperature has not been much lower than we have had it for a week before ; but we find that the degree of cold indicated by the thermometer, and that conveyed by our feelings, are widely different, for whenever there is a breeze of wind we find that it is much more disagreeable to walk about, when the thermometer is at twenty degrees above zero, than at zero itself in a calm. I do not mean to say, however, that this is any new discovery, on the contrary, I am aware that the same thing may be felt and observed, in any other climate as well as here ; but I have for some time past observed another fact, which, for ought I am aware of, may be also equally well known, but which certainly never struck me so forcibly before. It is this, that whenever the wind increases in strength, the thermometer rises, and vice versâ ; however, as we shall have many opportunities of observing the extent of this rule, or connection between the wind and temperature, I shall defer saying any thing more about it at present. The canal is now froze so firmly from one end to the other, that we can just only distinguish where it was, so that the ships are now as firmly fixed, as if they were a component part of the floe itself. In case, however, that the ice may break up by any unforeseen cause, anchors have been set in the beach, to which a cable is fast from each ship's larboard bow, and another from their quarter.

Another reindeer was seen this afternoon, which we immediately went after, and owing to the weather being thick at the time, we managed to surround him, and by that means got so near him, that he was at length shot. He was perfectly white, except one brown patch on the top of his rump; the carcase weighed, when skinned and cleaned, 147 pounds.

Friday, October 1st. — Another deer was killed to-day. A beautiful white bear was also seen to-day, but we were unsuccessful in our attack upon him, notwithstanding he approached so near to the ships, that we fired at him from them. Several shot struck him, however, in different parts of the body, as we could plainly perceive from the streams of blood that gushed from the wounds; but before we could re-load, he was out of gun-shot range from the ships. A large party of the officers and men immediately pursued him*, in expectation from the quantity of blood that issued from his wounds, that he would soon fall, or at least become so much exhausted that they would soon come up with him; in both these expectations, however, they found themselves disappointed, for the cold, in a short time, stopped the effusion of blood, and as none of the wounds happened to be in a mortal part, he succeeded in keeping out of gunshot distance from them. They supposed, however, that they would have ulti-

* All our dogs went after him also, but none of them would go very near him; for if they had, I have no doubt but he would soon make them suffer for their temerity.

mately come up with him, had they not been stopped from pursuing him by his swimming across a lane of open water that separated the sea-ice from that attached to the land. After getting out of the water on the opposite side of this channel, he was observed to be again of a perfectly white colour; but before he had been many minutes on the ice, his coat was changed again to the same crimson hue as before, so that it is probable, that although he escaped from his pursuers, that he will in the end die of the wounds he received. Although we have had evident proofs, from the number of their skulls that we found on this land, that bears are at least occasional visitors of it, yet as we have never seen any of them before to-day, it was supposed that they only came here in the summer time; persons went, therefore, out walking, not only singly, but often unarmed; a thing which, I presume, is not likely to happen in future, more especially as the bear seen to-day was first seen by a person, who, as I have just said, was walking out alone. On seeing the animal, he immediately returned with all speed to the ships, with the bear after him, which induced many to believe, that the animal was in pursuit of him; but, I think, it is most probable, that his scent had led him towards the ships, and that he would have come to them whether he had met the person in question or not: but be this as it may, it is certainly best to promulgate the idea, that he followed the man, as it may put others on their guard, not to go too far singly, at least without means of defence.

Wednesday, 6th. — Nothing occurred for some days past worthy of particular notice, except the gradual change in the state of the weather, which is getting colder every day: at four this morning, the thermometer was as low as eight degrees below zero. But we have now got the housing over the ships, so that the increased severity of the weather is not felt in the least on board, nor does it, indeed, put us to any inconvenience in our excursions on shore, except when there is a breeze of wind, which, as I have already remarked, renders the cold less tolerable to our feelings, although it raises the thermometer; but I may, perhaps, be going too far in saying, that it increases the temperature. Probably, a corresponding change taking place in the temperature of the atmosphere whenever a breeze of wind comes on, so many instances of it have now come under our observation, that we already begin to consider it as a general rule. Several deer have been seen during these five or six days past, but we were not fortunate enough to kill any of them: to-day, however, one of them, which happened to come close to the ships, was shot from the Griper; it weighed 170lbs.

Saturday, 9th. — Although the sun has not yet entirely left us, we receive now but little benefit from it, either in the way of heat or light; for ever since the housing has been put over the ships, we have been obliged to use candles the whole day, or properly speaking, as long as our allowance of these necessary articles last, which, I am sorry to say, is very inadequate, being only one candle (ten of which go to the lb.) every six days, to each officer, or a little more than an inch of candle a-day. When it is considered, then, that we are to be about three months deprived entirely of the light of the sun, and at least three months more deriving little or no benefit from it on board, I hope it will appear to every person, that I have not unnecessarily expressed regret at our not being more amply supplied with the useful article of candles. It is but just to observe, however, that as we have a light in the gun-room the whole day, no person has any occasion to complain of want of light, even if he was disposed to do so; but so far from that being the case, I have every reason to believe that every officer on board would cheerfully submit to any privation that might be deemed necessary for the good of the public service; and I have no doubt, should we ever happen to be situated under such circumstances as to put our zeal or endurance to the test, but my prognostication will be verified.

Sunday, 10*th*.—Seven deer were seen to-day, one of which we killed, and another was severely wounded, but, owing to the night coming on, he got away, after being pursued for several miles. The ardour with which he was followed very nearly led the party that went after him into a serious predicament, for they were so loath to give up the chace, that, before they thought of returning, the day was so far spent that they lost their way coming back. Two of them returned about six o'clock, in so exhausted a state, and so much affected by the cold, that we began to entertain serious apprehensions for the safety of the two remaining persons of the party who were yet absent. As it was now evident, from the report of those that returned, that the others lost their way, we commenced immediately to fire guns, set off rockets, and burn blue lights, in order to direct them towards the ships. About a quarter past seven one of them returned, but he was in such a state of insensibility, that we could not obtain any correct information from him respecting the other man, any further than that they parted about an hour before he came on board. One of his hands is very much frost-bitten, and he was altogether in such a state of pain, stupor, and confusion, that his answers to the questions that were put to him were, as I have just said, so incoherent that nothing could be learnt from him. It may easily be conceived, then, that if we were apprehensive before, we had double reason to be so now; for even the first two of the party that returned were very much exhausted, and, as to the person just mentioned, it is very clear that he could not have held out much longer, for both his body and mind had, as I above described, suffered very considerably from the severity of the weather. Unauspicious, however, as these circumstances were, we had strong hopes that, as the person who last returned had only parted with him who was yet absent, about an hour before, that he could not be far off; and, in order that no means might be left untried that could be deemed likely to direct him towards the ship, poles were set up, with lanthorns on their top, at different places, on the highest parts of the land around the harbour, and the firing of guns, setting off rockets, and burning of blue-lights, were continued on board as before. At length our endeavours were crowned with success, for at half past eleven o'clock the stray person returned; and, very much to our pleasure and surprise, had not suffered the least from the cold, notwithstanding he had been away upwards of four hours longer than any of the rest!

Thursday, 14*th*. — A wolf was seen to-day at the distance of about half a mile from the ships; he was of a white colour, and about the size of the Esquimaux dogs that we took home last year; some supposed that he was a little higher than them, but as far as I could judge, he was much about the same size, and not unlike them in shape, only that his legs appeared to be somewhat longer than their's. Four rein-deer were also seen to-day, but the weather being pretty clear at the time, we could not get near either them or the wolf unperceived; as the latter however appeared to be prowling about, as if inclined to keep nigh the ships, a small gun was taken on shore and set as a trap for him, by tying a piece of meat to a line affixed to the trigger, in such a way that an animal laying hold of the meat must inevitably receive the contents of the gun, that is to say, if it goes off; but that is a point, however, on which I am very doubtful, for we find of late that our fowling-pieces very frequently miss fire, from the moisture that freezes on the lock. They furnished the house to-day that has been built for the astronomical clocks, &c. and a shade has been constructed with spars and sails, which covers the boats, rigging, and stores that have been landed.* In order to detect any symptoms, or appearance of scurvy amongst the men, their gums were examined this morning, and I understand the same thing is to be done every Thursday, for the future. All hands are also to be mustered at divisions, at nine o'clock in the morning, and six in the afternoon every day, in order to see that the men are all clean and sober, two of the most essential things for preserving their health; this also affords an opportunity of examining what state their bed-places are in, which is done whilst they are on deck.

Friday, 15*th*. — No less than fifteen deer were seen to-day in one herd, but those who saw them were not so fortunate as to be able to kill any of them, from the reason that I mentioned yesterday, namely, that the persons who saw them could not get their muskets off at the time they were within shot of them.

Monday, 18*th*. — Eleven deer were seen yesterday, and upwards of twenty to-day, in one herd; out of those seen to-day we succeeded in killing one, which is much smaller than any of those that we killed before, weighing only a little more than ninety pounds, when skinned and cleaned. I have remarked, that all the deer that we have seen since we came to this harbour, sets off to the westward, when they are pursued, and even when not molested they are observed to be travelling in that direction.

* Parties have been employed also for some time past cutting turf, and bringing it down to the ships for fuel.

Monday, 25th. — Nothing of any importance has occurred for this week past, the weather has been, as might be expected, getting gradually colder, the thermometer has been some days ago as low as 17°, but we have not had any considerable fall of snow yet; in the vallies, indeed, there is a good deal of drift snow, but the surface of the land, in general, has very little more snow on it than there was when we came into the harbour. Notwithstanding the only part of the land where there was any considerable vegetation is now covered with snow, the rein-deer have not yet left it, for several large herds of them have been seen during this week past; but they all appeared, as I have already remarked, to be on their way to the westward, and whenever we approach them they set off at full speed in that direction, so that from this reason, and the uncertainty, and even difficulty of managing fire-arms with any dexterity, owing to the coldness of the weather, we have not succeeded in killing any of them. A wolf was seen to-day at a little distance from the ships; he was about the same size, and of the same colour, as the one seen some days ago: the general opinion, is indeed, that it is the same animal. A small white fox was seen also to-day, he seemed not to be quite so wild as the wolf, but unless they are caught in traps, I suspect that we shall find it a difficult matter to get nigh enough either of them to be able to shoot them: in the night time, however, I have no doubt but they come very near the ships, to pick up some of the refuse that is thrown on the ice, so that I am in hopes that we shall entrap some of them before the winter is over. I observed this afternoon two vertical columns of prismatic colours, about 15° on each side of the sun; they were about five degrees in length, their lower end touching the horizon. They preserved the same intensity of colour, for about an hour, that is from noon until one o'clock; they then began to vanish, and in less than an hour disappeared altogether. The only remaining occurrence of this day that I have now to mention, is, that a channel about three feet wide was cut all round the ships to-day, in order to take the pressure of the ice off them*, if such a pressure exists, of which I am myself very doubtful, for I am not aware that ice continues to expand after its formation, therefore if it does not, the ships cannot be pressed by it; but allowing even that such a pressure existed, I am inclined to think that it will be found a difficult matter to keep an open channel round them all the winter.

Friday, 29th. — A fox was caught last night in a trap set by the Griper; he is perfectly white, and is about the same size as the hares that were killed last month; his long bushy tail, indeed, gives him the appearance of being somewhat larger than them: but as his dimensions will most likely be taken, I shall forbear saying any thing more about his size at present. On being caught he displayed several of the cunning tricks peculiar to his tribe, for when he was taken out of the trap, he shut his eyes, and lay motionless, no doubt with a view of

* I understand that some cracking that was heard amongst the ice alongside the Griper lately, has given origin to the idea of pressure existing.

being taken for dead, so that when those who were around him got careless, he might watch an opportunity of getting off. Such an artifice might, and very probably does, enable these animals to escape from the bears and wolves occasionally; with his present captors, however, his wily tricks have little chance of affording him an opportunity of effecting his escape. He is not hurt in any way, for he was caught in an empty cask with a slide in one end of it, which fell, and shut him up in it immediately he laid hold of the bait within. It is probable therefore that they will be able to preserve him alive for some time, or at least until his habits are known, which I shall take an opportunity of mentioning hereafter, should he display any peculiarities deserving of notice. Very few deer have been seen for some days past, so that I am afraid, that we shall not be able to lay in such a good winter stock of these animals as was at first expected, for the daylight now lasts but a very short time, so that it would be dangerous to go any distance from the ships: there has been an order, indeed, issued some time ago, prohibiting any person from going out of sight of the ships.* Besides, the state of the weather now is not very favourable for long excursions, for the thermometer this evening was as low as 28° below zero, and we have generally a breeze of wind, which, as I have already remarked two or three times, renders the cold less tolerable to our feelings. We find that the wind is almost

* But if I am not mistaken, this order was issued in consequence of what happened on the 10th instant, and with a view of preventing a recurrence of the same in future.

invariably from the northward; but, contrary to what might be expected, we do not find that it is any colder than that from any other direction, nor does the thermometer even indicate any particular difference in this respect, for it is affected only by the force, and not by the direction of the wind. Columns of prismatic colours, similar to those described on the 25th inst., have been observed again two or three times since that day, at the same distance from the sun, of the same altitude, and indeed in every other way resembling those before-mentioned. The Aurora Borealis was seen also two nights ago to the southward, but it was too faint to deserve any description.

Tuesday, November 2d.—The weather has been milder during these two or three days past, than we have had it for some time before, for the thermometer has been for most part of the time at zero, which we now consider a high temperature; the sky during most part of the above period has been overcast, which may be the reason of the comparative mildness of the weather. We have not had any considerable fall of snow yet, but, I suspect, that during the hazy weather that we have lately had, some fell, although scarcely perceptible at the time, owing to its being in such small particles, and so dry that the lightest breeze of wind drifts it along, so that it is impossible to say whether the accumulation of it in some places is owing entirely to the drift, or is partly increased by new-fallen snow; I think it is probable, however, that the latter cause contributes in some measure to augment the local collections of it that we find to be daily accumulating in the vallies and ravines in our neighbourhood. The man (John Pearson, marine), belonging to the Griper, whom I mentioned, on the 10th instant, as having returned in a state of stupor and very much frost-bitten, has had this afternoon the four fingers of his left hand amputed, in consequence of the frost-bite that he received at that time. He has not lost the whole of the above fingers, but only the extreme phalanges, and part of the second of the three largest of them, and the two extreme and part of the third phalanx of the little finger. It is unnecessary to observe that every means was used at the time the man came on board, and, indeed, for several days afterwards, to restore life in the parts that were frost-bitten; and, considerable as the loss has been, it is but just to observe, that the treatment pursued has been productive of greater success than could at first have been expected, for the whole hand appeared at first to be in imminent danger, for when he came on board it was as hard as a piece of marble.

As the ships are now housed and secured, and the days getting so short that neither officers nor men can amuse or employ themselves by excursions to the country, two intended sources of amusement are about to be set on foot for the purpose of making the long approaching winter pass as cheerfully as possible. One of the sources in question which is a weekly newspaper, called "The Winter Chronicle, or New Georgia Gazette," has already commenced, for the first number of it came out yesterday morning; and the other object for amusement are Plays, for which they are now preparing. Of the last of these intended sources of amusement, I have no doubt but it will answer its end, that is, of diverting the men; but of the first I am not quite so certain of its answering its purpose so well, for I have seen one or two instances, and have heard of many more, where newspapers on board of ship, instead of affording general amusement, and promoting friendship and a good understanding amongst officers, tended in a short time to destroy both: for although the professed object and intention at first may be to afford entertainment and convey knowledge, yet for lack of materials to answer the expectations excited, jokes and reflections upon one another will at length be admitted to fill the columns: these will, by some, be taken in good part, and by others in a contrary way; consequently those who consider themselves offended will retaliate, perhaps, in less courteous language, on those whom they consider their annoyers; until at length the paper, instead of being the source of amusement and instruction, becomes the vehicle of sarcasms and bitter reflections. And should the conductor, or conductors of the paper have discretion enough to refuse admitting into their columns productions of this nature, yet they cannot repress the sentiments or opinions of the parties concerned, who, to make the matter worse, generally know one another; for, to be an anonymous writer on board of ship is but a thin veil to prevent a person from being known, for peoples' talents and turn of mind are soon discovered, when situated as people necessarily are, confined together at sea. Although I have thus far entered into a detail of what I have seen and heard of newspapers written on board of ship, it must not be understood that I am by any means inimical, or even augur any ill consequences from the "Winter Chronicle;" on the contrary, there is reason to hope, from the character of the person who is to conduct it, that it will afford amusement, and perhaps useful instruction; at all events, I presume, that such is the intention of it at present.

Thursday, 4th. — This being the last day that the sun was above our horizon this season, according to its declination taken from the Nautical Almanac, several of us went to the top of one of the adjacent hills to have a parting look at him; but the weather at noon being cloudy, nothing could be seen of the parting luminary but a faint light in the direction he was in.

Friday, 5th. — The officers performed this evening the farce called "Miss in her Teens," to the great amusement of the ships' companies; and considering the local difficulties and disadvantages under which the comedians laboured, their first essay did them infinite credit. Some of them, indeed, I believe had appeared on the stage before, but the majority of them never wore the sock or buskin, before this evening. The theatre was opened by a very appropriate address, spoken, and written purposely for the occasion, by Mr. Wakeham; and two songs, the composition of the same gentleman, were sung between the acts; so that by the united exertions of all those concerned, two hours were spent very happily on the quarter-deck, notwithstanding the thermometer outside the ship stood at zero, and within as low as the freezing point, except close to the stoves, where it was a few degrees higher.

Monday, 8*th*. — The weather was very clear to-day, so that we had several hours' twilight, nearly as clear as if the sun had been above the horizon in hazy weather. At noon, indeed, the sun must have been very near the horizon, by refraction, for the sky over it was very beautifully illuminated, of a bright reddish colour, which vanished gradually in its intensity towards the zenith. An experiment was made to-day on a piece of ice, similar to that which was performed at Petersburg at the marriage of the late Emperor of Russia. — I allude to the ice-guns that were used on that occasion. That which we made, however, hardly deserved to be called a gun, at least when compared with those in question, for the block of ice that was used was only about three feet long, two feet broad, and a foot and a half in thickness; and the bore, which was made with a two-inch augur, was about two feet in length; it was loaded with three ounces of powder, but when fired, instead of going off like the Russian ice-guns, it burst into a thousand fragments. Ice formed on salt-water is, from its porosity, very little calculated for an experiment of this sort; and if it were intended to withstand the shock of the explosion, the mass, I presume, ought to be larger than that which we used. It was, however, the thickest that we can as yet procure; but if there was any object in repeating the experiment, I have no doubt but we shall soon be able to get heavier ice; for that formed on the channel round the ship since Saturday, for it was not cut yesterday on account of its being Sunday, was found to-day to be eight inches thick.

Wednesday, 17*th*. — Nothing of any importance occurred for this week past, except that the weather has been getting gradually colder: yesterday it was as low as 42° below zero, consequently our mercurial thermometers are now of no use. The severity of the weather, however, does not confine the wolves to their dens, for their tracks are observed every day, at no great distance from the ships; and one of them was bold enough to-day to chace one of our dogs very close to the ships, or rather he followed the dog until that animal took refuge under the protection of the persons with whom he was walking at the time. The wolf, on this occasion, betrayed a considerable degree of cunning, in order to circumvent his intended prey, for he never moved whilst the dog was running towards him; but immediately he observed that the dog would not approach any nearer, he made towards him with full speed; and probably, had the dog had a great way to run, he would have overtaken him. At the same time that the wolf in question was chasing the dog, another animal of the same kind was heard howling at a little distance off, but the twilight at the time was so faint that he could not be seen. In the evening one of them came within seventy or eighty yards of the ship, and kept walking about within that distance for a considerable time, howling at short intervals during the whole time. Their howl is long, and somewhat lamentable to the ear; the only sound with which I could compare it, is the cadence, or terminating sound of a bugle-horn at a distance. What attracted them so much to-day we supposed to be the smell of some of the narwhal's blubber, that we killed in the summer, which we were boiling on the ice this forenoon. Between three and four o'clock this afternoon, a remarkable cloud was observed in the south-west: the centre of it, indeed, bore S. W. by S. (true). It diverged from a centre, at the horizon, in strait lines, or columns, which extended to a great distance over the surface of the sky: the lower edge of it, on each side, was very straight and well defined; and formed an angle of about 45° with the horizon. Directly over its centre, instead of straight lines, it had more the appearance of an immense volume of smoke than any thing else. The whole was compared by our gunner to a powder-magazine in a state of explosion; which those who had an opportunity of seeing such a sight, thought a very apt comparison; for the reflected rays of the sun, which illumined that part of the sky behind the cloud, gave it very much the appearance of an immense explosion. It is probable that this remarkable cloud had some connection with the Aurora Borealis; for, after it had vanished, which took place about six o'clock, that phenomenon was seen in the same part of the heavens that the cloud occupied: it made its appearance, indeed, before the cloud disappeared entirely, but not before it had lost its radiated form, and dispersed so much that nothing particular could be seen about it.

Tuesday, 23d.— The weather, for this week past, has been very boisterous, during most part of the time; within these two days, in particular, it blew so strong that there has been no communication between the two ships, although they are only about eighty yards from one another, on account of the clouds of drift snow that are carried along by the wind. I have already remarked so often the effect the wind has in raising the temperature of the atmosphere, that it will perhaps be considered tautology to notice the same thing again: allowing even this to be the case, I cannot help observing in this place, however, that the same thing occurred, on this occasion, in a more striking manner than I have ever observed it before; for, on the evening of the 19th inst., the wind, from light airs, died away to a perfect calm; and, as the wind diminished, the thermometer continued to fall, and at midnight was as low as 47°. During the whole of the succeeding day the wind was never stronger than what is termed a light breeze; and the consequence was, that the thermometer never fell below 40°; but on the 21st it came on to blow strong, and has continued to do so ever since; and the effect has been, that the thermometer from that day, at noon, until this time, has never been above 25°, notwithstanding the wind, during the whole time, has been from the northward. Severe as the weather has been during these few days past, the wolves still continue to prowl about, for they are often heard howling at night in the neighbourhood of the ships: I have said at night, perhaps, improperly, for ever since the sun left us, and until it returns, it may be said to be one continued night; but, as it is most convenient to distinguish the different parts of the twenty-four hours, according to the way in which we have been accustomed to do, I shall still make use of the common distinctive words, of morning, noon, evening, and night, in the same manner as if these distinctions were apparent in nature; and I may remark, that it is not more incongruous to continue these appellations now, than making use of them in the summer time, or when the sun is never below the horizon.

Wednesday, 24th. — Another play was performed by the officers this evening, which amused the people very much, and, I believe, that it is intended to perform one every fortnight during the winter, if the weather does not get so cold as to prevent it. The weather has of late, indeed, been very severe, but when there is no wind, we can take exercise in the open air without any inconvenience, although the thermometer is generally between 40° and 50° below zero. A person cannot, however, make much use of his hands in the manner in which they are obliged to be covered, to prevent being frost-bitten: they have, therefore, left off cutting the ice round the ships, having found that it was impossible to continue that operation with safety to the men; two or three of them indeed, got their toes slightly frost-bitten, during the last days they were employed at it. We have the satisfaction to find, however, that the discontinuation of cutting the channel above mentioned, has not yet been, nor do I think it is likely to be productive of any bad consequences; on the contrary, there is reason to expect, that the snow which is accumulating round the ships will be of considerable benefit to us, in the way of keeping them warm, and in order to do this more effectually, they have banked the snow up against their sides all round, except at one place, where a hole is to be kept open in the ice in case of fire.

Monday, 29th.—A very interesting and curious fact was observed this evening, which tends to subvert a point that I believe has hitherto been received as a general law, which is, that mercury does not freeze in a higher temperature than 39 or 40 degrees below zero. The instance in question is simply thus, that the mercury used by some of the officers this evening as an artificial horizon whilst taking lunar observations, was found, after being four hours exposed in the open air at the temperature of 36 degrees below zero, to have frozen into a solid mass. The novelty of the thing immediately excited attention, and in order to be perfectly satisfied that the temperature of the atmosphere was not lower than what was indicated by the thermometer used for registering the temperature on board, another thermometer was tried, and it only fell also to 36°. The only way in which I can account for this strange deviation from the general law, is, that the mercury had become amalgamated with the lead, of which the artificial troughs generally used are made. *

Tuesday, 30th. — The same thing was observed again this evening with regard to the mercury, for it became solid at the temperature (by a spirit thermometer) of 36° below zèro. I do not mention this, however, as a matter of surprise, for it was the same mercury that was used last night, consequently it ought of course to freeze again at the same temperature.

Wednesday, December 1st. —Between seven and eight o'clock this evening, four Paraselenæ, or mock moons, were observed, each at the distance of about 21½° from the moon. One of them was situated close to the horizon, and another perpendicularly above it; the other two were one on each side of the moon, in a line parallel with the horizon. Their shape was somewhat like that of a comet, but incomparably larger, having their tails on that side farthest from the moon; their colour was slightly prismatic, the side of them that was nearest the moon being of a light orange colour, which vanished gradually into a yellow towards their tail.

Shortly after they were seen, a halo, or luminous ring, having the moon for its centre, made its appearance; the radius of this ring was equal to the distance between the Paraselenæ and the

* That some impurity in the mercury is the cause of its freezing at such a low temperature is obvious, I think, from this circumstance, namely, that the mercury in the mercurial thermometer did not freeze even at 38°, for the temperature of the air was registered by it until it exceeded that cold.

moon, consequently it passed through them. At the same time that the ring appeared, two yellowish coloured lines joined the opposite Paraselenæ, and bisected each other at the centre of the circle, thereby dividing it into four equal quarters. These lines, or columns, as well as the halo, or ring, and the Paraselenæ, or mock moons, were at different times of different degrees of brightness; and above the halo, that is, between it and the zenith, there appeared occasionally a segment of another halo, which touched the upper edge of that above described, or rather the Paraselene that occupied that part of it. These phenomena, if I may so call them, continued for upwards of an hour, and during that period frequently varied, as I have already said, in the intensity of their colours, but every part preserved invariably the same shape, although at times, some parts, particularly the upper segment and the cross that divided the halo, became so faint as scarcely to be visible.

Thursday, 2d. — A Halo, with Paraselenæ, and a cross similar to that above described, were seen again this evening, nearly about the same time. It is unnecessary to enter again into a detail of their appearances, as the above description answers in every respect to that seen to-night.

Wednesday, 8th. — Nothing occurred for this week past deserving of any particular notice; the weather has, to our surprise, been much milder than we had reason to expect from the month of November, for the thermometer, since the beginning of this month, has seldom been lower than 30°, and the average cold has not been greater than 20° below zero. What little wind we have had has been generally from the northward; but I do not mean to imply from this, however, that it has been more so this month than the last; on the contrary, I believe the reverse would be nearer the truth, for it was almost invariably from the northward during the month of November. I omitted to mention, at the time it happened, which was a few nights ago, that the fox caught by the Griper has made his escape, by the chain with which he was made fast getting loose. He was seen next morning close to the ships, and the mark of the chain has been seen on the snow, at no great distance off, several times since; but I think it is probable, unless he is again entrapped, that he will soon fall a prey to the wolves, for he must be so much encumbered with the chain that he has carried off with him, that he will not be able to escape from them should he be pursued, and it must also be a great hindrance to him in the way of procuring his food.*

At the time he was caught, I said very little respecting him, any farther than merely a few words, stating his size, and general appearance, in hopes that I should, as I remarked at the time, be able to give a better description of him at some future period, when his habits, &c. would be

* We have reason to suppose that mice constitute the principal part of their food, for we have seen several of these animals during the winter, and their tracks are very numerous on the snow. They are perfectly white, and are rather larger than the common mice. Their shape indeed is quite different, for they are short, thick, and flattish, and their tail is not above half an inch in length.

better known. I must confess, however, that even now, I can add but very little to what has been said of him at the time he was taken. He became daily more domesticated, and was latterly so tame, that a person might handle him with great freedom, without running any danger of being bitten; he ate any kind of food that was offered him, but what he chiefly subsisted on was bread and peas.

Sunday 19*th*. — These ten days past have been as barren of events worthy of notice as any period of equal length since the commencement of the winter, for all nature appears, if I may use the expression, as if she had gone to rest, for darkness has spread her sable mantle over all the surrounding scene; and the occasional howlings of the wolves, and the whistling of the wind, are the only two objects that interrupt the perpetual silence that reigns over these dreary regions. The plays, however, and such other sources of amusement as are within our reach, have hitherto made the time pass very cheerfully, and I hope that they will continue to do so.

Tuesday, 21*st*. — This being our shortest day, or, more properly speaking, the day on which the sun is farthest from us, several of the officers went out on the ice at noon with books to determine whether it was possible to read by the twilight, and, surprising as it may appear, yet we found that the smallest print could be read by it. The book that I took was a small (pocket) Common Prayer-Book, (which was the smallest print I could find,) and, by facing it towards the south, I could read it very distinctly. As the portion of it that

M 2

presented itself by chance on this occasion contains a good moral lesson, I hope it will not be considered an idle or impious thing to quote the sentence that happened to be the subject of experiment. It was the first verse of the forty-sixth Psalm: *God is our hope and strength: a very present help in trouble.* In addition to what has been said, I ought also to mention that the weather at the time was rather cloudy, so that very few stars could be seen, and the moon's declination was about 15½° S., consequently below the horizon; therefore the twilight was the only source from which we could receive any light at the time. My object in being so minute in detailing this circumstance is simply to give an idea of the degree or quantity of light that we still receive from the sun. It must not be understood, therefore, that I mentioned it as any thing extraordinary or unexpected; for even if such were my design, I should be only exposing my own ignorance, since it is known to every person that the twilight does not cease until the sun is eighteen degrees below the horizon, or passed the imaginary line called the crepusculum.

I have omitted to mention until this time, that, ever since we came into this harbour we have used no other water except that which is obtained by the melting of snow; and yet we have not found any of those bad effects from it that are mentioned by Captain James in his disastrous voyage in search of the north-west passage in the year 1631; for he says, that the snow-water made himself and his people so short-breathed that they could hardly speak. His own words are, "It made us so short-"breathed that we were scarce able to speak." What Captain James attributed to the snow-water was most probably one of the incipient symptoms of scurvy, or some other complaint, brought on by the cold and comfortless situation in which they passed the winter in Hudson Bay. I ought perhaps to defer, however, saying any thing on this subject until we have passed the winter ourselves, in case we should be so unfortunate as to find out that his report was true; but until then I shall have some doubt whether snow-water does produce that effect.

Thursday, 23d. — The officers performed the play called "The Mayor of Garratt" this evening, and after it a piece wrote purposely for the occasion, by Mr. Parry, called the "North-West "Passage, or the Voyage Finished." I believe the object of this piece was to point out to the men the probability that there is of our accomplishing the discovery of the north-west passage, and the rewards and honours that will be heaped upon all on returning home, after performing such an extraordinary service. And, as far as I was able to judge, it appeared to answer remarkably well the purpose it was intended for. The thermometer in the open air at the time of the performance was at 32°, and on deck, even where the people were sitting, it was as low as 19° during the whole time; but the pleasure they derived from seeing a scene exhibiting their own character in so favourable a point of view, completely overcame any inconvenience they may have suffered from the state of the weather.

Although it may perhaps to some appear a frivolous anecdote what I am about to mention, yet I cannot help noticing it, as it tends to show the favourable reception with which the dramatic piece in question was received, and at the same time exhibits in a very noted manner the misapplication of words by men who make use of terms or expressions which they do not thoroughly understand themselves. Whilst the curtain was down between the first and second acts, all the men were conversing together, extolling the merits of the new play, when the boatswain, wishing to pay a higher compliment to it than any other person, said that it was much superior to fine or excellent (the epithets of approbation used by the seamen); that it was "in fact, real philosophy!"

Saturday, 25th. — Notwithstanding our sequestered situation, and the climate in which we are situated, we spent Christmas-day as happily as we could do in England, with the exception of being amongst our friends. Indeed, the only thing that could give us any concern, was their not knowing that we are so comfortable. As far as meat and drink were concerned in making us comfortable, we had certainly every reason to be so, for we afred most sumptuously, had excellent roast beef and venison, and plenty of good port wine, and above all, good health to enjoy these luxuries.*

* The weather to-day was what we are now accustomed to call mild, the thermometer being only 24°; a temperature in

Saturday, January 1st, 1820. — The new year ushered in without any remarkable event to distinguish it particularly: the cold has not, as we expected, been at all severe; for the thermometer at midnight last (that is at the moment of the commencement of the year) was only 5°. About 11 o'clock this forenoon a very beautiful halo, 45° in diameter, was observed round the moon. It was intersected by two luminous columns of a yellowish white colour, which crossed each other at right angles over the moon's disc. The breadth of this cross, or rather the columns that formed it, were equal to the moon's diameter, in her immediate vicinity; but, as they receded from her, they became narrower, so that at the place where they touched the halo, they had tapered to such a small point that they were scarcely visible. In those points of the halo, where they terminated, were luminous spots, or paraselenæ: the two horizontal ones, or those situated in that part of the circle where the horizontal column of light ended, exhibited in the prismatic colours very beautifully, and each of them had a long tail proceeding from them, similar to that which I described on a former occasion, when mentioning the appearance of a phenomenon of the same kind. The luminous spot, or paraselene, in that part of the halo immediately above the moon, was of a very faint colour, when compared with the two just mentioned, and the fourth one,

---

a calm day such as this was, is not at all inconvenient. I had, indeed, as pleasant a walk to-day, for upwards of an hour, as if it had been in Hyde Park.

that is to say, if it existed, was hid from us, owing to its being (as well as a segment of the halo) below the horizon, the moon's altitude being only about 18°. The halo itself was not equally bright all round, for in those parts that were equidistant, that is 45° from the paraselenæ, it was of a very faint colour, and from these points towards the paraselenæ it became gradually brighter. Like the Aurora Borealis, its intervention did not obstruct the light of the stars that it chanced to pass over, for the planet Mars happened to be situated in the brightest part of the horizontal luminous column, and yet it appeared as bright as usual; its reddish colour seemed, indeed, to be a little increased in its brilliancy. This halo, as well as that described last month, happened about the time of full moon. A hole was cut through the ice to-day, to ascertain the thickness of it, which was found to be four feet one inch, exclusive of the snow that was on it.

Sunday, 2d. — Another halo was seen about the moon this forenoon, similar in every respect to that described yesterday, except that there was a segment of another halo touching its upper side. The colour of this segment was much lighter than that of the halo itself. The moon's altitude at the time the halo was seen, was 17°, consequently a segment of it was, as I mentioned yesterday, below the horizon.

Thursday, 6th. — The officers performed the farce called "Bon Ton" this evening, in a lower temperature than perhaps any thing of the kind had ever been done before, at least by Europeans; for a thermometer, hung up in front of the stage, stood at 12°, and some parts of the theatre, if I may use that word, must have been considerably colder, for the stoves and hot shot with which it was warmed, was much nearer the place where the thermometer hung up, than the after-part of the deck where the people sat. The thermometer outside the ship at the time was only 27°; but there happened to be a fresh breeze of wind, a circumstance that rendered the cold, as I have often observed, less tolerable when the temperature is comparatively high, than we find it in the severest frost during calm weather.

Wednesday, 12*th*. — A very noted instance of this occurred indeed to-day, for I was out walking this afternoon when the thermometer was 51° below zero, and, owing to the weather being calm at the time, I felt no more inconvenience from it than if it had been at zero in a breeze of wind. A small quantity of strong brandy was exposed in the open air this afternoon for the purpose of experiment. It had not been above ten minutes on deck when it began to congeal, and in the course of half an hour it became of the consistence of honey, and not unlike it indeed in appearance. It never became harder than this, although left on deck for upwards of an hour; it was tried again in the evening, and after being exposed about an hour longer to the same temperature, we found the only difference it produced was, that it became dryer, being in consistence and appearance somewhat like brown moist sugar. The freezing did not appear to alter either its taste, or strength, in the least; we tasted it in its frozen state, without suffering any inconvenience from it, except a little smarting of the tongue.

Saturday, 15th. — Between seven and eight o'clock this evening, the Aurora Borealis was seen forming a beautiful arch, coincident with the plane of the meridian, and extending from the southern horizon, across the zenith to the northern horizon. After remaining stationary and of this shape for about ten minutes, it then formed an ellipsis of great extent, whose transverse diameter was also parallel with the plane of the meridian, and situated on the east side of it, and in such a position that the west side of the ellipsis reached the zenith. It remained of this form only a few minutes, and then assumed a variety of shapes, which were constantly varying, being chiefly shooting in streams from the southern horizon towards the zenith.

Wednesday, 19th. — One of our dogs had a severe fight with a wolf this morning, at the distance of between two and three hundred yards from the ships; it was so early in the morning, however, that they were not seen at the time, but in the course of the forenoon, the place where the conflict happened, was soon, and indeed easily found out, from the blood and tufts of hair left on the snow. It is impossible to say which of them was beat: I think, indeed, that they parted by mutual consent, for both of them must have suffered considerably: what the dog has sustained there is certainly no question about it, for we have seen the extent of the damage, which is a severe laceration of the integuments of the lower jaw and fore-part of the throat: there appears, indeed, to be a piece taken out of that part of the neck over the root of the tongue. Although we have not actually seen the wounds that the wolf received, yet there are two or three circumstances which lead us to suppose, that he suffered at least as much as the dog: for, in the first place, the dog is a very powerful one, and certainly much superior in point of strength to the wolf; and, in the next place, we found a considerable quantity of blood at a place, where the latter animal had lain down, about a mile from the ships, from which we may conclude that he had received some serious wounds, since the blood was not staunched after having gone that distance in such weather as this. We were somewhat at loss at first, when the dog came on board, to know what animal he had been fighting with, for we had no reason to think that it had been with a wolf, since a dog belonging to one of the officers of the Griper has been seen frequently with a wolf, that has been in the habit of coming within sight of the ships for several days past; indeed, the dog in question had been away the greatest part of last night and this morning, as we suppose, with a wolf. The only way therefore in which I can account for the favourable reception with which one dog has been received, whilst another has been so roughly used, is thus: that the latter may have fallen in with a male wolf, at the same time that the former may have been paying his court to the female; besides, the Griper's dog is mostly of the same colour as the wolves themselves, and might therefore very possibly be mistaken by them for one of their own species; but our dog, being perfectly black, could not be easily taken for an animal of their own kind. I mention these circumstances, however, as a mere matter of opinion, and I have no doubt but it will be considered, that I have said more about the subject altogether than it deserved.

Thursday, February 3d.—Nothing of any importance occurred for this fortnight past; the weather has been for most part of the time more boisterous than we have usually had it during the first part of the winter, the thermometer has therefore never been very low; for, from the 20th of last month, until two o'clock this afternoon, it had never been below 40°; this evening however it came on a calm, and the thermometer before midnight fell as low as 44°. For some days past we have had so much light about noon, that both officers and men generally went to the mast-head to look out for the sun; for although we were perfectly aware of the time on which it ought to reappear, according to its declination, yet as the Dutch navigator, Barentz, saw it at Nova Zembla several days before it ought to be seen, in the latitude in which he wintered, we had reason to suppose that whatever effect refraction might have there, the same might be expected to take place here. Notwithstanding our vigilance, we always found, however, that although it must have been very nigh the horizon for some days past, that it never appeared above it until to-day.* As the

* It deserves to be mentioned, that although we have not seen the sun so long before the time it ought to be seen as Barentz did, yet that its reappearance to-day is three days

forenoon was very fine and clear, we made sure of seeing it; several of us were therefore in the maintop about half past eleven, to welcome its return, and at twelve, or rather a few minutes after, we had the pleasure of seeing the glorious luminary again, after an absence of ninety-two days. It is more easy to conceive than describe the pleasure that every person felt on this occasion, at again seeing that heavenly agent, which is to set us free from confinement. But I consider, that to do justice to this subject, and to the sensations excited by so sublime and joyful a sight, would require my entering into rhapsodies, more suitable to the effusions of a poetical imagination, than the unadorned language of a plain narrator; I shall therefore avoid saying any thing more about the matter. During the time the sun was above the horizon *, a vertical column of a beautiful red colour extended from it towards the zenith, the colour of it was most brilliant near the sun, and diminished gradually as it went upwards. It was observed also, that

---

sooner than it ought to be seen in this latitude, according to its declination; but when we consider the density of the atmosphere in these regions, and consequently its increased refractive power, we ought not to be surprised, but, on the contrary, rather expect to find that the sun would reappear some time before it got within 90° of us, after allowing for the ordinary refraction.

* There was a little thin haze in the horizon, so that the sun's disc was not well defined; from this circumstance one or two persons who were inclined to be sceptical, doubted even the sun being above the horizon at all; but characters of this sort will always appear in subjects that admit of a doubt.

it was not always of the same brilliancy, but that it twinkled so that the upper part of it vanished altogether for a moment; it then instantaneously brightened up as splendid as before; this twinkling went on in quick succession, during the whole time the column appeared. Its breadth was about equal to the sun's diameter, and its height, or altitude, when in its greatest splendour, was between four and five degrees.

Friday, 11th.—The dog belonging to one of the officers of the Griper, which has been mentioned some time ago, as having been in the habit of paying visits to the wolves, or at all events on being on very familiar terms with them, has been missing since the 2d inst. He was supposed, for the first day or two, to have remained only a little longer than usual to gratify his amorous propensities, and that, after his desires had been satiated, cold and hunger would induce him to return. But the length of time that he has now been away, leaves, I think, very little hope that we shall see him any more. It is most probable that they decoyed him into one of their dens, and there destroyed him; some, however, are of opinion that he lost his way in returning to the ships, and ultimately perished by the cold; but as it is a subject not worthy of any great speculation, I shall not say any more about it. It is possible, indeed, that when the snow melts in the spring, we shall fall in with some remains of him that will tend to show the manner in which he was lost. The weather to-day, and for some days past, has been very fine; from ten o'clock in the forenoon, until two in the afternoon, there is generally a zone or belt, of a beautiful red colour, all round the horizon, from the S. E. round by north to the S. W. The breadth of this ring is from four to five degrees ; it is brightest near the horizon, and its colour diminishes gradually towards its upper edge, where it terminates in a pale yellow. The colour of the sky above this belt is of the finest blue, which increases gradually in its intensity, or darkness, towards the zenith. The Aurora Borealis has been seen for some nights past, but never very brilliant ; the electrometer has been tried, but it was not affected by it, nor has any effect been produced by it on the most sensible of our azimuth-compasses.

Monday, 14*th*. — The thermometer this afternoon fell to 54° below zero, which is the greatest cold that we have yet registered, or indeed that we have any well authenticated account of any one else having registered.* The weather at the time was perfectly calm, and although certainly cold, it was so far from being intolerably so, that we walked about in the open air without any inconvenience, and without any additional clothing more than we have been accustomed to wear throughout the winter. I am of opinion, indeed, that a much greater degree of cold might be endured in calm weather without suffering any bad effect from it, for the feelings does not appear by

* M. Haüy indeed mentions that it is recorded in the Transactions of the Academy of Petersburg, that a temperature of 57° below zero had been registered once in some part of Siberia.

any means to be so sensible after the thermometer has fallen to between 30° or 40° below zero.

We had a good instance to-day of the effect that different colours have in reflecting heat, for the piece of board on which the thermometers were suspended had one side of it painted black, and the other side white, that is of the colour of the wood itself, and it was observed that the thermometer suspended on the black side, never fell lower than 52°, while the one that hung on the white side of the board stood at 54°. * I remarked also at this time that the smoke from the ships rose quite perpendicularly, (there being no wind at the time,) so that a low temperature alone does not appear to be sufficient to produce the phenomenon of smoke falling to the ground as some have observed, but which I must confess I have never seen myself, although I have frequently, during this winter, looked out for the thing. I have observed, indeed, two or three times, that the vapour from the coppers, when they were melting snow, condensed, and fell immediately it came into the open air; but this is easily accounted for, nor could indeed any thing else be expected than that aqueous vapour would, on coming into a temperature of thirty or forty degrees below zero, immediately condense, and consequently fall.

Tuesday, 15*th*. — At six o'clock this morning

* As the piece of board on which they (thermometers) were suspended, was set up on the ice at a considerable distance, (perhaps from 80 to 90 yards) from the ship, we are certain that this difference could not be caused by any locality, or substance that was near it.

the thermometer was as low as 55°, but a light breeze having sprung up shortly after, it soon rose to 50°. As I considered this day to be one of the coldest that we are likely to have this winter, I made an experiment, which, although trivial, deserves to be mentioned, as it exemplifies in a very simple manner the rapidity with which water is frozen in such a temperature, as we have had to-day. The experiment in question is thus: I took a quart bottle, full of fresh water to the maintop, and there poured it through a small cullendar, when it was found that by the time the drops of water had fallen to the roofing over the ship, they had congealed into irregular spherical masses. The height between the main-top and the place on which they fell was 40 feet 8 inches. *

Thursday, 17*th*.—The thermometer in my cabin last night was as low as 10°, and the average height of it there for these ten days past has been from 15° to 20°; in the day time, indeed, it sometimes rises to 24°, but seldom ever above that.

Thursday, 24*th*.—Nothing of any importance occurred for this week past; but an event took place to-day rather of an unpleasant nature, for at a quarter past ten in the forenoon, the house on

* I ought to mention, however, that the water did not fall quite perpendicular, owing to a light air of wind that existed at the time; consequently it must have taken more time in falling than a body moving freely would take in describing the same space; for according to the rule, that, "the spaces described by a body falling, increase as the squares of the time increase," it would appear that the water in question froze in less than two seconds.

shore was observed to be on fire; every person ran immediately to put it out; but the mats with which the inside of it was lined were so dry, that it was found impossible to extinguish it, or rather to smother it, for, as we had no water, the only thing that we could substitute for it was snow, which was thrown on it in great abundance, but with very little effect; for, notwithstanding the violence of the fire, it melted but very little of the snow. But although it did not extinguish the fire, it answered another purpose, almost equally beneficial, for by covering the different astronomical instruments, &c., they were secured from the fire, and after this important point had been accomplished, the roofing was pulled off, and in a few minutes after the fire was extinguished. After the snow was thrown out, it was found that very little damage had been done to any of the instruments; the astronomical clocks, which were the most valuable articles there, were fortunately in the cases as they were landed, which secured them completely. A repeating circle was, indeed, the only instrument of any importance that was injured; and the only damage it sustained was its levels having got broke, most probably by the boiling of the spirits that they contained. A pair of mountain barometers, and two or three thermometers, were, I understand, the only instruments that were destroyed. I ought to mention, however, that several articles of wearing apparel, (that had been taken there to get washed,) were consumed, and three or four fowling-pieces, that had been there undergoing some repair, had their stocks very much disfigured, and one or two of them rendered unserviceable altogether; but, upon the whole, I think much less damage was done than we had at one time reason to expect, for the conflagration at the time the roofing was taking off, gave little hopes of any thing being saved. Considerable as the fire was, its influence or heat extended but a very little way, for several of the officers and men were frost-bitten, the two men in particular, who were in the house at the time the fire commenced, suffered very severely; one of them, indeed, is in great danger of losing some of his fingers, for, notwithstanding every effort was, and is still making to restore them to life, most of them are, as yet, without the least sensation. Some idea may be formed of the state they were in when he came on board, from this circumstance, that when they were immersed in a small tub of cold water for the purpose of thawing them, the cold they communicated to the water was so great that a thin film of ice was immediately formed on its surface. This may appear to some to be so extraordinary, as to be almost incredible, and I have no doubt that I should be apt to disbelieve it also, had I not been an eye-witness of the thing myself; but this was certainly one of the coldest days I ever experienced, for it blew very fresh, and the thermometer was at the time we were out at 43° below zero; what must therefore be the effect of such a cold on a man having his bare hands exposed to it for an hour, as was the case with the man in question? The way in which the fire broke out at first, was by some clothes which were hung up close to the stove having caught fire, which communicated it immediately to the dry mats with which the inside of the house was lined.

Monday, 28th. — We had a portion of the 2d, 19th, and 22d articles of war read on the quarter-deck to-day, and after that a long order relating chiefly to some difference between two of the officers some days ago.

Wednesday, March 8th.—Nothing has occurred for this week past deserving of particular notice, except haloes and parhelia, which have been seen at different times round the sun; their usual distance, or I may say, indeed, their almost invariable distance from it is about 22½°; although from their edge being sometimes but badly defined, it is found at times to be a few minutes, and sometimes even a degree less. The most beautiful phenomenon of this kind that I have yet seen was observed this afternoon; the parhelia were so bright, that had the sun not been in sight, either of them (for there were two) might be supposed to be it, behind a thin cloud. They were parallel to the horizon, at the usual distance from the sun, and situated so that a straight line drawn from the one to the other would pass through the sun. The side of them that was nearest to it was of a bright reddish colour, which vanished gradually into orange, and that again into yellow; but instead of the rest of the prismatic colours following this, as usual, in succession, the next colour was a very brilliant white, which occupied the centre of the parhelia. The halo was also very beautiful, and presented all the prismatic colours faintly.

The weather, for two or three days past, has been much finer than we have had it since the commencement of the winter, for the thermometer was for some hours yesterday, and the day before, above zero; and at two o'clock yesterday afternoon, when placed in the sun under the stern of the ship, it rose to 35.

Tuesday, 14*th*.—One of the men who was frost-bitten when the house was burnt a fortnight ago, had a part of three fingers of the left, and two of the right hand amputated to-day, in consequence of what he suffered at that time, having destroyed life in the joints that were removed. Whatever the process is that destroys vitality by means of cold, its effects on the parts that are destroyed are very different from that produced by sphacelus, or mortification of any other kind, that I remember having ever seen; for neither the size, nor the texture of the parts in question, were in the least altered, except that the skin and nails came off a few days ago.

The destruction of the skin, or rather the detachment of it, has almost invariably taken place in every case of frost-bite that has occurred since the beginning of the winter. Of the mode of treating them, although our practice has been very considerable, I am not aware that we can throw any additional light on the subject. Friction, with snow at first, and afterwards immersion in cold water, until sensation is restored, appears to be the best applications to begin with; and when cold applications did not subdue in a short time, the inflammation that afterwards occurred, I always observed that cataplasms were the most efficacious remedies.

Thursday, 16th. — The weather, for these ten days past, has been, generally speaking, very windy, which we attribute, as is customary, to the approach of the equinox. The temperature of the air still keeps very low, for the thermometer, to-day, at noon, in the shade, was 21° below zero; whilst, in the sun, at the same time, it rose to 29°, making the extraordinary difference of 50° between the sun and the shade. The officers performed this evening the last play that is intended to be acted this season; and after it, was spoken a very appropriate epilogue, written for the occasion by Mr. Wakeham.

Monday, 20th. — A large white bird was seen to-day by two of our men, who were on shore; it is generally supposed that it was an owl; but the men themselves think that it was a glaucous gull, or burgomaster as they call it; and as one of those who saw it has been often in Greenland, and consequently must have frequently seen these birds, some deference is certainly due to his opinion, however much we may be surprised to find a bird of this kind in these regions so early.

Thursday, 23d. — A hole was made to-day through the ice, about a cable's length from the ship, for the purpose of ascertaining its thickness, which was found to be six feet six inches, exclusive of six or seven inches of snow that lay on its surface. Although the temperature of the air is still much below the freezing point, it may be presumed, I think, that the ice will not increase much more in thickness this season, for the influence of the sun is now very perceptible from noon until two o'clock.

Monday, 27th.—The people have been employed for some days past bringing stones down from the hills to the beach for ballast. This way of employing them happens to come very opportunely, for some cases of scurvy have lately made their appearance; but it is to be hoped, that since the weather now permits their being employed in the open air, the disease will be prevented from spreading any farther. We found a fox to-day (dead) in one of the traps that are out; he is about the same size, and in every respect similar in appearance to the one caught by the Griper in the winter time. The weather, although fine, still keeps cold; for the thermometer, at four o'clock this morning, was as low as 33 below zero, and for some days past it has not, at any time of the day, been higher than 18°.

Saturday, April 1st.—Paucity of events induces people sometimes to record things that are often very trivial, and of this description, I have no doubt but many would consider the following circumstance; but as it throws some light on a point that lay in obscurity, I shall insert it. The circumstance in question is concerning a stone that was found to-day about three miles inland from the ship, having the letter P cut on it. As we had every reason to suppose that no civilized person had ever been on this island before ourselves, and as but few had been in the habit of going in the direction where the stone was found, it excited enough of curiosity to cause an enquiry to be made, if any person in either ship had cut the letter in question; when it was found, that one of the men belonging to the Griper, who was of the party that lost their way in the month of September last, recollected his having, during the time they were away, cut the letter P, which is the first of his name (viz. Peter Fisher), on a stone, whilst he was sitting down resting himself. From this circumstance it would appear, that the party in question, instead of going, as some of them thought, a great way inland, must have gone to the eastward, at no great distance from the coast, for the distance between the place where the stone was picked up, and where the ships then lay, is upwards of twenty miles, so that their going and returning over that space would occupy no inconsiderable portion of the time they were away.

Wednesday, 5th.—The weather to-day, and for some days past, has been remarkably fine: the thermometer in the sun this afternoon rose as high as 46°; in the shade, however, it still keeps low; at four o'clock this morning it was 24° below zero, and even at noon it was 12°.

In speaking of the scurvy having made its appearance last month, I omitted to mention that several cases of it occurred also in the Griper about the same time, one or two of them with symptoms rather more unfavourable than any we had here. In consequence of this, and their having a greater proportion of cases than we had, it was deemed expedient to remove the men's bed-places, and to substitute hammocks for them, as it was supposed that the dampness occasioned by the steam of their victuals, and breath, &c. condensing in their bed-places, from the smallness of their deck, had been conducive to the increase of the disease. What share of influence this alteration has had in producing the favourable change that has since taken place, I will not venture to assert; but I have pleasure in stating, that all those who were ill in both ships are now recovering fast; and, indeed, with the exception of one or two, are all quite well.*

Sunday, 9th. — Haloes and parhelia have been seen at different times since the beginning of this month; but as none of them differed in any way from those that have been already described, I have omitted saying any thing about them. One was seen to-day, however, which differed very materially from any that we have hitherto seen. It first appeared at noon, and continued visible until six o'clock in the evening. It exhibited the greatest display of colours about one o'clock. It consisted of one complete halo, 45° in diameter, and segments of several other haloes; the most perfect of them was immediately above it, where their peripheries touched: the other segments were one on each side of the halo, not unlike parts of a rainbow resting on the horizon; and two above it, that is, between it and the zenith. Besides these, there was another complete ring, of a pale white colour, which went right round the sky, parallel with the horizon, and at a distance from it equal to the

* Their speedy recovery on board of us, may be attributed in a great measure to some mustard and cress, which Mr. Parry took great pains to grow in his cabin for them.

sun's altitude. Where this ring or circle cut the halo, there were two parhelia, and another close to the horizon, directly under the sun ; this was by far the most brilliant of the parhelia, being exactly like the sun slightly obscured by a thin cloud at its rising or setting. With respect to the colours of the other parhelia and haloes, I may say of them in general, that they were prismatic, and showed them more or less to advantage, according to the state of the weather: when there was a little snow falling, as was frequently the case during the day, the different colours shone with the greatest splendour. I have always observed, indeed, when these haloes or parhelia are seen, that there is a little snow falling, or rather small *spiculæ*, or fine crystals of ice.

Friday, 14*th*.—One of our dogs, which had been with a wolf for these three days past, returned to the ship this morning, without having suffered any injury from its ravenous companion, which we suspect to be a she-wolf, from the intimacy that appeared to subsist between them. On Wednesday, a party of us were within a hundred yards of them, when another dog that we had with us ran up to them; but he appeared to be a very unwelcome visitor, for she gave him a few rough shakes, which soon sent him back howling. She was about the size of a Newfoundland dog, and not unlike one in shape, only that her tail was longer, for it reached the ground. The weather is fine and clear ; but, considering the advanced state of the season, it is much colder than we anticipated to have it at this time ; for the thermometer has been for several nights past as low as 30° ; and the average temperature throughout the whole day is 20° below zero.

Thursday, 20th. — There has been a considerable fall of snow to-day ; and it fell in flakes, which is different from any that we have seen since last summer ; for what fell during the winter, used always to be something like fine powder. The weather, since this fall of snow, has become much milder than it was before ; this afternoon the thermometer in the shade rose as high as 4° above zero, the wind at the time being from the southward and eastward, which we always find to be the warmest wind.*

Wednesday, 26th. — The weather continues to improve ; the snow that was on the roofing of the ships all melted off to-day ; and on shore, where the black turf appears through the snow, the edge of the snow has dissolved a little ; and the plants that are uncovered in these places, are already beginning to bud. The ground, however, is more generally covered with snow, than it has been since the beginning of the winter ; for the snow that fell lately has been, as I have already mentioned, moister than usual, so that it has not blown off as it used to do. The wolf has been frequently seen of late, and the dog that I have before-mentioned continues to pay her his visits : he generally, indeed, remains with her for two or three days

* It is only within this month past, however, that we have found that the S. E. wind has been warmer than any other ; for it may be remembered that I remarked during the winter that we found no difference in point of warmth from whatever direction the wind was.

at a time. They keep, for most part of the time, within sight of the ships; but she is so wary, that it is impossible to get within gun-shot of her; and the traps that we have are too small to hold her, — for some animal, which we suppose to be a wolf, has been in them once or twice, but yet managed to get away.

They have, within these few days past, been surveying the provisions, fuel, and stores of the Griper. They have not yet finished, so that the report of survey is not yet made out. I understand, however, that the frost has done some damage to their lemon-juice, by bursting many of the bottles. This, indeed, is a thing that has occurred to our own, and with which we have been acquainted for a long time past; for, in many of the lemon-juice cases that were opened during the winter, several bottles were found broken.

Thursday, May 4th. — An order has been issued to-day, stating that the officers and men of both ships are to be reduced to two-thirds' allowance of all sorts of provisions, except "meat, and sugar for cocoa," on the 8th instant. Whether this regulation is in consequence of any deficiency that has been found by the late survey or not, I am unable to say, as the order did not state the reason; but certainly there must be good reasons for adopting such a measure, particularly at this time, when active employment is about to commence. The weather is now improving daily; the thermometer, about midnight, generally falls as low as zero, but during the day it is, for the most part of the time, from 10° to 15° above it;

and on the 30th of last month it rose to 32°, which is the greatest heat that we have experienced since we came to Winter Harbour.

The people have been employed, during these two days past, clearing away the snow that was banked up against the ship's sides at the beginning of the winter; and, after it is cleared off, it is intended to cut the ice round the ship, for it is not considered safe to put ballast into her whilst fast in the ice.

In that part where they have cleared away the snow, we had an opportunity of observing that the ice has not increased in thickness from its upper surface during the winter; for the surface of the ice on the channel that they used to cut round the ship was exactly in the same position, with respect to her sides, as when they left off cutting it; and the ice on the edge or bank of this channel was a few inches higher than it, just the same as it was before it was covered with snow. My reason for mentioning this circumstance, is, because an opinion was some time ago entertained that a considerable part of the floe-ice was formed by the snow which fell upon it, consolidating on its surface; and, certainly, there was very good foundation for supposing this to be the case, for the water obtained from the floe-ice, when dissolved, we never found to be any more than slightly brackish, and that which we found in the pools on its surface was so fresh, that we used to water the ship from them. It is evident, however, from the foregoing circumstance, and many others that might be adduced, if necessary, that the ice is formed from the water, and not from the snow, although there can be no doubt but the latter adds very materially to the thickness of the floes. Since the first of this month, the sun has been seen above the hills at midnight, so that we have now lost the natural distinction of day and night; however, for the sake of perspicuity, I shall continue to use these terms.

Wednesday, 10*th*. — Nothing has occurred for this week past deserving of notice, except the gradual improvement in the state of the weather, and that, indeed, is very slow; for the thermometer, even now, fell at midnight to zero; the progress of vegetation is, however, beginning to be very perceptible. The people have been employed, as above mentioned, cutting the ice round the ship. The average thickness of it is about seven feet, which I think may be presumed to be the general thickness of all the ice on this harbour, and perhaps, indeed, of all the ice that has been formed off this coast during the last winter.

Friday, 12*th*. — At two o'clock this afternoon the thermometer in the shade rose as high as 18°, although the wind at the time was from the northward; we had besides to-day another instance of the approach of summer, which is that of a ptarmigan having been seen. Its plumage, with the exception of the tips of the tail feathers, was perfectly white, and these were of a jet-black colour.

Saturday, 13*th*. — A ptarmigan was shot to-day, which is supposed to be that seen yesterday, as it was found near the same place; it was in very good condition, from which we might infer, if we were in doubt about the matter, that it had been living in a better country than this during the winter. But, I believe, every one is perfectly satisfied that they migrated to the southward at the commencement of the winter, for if they lived in this country we must have surely seen some of them during these eight months past; besides, if we had no other ground to reason upon than the myriads of them that are found in the neighbourhood of Hudson's Bay during the winter, it might be inferred that they migrate thither during that season.

Monday, 15th.—Several ptarmigans have been seen by different persons yesterday and to-day, and their tracks and excrement are met with so frequently on the snow, that there must be a great many of them already arrived. I have seen four of them to-day on the wing coming from the southward. A snow-bunting and a raven were also seen to-day. One of the parties that were out observed a curious scene between the latter and a wolf: when the raven had lighted, the wolf managed to get within a few yards of him unperceived, but immediately he (the wolf) observed that he was seen by the raven, instead of running direct on to him, he began to go round him, at the same time closing upon him so gradually as to be scarcely perceived; but before he had accomplished his object, the party got so close to them as to set them off. Several tracks of rein-deer were seen yesterday leading to the northward: they were supposed to be fresh tracks by those who saw them, but the tracks that they left on the snow before the winter set in are yet in some places so perfect, that some doubts are yet entertained whether those in question are not old tracks. For my own part, I consider it quite unnecessary to offer an opinion on the subject, for if they are fresh tracks, it is more than probable that in a very short time we shall have unequivocal proofs of the return of the deer. The weather has been very mild for these two days, but the thermometer in the shade has not been above 20°, but it is above the freezing point in the sun every day in places that are sheltered from the north wind, and having a southerly aspect. As soon as the weather is likely to become permanently fine, I understand that it is intended for a party to go over land to the northward, to ascertain, if possible, the breadth of this island, and to see what state the sea is in to the northward, together with such other remarks as they may be able to make. For the greater convenience of carrying the provisions, tents, and other baggage they are to take, a light cart is making, which the men are to draw. The tents (two in number) are made of blankets, and are to be set up on boarding pikes, which, in case of its being necessary to make defence against any animal, will be found useful weapons. The provisions are packed in such a way that, in the event of the cart breaking down, or its being from any other reason necessarily abandoned, that they may carry them on their backs. I shall forbear saying any more about the subject at present, as I expect a few days will enable me to give a full account of the equipment, &c. of the party.

Wednesday, 17*th.* — Several of the people who have been out on excursions at different times during this week past, have experienced on their return severe pains in their eyes, or, as it is commonly called, snow-blindness. It first commences by a sensation somewhat like that which is felt when sand or dust gets into a person's eyes: indeed those who were first affected could hardly be persuaded but that their sufferings proceeded from something of that sort, for the general complaint was that sand or dust got into their eyes. The true cause is now, however, perfectly well known, and to prevent the recurrence of the complaint, all the men before they go out are ordered to wear a piece of crape, or some substitute for it, over their eyes. All the cases that have yet occurred of this complaint recovered in two or three days by keeping the eyes covered, and bathing them occasionally with some cooling lotion; that which we have used is what is commonly called the sugar of lead (*Cerussa acet.*) Notwithstanding all the cases that we have hitherto had of this complaint yielded easily to the topical application above mentioned, some of them had their eyes highly inflamed, and, as I have already said, exceedingly painful, insomuch that one or two of them could hardly be persuaded, the first day, but that they would lose their eye-sight.

Several grous (*Ptarmigans*) have been killed within these two or three days past, and we are now perfectly certain that there are deer on the island, although we have not yet seen any of them.

They finished cutting the channel round the ship to-day, and immediately she was relieved from the ice, she rose about a foot and a half forward, and a foot aft; which was contrary to what was generally believed would take place, for it was supposed that she was buoyed up by the ice. A little reflection, however, would show that the reverse must have happened, for all the fuel and provisions that have been consumed for these eight months past must have necessarily lightened her very considerably; consequently, the ice, by maintaining her in the same position that she occupied at the commencement of the winter, would tend to keep her down, or, in other words, force her to draw more water than was necessary to float her.

Thursday, 18*th*. — The weather continues to improve daily. I need only mention as a proof of this the following instance, which is, that the Griper's housing was taken off her to-day, and I believe ours is kept on merely because the survey on some of the stores, &c. is not yet completed.

Wednesday, 24*th*. — Nothing has occurred for this week past deserving of notice, except I was to give a diary of the gradual change in the state of the weather, which, as I have frequently mentioned of late, continues to improve. The thermometer to-day, in the shade, has been from eight o'clock in the morning until midnight above the freezing point, so that in the sun the snow and ice must be dissolving very rapidly. Within these two or three days past, little pools of water have been formed on the snow, in different places where earth had drifted over it. This is particularly exemplified on the snow between the two ships; for the sand and sweepings of the decks, that used to be thrown overboard, drifted there, and the snow in that space is now completely honeycombed, if I may use the expression. The reason of this is obvious, being caused by the sand and sweepings just mentioned absorbing the rays of the sun, and by that means acting on the snow; and the same reason will account for the pools of water that are met with on the snow, on the land, where it is mixed with earth. Another circumstance occurred to-day, that shews, if possible, in a stronger degree, the change in the weather, which is, that we had two showers of rain to-day, one in the morning, and the other in the evening. This is such an extraordinary phenomenon in these regions, that when the first shower was reported, we all ran on deck to see it, and some were not even satisfied with seeing it, but were so much taken with the novelty of the thing, that they went outside to receive a little of it.

Saturday, 27th. — Two ivory gulls were seen to-day, from which we may infer, that there must be open water at no great distance off. Among the many instances that I have lately mentioned, of the great change that has taken place in the state of the weather, nothing can more clearly shew this, than a circumstance that occurred this afternoon, which is, that two musquitoes have been caught. They were rather smaller than those of tropical climates, but resembled them in every other respect. A great part of the hills is now uncovered of their winter garb, and vegetation is in some places well advanced. From this circumstance we have been induced to manure, and delve two or three pieces of ground, in which are to be sown radishes, onions, and some other seeds of culinary plants, that were supplied to the ship.

Thursday, June 1*st.*—The expedition that I mentioned some time ago, that were getting ready for travelling overland to the northward, is intended so set off this evening. It is to consist of five officers, and seven men, whose names are as follows, viz.

Lieut. W. E. Parry	- -	Hecla.
Capt. E. Sabine, R. A.	-	ditto.
Mr. Alex. Fisher, Assistant Surgeon		ditto.
— Jo. Nias, Midshipman	-	ditto.
— And. Reid, ditto	-	Griper.
Serjt. Martin, R. A.	- -	Hecla.
—— M'Mahon, R. M.	-	ditto.
Wm. Dick, seaman	- -	ditto.
Rich. Drew, ditto	- -	ditto.
Jo. Kately, marine	- -	ditto.
P. Fisher, seaman	- -	Griper.
Benj. Scrivener, ditto.	-	ditto.

As I am appointed to be one of this party, I must necessarily omit saying any thing concerning the occurrences that may happen on board, until our return; therefore, what immediately follows, will be a diary of every thing worthy of notice, that comes under our observation in the course of our excursion. The object of the expedition I have already mentioned, being that of determining, if possible, the breadth of this land, and if that can be accomplished, to see what state the sea is in to the northward. Some minor objects might also be enumerated, that make it desirable that such an excursion should be undertaken; for Europeans have seen so little of the interior of Arctic lands, that, had we no other object, that alone would be a sufficient motive for undertaking such a journey, more particularly as it happens to be a time when nothing else can be done, for although the weather is very fine, the ice on the harbour is dissolving but slowly, so that there is no immediate prospect of an open sea. We are to take three weeks' provisions with us, two tents, and several bundles of dry wood for fuel, these articles, being, as it were, public property, are to be carried in the cart.* Every officer and man are to carry besides a certain number of articles, (for their own particular use,) of which a list has been made, in order to furnish themselves accordingly. These are a blanket, a spare pair of shoes, two spare pair of stockings, a flannel shirt, and a number of smaller articles, that hardly deserve to be specified separately; let it suffice, that the whole of every individual's private baggage, weighs from eighteen to twenty-four pounds. We carry it in knapsacks; the officers have one each, and the men a knapsack between every two. Besides the articles above-mentioned, we have three fowling-pieces, and two pistols, with a considerable quantity of ammunition, by means of which, we may presume, on being able to add a little to our stock of provisions on our way.

* The weight of every thing on the cart was altogether about 800 lbs.

Being thus equipped, we started from the ships at a quarter of an hour after five o'clock in the afternoon. We were accompanied to the beach by almost every individual in both ships, where they gave us three hearty cheers, which we returned with equal spirit. The major part of the people now returned on board; sixteen officers and men, however, who were anxious to give us, if possible, a more convincing proof of their zeal towards the enterprize we were undertaking, accompanied us for about five miles, carrying our knapsacks, and drawing the cart. On their parting, another volley of cheers was interchanged. We now proceeded on by ourselves, until a quarter past eleven o'clock, when we stopped, pitched our tents, and supped, or, according to our intended arrangement of time, dined; for as we are to travel at night, it will be best, I think, to name our meals according as they occur with regard to our time of rest. The reason that we are to reverse the order of time, or, in other words, to sleep in the day and travel at night, is because the day-time is the warmest, and consequently the fittest for resting to people provided as we are with no other covering than what we wear, except the tent, and a single blanket each.

Friday 2d.—We had every thing packed up again at a quarter before one o'clock this morning, and resumed our journey. In the Donkin's preserved meat-case that was emptied at dinner, we put a slip of parchment, on which was written a brief account of the party who left it, and deposited it under a small pile of stones at the place where we dined. Shortly after we started, this morning, we came to a small lake about half a mile in length, and two hundred yards in breadth; a considerable part of it was clear of ice, which led us to suppose that two Eider ducks that flew past us, a little while before we came to it, had come from it. Soon after we passed this lake, we saw several ptarmigans, and in the course of the night shot seven of them as we went along. Between two and three o'clock in the morning, we got to the north-west end of a range of hills, which terminate the view to the northward from Winter Harbour. From the top of these hills we could see the ships' masts very plainly with the naked eye, the distance being, as near as we could judge, ten or eleven miles. From these hills also we had a very extensive view of an immense plain extending to the northward and westward of us. It was completely covered with snow, and so level, that, had we not been convinced that it was considerably higher than Winter Harbour, we should be apt to suppose that it was the sea; but as this objection could not be started against its being a large lake, some were of opinion that it was so; on approaching the border of it, however, we were soon satisfied that it was only a level plain. Our route from the time of our leaving the ships, until we came in sight of this plain, was over ground, generally speaking, pretty even, but gradually ascending: its surface, for most part of the way, was at least more than two-thirds covered with snow. Soon after we got to the confines of the plain above-mentioned, we saw a reindeer, and a fawn coming across it from the southward,

The fawn appeared to be very young, at least if I may judge of its age by its size, for it did not look to be much larger than a full grown cat. It could run however very fast, for one of our party who went a little distance after them, found that he had no chance of coming up with them by dint of running. The fawn appeared to be rather of a darker colour than the doe; the latter did not differ in this respect from those that we killed in the beginning of last winter.

We continued our journey until six o'clock this morning, when we again pitched our tents, supped, and laid down to rest, leaving an officer and a man on watch, to keep a look-out, in case of our being taken by surprise, by any wild animal, &c. Soon after we pitched our tents, an accident occurred to our thermometer, owing to the carelessness of one of the men, who let something fall upon it, which rendered it useless. The ground was frozen quite hard when we laid down, but the heat of the sun was so very powerful during the day, that we found no inconvenience from cold in our tents, but from being as yet unaccustomed to bivouacking, few of us got any sleep; we rested however very comfortably.

We found by meridian altitude, our latitude to be 75° 00′ 37″ N., and longitude, by chronometer, 10′ east of Winter Harbour, so that we must have travelled over fifteen or sixteen miles of ground, since we left the ships; the difference of latitude alone between them and us being thirteen geographical miles. At four o'clock P. M. we all got up, and prepared for resuming our journey. We breakfasted on biscuit, and a pint of gruel, each made of salop powder, which we found to be a very palatable dish. Immediately after breakfast, a party, consisting of an officer, and two men, who accompanied us for the first day's journey, returned to the ships. This escort consisted properly of three men, but we found the snow so soft inland, that it was deemed necessary to take one of these men with us*, so that our travelling party now consists of thirteen persons, instead of twelve, as was originally intended. We started again at six o'clock in the evening, and continued our journey until half-past ten P. M., when we again pitched our tents, dined, and rested between three and four hours; for we had a very heavy pull all the afternoon, our march being along the skirts of the plain before-mentioned, which as I have already remarked, is so deeply covered with snow, that it required the united exertions of all the officers and men of the party to drag the cart through it. The only animals we saw in the course of our journey this evening, were a few ptarmigans, and a white owl. The latter was so shy, that we could not get near it, and of the former we got only one or two, the assistance of all of us being so indispensably necessary for getting the cart along, that we had but little time for sporting.

Saturday, 3d.—We resumed our journey again at half-past two o'clock this morning, the weather being hazy, with a light breeze of wind from the southward. Soon after we started, we came to the

* His name is Benjamin Hadman, seaman.

side of a hill, on which we found small pools of water, from which we filled our canteens, having been hitherto obliged to melt snow to procure that necessary article. As we went along we fell in with a reindeer (without horns), which at first was exceedingly tame, for he came within twenty or thirty yards of the party who first saw him; they happened unfortunately however to have no fire-arms with them, and by the time those who had come up with him, he became more wary: he was fired at, however, but without success. We pitched our tents again at six o'clock A. M., supped, and at eight retired to rest, under the protection, as I have already remarked, of an officer, and a man on watch; but as this precaution is to be always adopted whenever we stop for that purpose, it will be unnecessary to mention the thing hereafter. In order to give every person as much rest as possible, every officer and man, indiscriminately, are to keep watch in their turn, so that the men will not have above an hour's watch each, every night, and the officers rather better than an hour and a half.

Our latitude by meridian altitude at noon was 75° 6′ 52″ N., and longitude, by chronometer, 20′ 48″ E. of Winter Harbour, or rather of where the ships lie.* We resumed our journey again at a quarter before six in the afternoon, and continued on the march until a quarter past eleven, when, as usual, we pitched our tents and dined. Our

* Azimuths were also taken, by which we found the variation here to be 129° 22′ 59″ E.

route this evening was over as barren a track of land as I ever saw, for there was not a single vegetable production of any kind to be seen, except lichens. The surface of the country over which we passed, was, generally speaking, even, but in many places very rough, being covered with loose stones, over which we found considerable difficulty in dragging the cart: but the greatest obstruction that we have yet met with, was in getting it across a deep ravine that we had to pass. A little way to the northward of this ravine we passed a piece of ground that was covered with patches of red sandstone, in a very disintegrated state. We saw no animal of any kind during our march this evening, nor even the traces of any, except here and there the tracks of a fox.

Sunday, 4th. — In describing the occurrences of yesterday, I omitted to mention that we left the border of the extensive plain along which we came the evening before; how far we are from it at present it is impossible to say, as the weather is hazy, and has been so indeed for most part of the time for these four-and-twenty hours past. At the place where we dined last night, we left a tin canister, containing a piece of parchment, on which was written a short account of the party who left it. We built over it a pile of loose stones, about three feet high. We started again a quarter of an hour before three o'clock this morning, and continued on the march until twenty minutes after seven. Our route was over a plain so completely covered with snow, that the eye looked in vain for land in any direction*, except to the westward, where an extensive range of mountains, (which from their appearance we usually call the Blue Mountains), terminate our view. This range appears to run nearly north and south, for our route during these two days past have been parallel with them, and at the distance, as near as we can estimate, of twelve or fifteen miles from them. Between five and six o'clock this morning a breeze sprang up from the southward, of which we availed ourselves in a way which I never saw wind made use of before; for we got one of the tent-blankets rigged out on the cart as a sail, which made our caravan truly characteristic of our travellers, for certainly none but seafaring people would ever think of such a contrivance; the benefit that was derived from it however exceeded the hopes even of those who suggested it. The weather being cloudy, we had no observations at noon. We did not resume our journey this evening until half past seven o'clock, owing to the weather being very unfavourable, for it blew very fresh, snowed, and drifted the whole day, which made the tents for the first time rather uncomfortable; and, to add to this, one of the officers of the party was taken ill with a complaint in his bowels, which rendered it necessary to have him carried on the cart for the greatest part of this evening's march. We had the sail on the cart again for some time, and found it, as before, of considerable ser-

* To give an idea of what little space there was clear of snow, I need only mention that the only spot that was clear of it, was that on which we pitched our tents, and it was so small that they covered the whole of it.

vice whilst we went before the wind; but this was not always practicable, as we had at different times to cross ravines, and other places that obliged us sometimes to deviate from our true course. The direction of all the ravines that we crossed this evening was from east to west; one of them was very large, having its southern side very abrupt, and the opposite slanting gradually.

Monday, 5th. — The weather became so foggy after ten o'clock last night, that we could not see distinctly above fifty or sixty yards before us, so that we were obliged to steer our way by compass; that indeed we found no great difficulty in doing, but owing to the ground being so completely covered with snow, we could not find a single spot clear of it to pitch the tents on at our usual time of resting, and we were at last obliged to be content with a sort of pavement that we made of loose stones to place them on. Fatigue however made it as soft to us as a bed of down, for we rested from a quarter after one o'clock this morning, until half past five, as comfortably as possible. After dinner this morning we drank His Majesty's health, in honour of the anniversary of his birthday. We were rather behind hand in point of time in paying this compliment, but as the circumstances already stated prevented our dining earlier, we may hope to be excused for our delay. Our trip this morning was, comparatively speaking, but short, for we did not start until a quarter before six o'clock, and we stopped again at eight. Our course was across a level plain, covered with snow so completely, that, had the weather been clear last night, I believe that we should find some difficulty to get a spot clear of snow to pitch our tents on. The place where we stopped this forenoon was the best spot for our purpose that we met with since we left the ships. It was at the bottom of an open ravine, where we found abundance of water, and fine dry ground to lay upon. We found the latitude of this place by meridian altitude to be 75° 22′ 43″ N., and longitude, by chronometer, 25′ 57″ west of Winter Harbour. We built at this place a circular pile of stones, about eight feet high, in the centre of which we deposited a small cylinder containing a slip of parchment, similar to those already mentioned that were put in the tin canisters. We resumed our journey at half past five o'clock in the evening, with a fine breeze of wind from the southward, and beautiful, clear weather. The wind being fair we set sail immediately we got out of the ravine. At about four miles from the place where we started from, we came to another ravine, and between three and four miles farther on we crossed a second, both of which I remarked had their south side (for they ran east and west) abrupt, and the north side sloping like those already mentioned. This conformation I am inclined to think is owing to the snow that collects in the north side of them, for we could not see the ground on that side, whilst on their south side the surface of the ground was always visible.

We steered our course to-day entirely by compass, for our route was over a level plain, so completely covered with snow, that no remarkable object could be seen at a distance to be guided by. The way in which we managed it, therefore, was putting the compass on the snow until we got our eye fixed on some particular object, four or five hundred yards on, in the direction we wanted to go, and when we got there, taking a fresh mark in the same way. This was always done by two persons who went on before the rest, so that those who dragged the cart never had any occasion to stop; indeed, as a proof that there was no time lost, we estimated that we walked over more ground this evening, than we did at any one spell since we first started; the ground being even, and the wind in our favour, contributed certainly very much; besides, we were a considerable time on the march, for we did not stop until midnight.

No living creature of any kind was seen to-day; we saw however the track of a deer, and several foxes' tracks. The blue hills before mentioned were in sight the whole day. In our route to-day we thought that we approached them a little, but I do not think that we have been at any time within four leagues of them. About an hour before we halted this evening, (*i. e.* at eleven o'clock,) we descried a range of hills extending from north by east to the eastward, which we hailed with as much pleasure as mariners do land on first seeing it; for the monotony of the plain that we have been travelling over for these two days past, has been uninteresting in the extreme. How far these hills are off we can as yet form no certain estimate, but to have some object in view, let it be ever so distant, affords some satisfaction to the mind. Besides, I am in hopes that we have already reached the extremity of the plain that we have been travelling over lately; for where we pitched our tents this evening, there are two or three eminences that are not covered with snow.

Tuesday, 6th. — We started again at four o'clock this morning, and in less than half an hour got to the top of one of the eminences above mentioned, where, very much to our surprise, we found the land descend rapidly, as near as we could judge, between three and four hundred feet; from the foot of this declivity it sloped more gradually for the space of three or four miles, where it terminated in a large plain, of which we could see no end to the northward.

This was the impression we received when this prospect opened first to our view, but after a few minutes' observation, we were satisfied that this plain could be nothing else but the sea, for, on viewing it with a telescope, we could see several pools of water on its surface, and along the edge of it there were hummocks of ice thrown up on the beach, the same as on the south coast of the island; in fact, nothing now remained to convince us of its being the sea, except tasting the water, and that test we were determined to add also as soon as we reached it. Before we could accomplish this, however, the weather became thick, and began to rain a little, with a fresh breeze of wind from the southward. In order, therefore, to secure a dry spot to pitch our tents upon, we were obliged to stop at six o'clock, being then, as near as we could judge, about two miles from the coast. To shelter ourselves from the wind, which was, as

I have already observed, very fresh, we built a wall between five and six feet high, and seven or eight long to windward of the tents. In a valley close to us, there was a small lake of open water which appeared to be frequented by wild geese, for we saw eight of them flying about in its neighbourhood. The under part of their body, from the breast backwards, was of a dull white colour, all the rest of the body was dark. As the wind still continued to blow pretty fresh, and the ground being covered with snow that had fallen during the day, we did not move with the tents in the evening, but at six o'clock, P. M., a party started to examine the coast more particularly, and at eleven o'clock they returned perfectly convinced that this is the sea; but the ice was so thick, that they could not, with the means they had, penetrate through it. In order, however, to leave no room for any person, let him be ever so sceptical, to doubt on this point, it is determined to remove the tents early to-morrow morning down to the beach, and then to employ all hands in making a hole through the ice. It is desirable also to determine the latitude and longitude of this part of the coast, for the state of the weather to-day prevented our obtaining either. With respect to the nature of the country on this side of the island, there is as little to be said in favour of its fertility as any part of it that we have yet seen; in fact, it is as barren as it is possible for land to be: even the hardy poppy that abounds on the south side of the island, in the worst soil, is not to be seen here. The only mineral that we have yet seen on this side, is sandstone of a whitish colour, and generally of a slatey nature.

Wednesday, 7th. — We packed up the tents and set off for the sea-side at a quarter before two o'clock this morning, and at twenty minutes after four pitched them again on the beach, under the shelter of some high hummocks of ice that were thrown up there. As the weather was inclement at the time, we did not begin to dig the hole through the ice until the afternoon. It fortunately, however, cleared up for a little while at noon, so that the meridian altitude of the sun was obtained, and, in the afternoon, sights were taken to determine the longitude, and azimuths for finding the variation. The results of these observations were as follows, viz. lat. 75° 34′ 47″ N. long. 12′ 18″ E. of Winter Harbour, and the variation of the compass 134° 32′ 20″ east.

We had reason to consider ourselves very fortunate in having been able to determine these points in so short a time, and in so unfavourable weather. We were no less successful in cutting through the ice, for although we had no other instruments but the boarding pikes to dig with, we succeeded in getting through it by ten o'clock, P. M. Its thickness exceeded any floe ice that we have seen in these regions before, being no less than fourteen feet four inches, and it likewise appeared to be of a firmer texture than what we have usually seen before, being as blue as any berg-ice, and equally as compact. The water that rushed through it did not taste very salt; it was sufficiently so, however, to distinguish it to be that of the ocean, so that we had now all the proof that could be adduced, that we had reached the sea, and by that means fully accomplished the object of our expedition.

And as we may fairly claim the honour of being the discoverers of this coast, Mr. Parry took this opportunity of establishing our right to that honour, by naming the different remarkable places that were seen on this occasion. The hills that I mentioned as having been seen on the night of the fifth instant, bearing then, from north by east, to the eastward of us, appear now to be a separate island, which he has named Sabine Island. The northern extremity of the blue hills that have been so frequently mentioned in the course of our journey, he has done me the honour of naming after me, Cape Fisher. It bore N. W. of us, distant, as near as we could judge at the time, six or seven leagues; from the view that we had of it, it appeared to be very bold, and of a considerable height. The point on which we pitched our tents, he named after one of the gentlemen of the party, Point Nias, and another point of land, a few miles to the eastward of this, he named Point Reid, after another gentleman of our party; and a large bay, lying between Cape Fisher and Point Nias, was named after the ships, Hecla and Griper's Bay. These were the different places that were distinguished with names on this occasion, and as the weather was fine and clear in the evening, we had a very excellent view of them, and angles were taken, from which their situation will be correctly laid down in the chart, or rather the map of our travels. Before I conclude my diary of this day's events, I must mention one circumstance more, which, although trivial in itself, deserves to be noticed, inasmuch as it tends to shew, that although this shore is at present blocked up with such heavy ice, yet that there are times when there is open water here. The circumstance that I allude to is a piece of fir-wood seven feet and a half long, and about the thickness of a man's arm, that was found between seventy and eighty yards (inland) from the hummocks on the beach, and at least five and twenty or thirty feet above the level of the sea. Most part of it was buried in the ground, and it appeared, indeed, to have lain there for a considerable time, for the earth had penetrated in between the fibres of it, so that when it was dug up it separated into distinct filaments, according to the grain of the wood.

Thursday, 8*th*. — We packed up our tents at half-past two o'clock this morning, and took the cart up to the top of an eminence about half a mile from the beach, where we had determined yesterday to build a monument; but, owing to the weather being so bad in the forenoon, and the cutting of the hole in the ice occupied so much of our time in the afternoon, that we were obliged to defer it until this morning; it did not delay us long, however, for there were so many stones on the spot that we had selected, that we finished it by four o'clock. It is of a circular form, and of the following dimensions, namely, twelve feet in diameter at the base, and about twelve feet high. In a small apartment that we made in the centre of it, we deposited a tin cylinder containing a slip of parchment, on which was written a brief account to the same purport, as I have already mentioned, that was on the papers that we left at other places where we halted. Along with the cylinder we also left a sixpence coined in 1817, a penny-piece, bearing the date of the year 1797, and a half-penny dated 1807, and several naval uniform buttons were likewise put there by some of the men.

I mentioned two days ago, that the stone chiefly met with on this side of the island, is sandstone, and of this we had to-day a very convincing proof; for the point on which we erected the monument being our farthest north, we were all desirous of taking something back from it; and, as nothing was to be found on it but stones, our choice was necessarily confined. But we had no idea, until we began to examine the place, that it afforded so few varieties; for, after the most diligent search, nothing was to be met with but sandstone, except one small piece of granite, which we divided into specimens.

The object of our expedition being now accomplished in every respect, we began our journey back at four o'clock in the morning. As our route to the northward was on a tract so barren of interest, it is intended not to return in that direction, but to go to the blue hills so often mentioned, where we may expect to meet some variety, and as they run nearly north and south, our going along them will not take us much out of our way; and even if it would, we have plenty of provisions to return with. Our course, therefore, after we started this morning, was to the southward and westward, for a considerable part of the way along the south-eastern coast of Hecla and Griper's Bay. The weather was so cold that it froze the water in our canteens, and one of them was burst in consequence. We pitched our tents again at seven o'clock, on the side of a dry sandy hill, the top of which we found to be full of holes, like a rabbit warren; most probably fox burrows. At this place also we found a ptarmigan: so that we may already say, that we have met with more to interest us than we did during the last three days of our journey to the northward. The latitude of this place we found, by meridian altitude, to be 75° 33′ 55″ N.; and longitude by chronometer 1′ 23″ 5, W. of the ships.

We resumed our journey again at half-past five o'clock in the afternoon, and continued on the march until half past eleven. Our route during this day's journey was for the most part over plains, the greatest part of which were covered with snow: as we came along, however, we found that the parts that were clear of it, improved very much in their appearance; for vegetation was, in some places, well advanced, especially in those places where the ground was moist from the dissolution of the snow. In course of our journey, this evening, we shot a ptarmigan, and saw two geese of the same kind as those that were seen on the 6th instant.

Friday, 9th. — We started again a quarter after three o'clock this morning, directing our course more to the southward, in order to keep on a ridge of rising ground, that is almost clear of snow, and leading to the Blue Hills. As our route, for most part of the way, was over such good travelling ground, we got, by seven o'clock, to the foot of these hills; where we pitched our tents on the top of a fine dry eminence; from which, we had a tolerable good view of the plain to the northward aud westward of us. We shot three ptarmigans at this place, two of which were hens, and had the colour of their plumage so much changed, that a person would hardly suppose them to be the same kind of bird as those that we killed about a week ago; for the belly was the only part of them that was white; the head, neck, back, and upper side of the wings, and the tail, being nearly of the same colour as a partridge. The cock was perfectly white, as before. In the course of our trip, this morning, we saw, for the first time this season, a running stream of water; and we passed several large pools of it in the ravines that we crossed. We found the lat. of the place of our encampment to-day, by meridian altitude, to be 75° 26′ 43″ N. and long., by chronometer, 53′ 37″ 5 W. of Winter Harbour. The weather, to-day, was extremely fine, with a light air of wind from the southward and westward. The men employed themselves, during their respective watches, to-day, washing their flannels, stockings, and such other articles as they had dirty; which were all perfectly dry by half-past five o'clock in the afternoon; the time that we started again. Our route this evening was sometimes across plains and valleys, and at other times, over hills; in the former, we find it now rather heavy travelling; for the snow is melting so rapidly, that the land is, in these places, completely saturated with water. The progress of vegetation is astonishingly quick: the sorrel is already so far advanced, that we picked enough, during our march this evening, to afford us some refreshment. The ground that we came over to-day must be, at times, well stocked with deer; for we passed a great many of their horns; and their old tracks were very numerous. We killed two ptarmigans in the course of the evening, and two or three more were seen. Between nine and ten o'clock the weather became hazy, with occasional light showers of snow: we continued on the march, however, until a quarter before eleven o'clock.

Saturday, 10*th*. — We resumed our journey again a quarter before three o'clock in the morning, and continued on the march until a quarter after seven. Our route was, as I mentioned yesterday, over hills and plains; we also crossed several ravines, some of which we found a little difficulty in passing, especially one or two, for the snow in them is now so thoroughly soaked with water, that the cart sunk into it up to the naves. The weather was so thick this forenoon that we could see no great distance, and even if it were clear, I believe our view would not be so extensive as we thought it would when we saw these hills at a distance; for they are so nearly of a height, that every little rising obstructs the prospect from one over the other. The plains on their top are yet almost entirely covered with snow; we came across one of these this morning, that was several miles in extent, which had scarcely a single black spot on it. The only animals we saw during this march were four arctic gulls (*Larii Parasitici*) flying to the eastward. Our latitude by meridian altitude today was 75° 20′ 54″ N.

We started again at half-past five in the afternoon, but the weather was so bad that we were obliged to halt again at half-after nine; for it blew very fresh indeed from the south-east, and snowed so incessantly that it was impossible to see distinctly thirty yards before us. We were fortunate, however, in getting a good place to pitch our tents in, for we got into a very deep ravine that afforded us excellent shelter, and there happened to be plenty of slatey sandstone in the same place, with which we paved the floor of our tents. In the north side of this ravine there was an immense accumulation of snow; great pieces, or avalanches of it, which had broken off, were lying at the bottom of the ravine. I have hitherto omitted to mention that, since we got into the neighbourhood of these hills, and particularly since we got on them, we have found a considerable difference in the mineralogical productions of the parts that we have travelled over, sandstone is indeed the predominant mineral, for all the fixed rocks that we have seen are entirely composed of it; but we frequently meet with pieces of granite, quartz, and felspar, and sometimes hornblende. The sandstone is remarkably schistose, being frequently as thin as roofing slate; solid blocks of it, indeed, are rarely to be met with of any considerable size.

Sunday, 11th. — The weather cleared up this morning, the wind having veered round to the N. W. We therefore packed up our tents and resumed our journey at five o'clock. Our first outset was up the south side of the ravine in which we slept last night; this we found to be an undertaking that required all our exertions, for it was so steep, that it took us nearly three-quarters of an hour to get the cart up. Our route afterwards was for about three hours over a plain covered with snow. It appeared to be of a considerable height, for we had a very extensive view from it in every direction. After we got to the end of this plain, a very romantic prospect presented itself to our view all at once; for we beheld at the foot of the plain, and about two or three miles to the south-eastward of it, a very extensive sheet of ice, with an island about three-quarters of a mile in length, rising abruptly from the middle of it to the height of six or seven hundred feet. The shores of this lake, or gulf (for we were unable at this time to say which it was) appeared to be very rugged and precipitant, particularly on the north-west side, or that which we were on. We continued to approach it until ten o'clock, when, going down the side of a steep and rough hill that lay on the north side of it, the axle-tree of the cart snapt in two, in the middle. As this was an injury that we had no possible means of repairing, it required no time to consider what was to be done; we therefore got every thing immediately taken off it, and carried down to a valley at the foot of the hill. It was at first intended to break the wheels up for fire-wood, but on reconsideration it was found that the body of the cart would afford as much fuel as we were likely to require; the wheels and axle were therefore left, for future travellers (if any should pass that way) to see that they were not the first adventurers that passed over these rocky mountains. Although the loss of the cart was a thing by no means to be wished for, yet we did not consider it in any way in the light of a disaster; for what provisions remained we found to be no more than what we could manage to carry very well, when properly divided amongst officers, and all.

Had the accident occurred indeed when we were on the north side of the island, it might have put us to some inconvenience, but we have reason to think, that, instead of its retarding our progress at present, we shall get on much quicker without the cart, for the ground has been getting gradually worse for travelling every day for some time past, and there is every chance of its continuing to do so.

From the top of the hill on the side of which the cart broke down, we could see "Table Hill," or at least, a hill which we have every reason to suppose from its bearing and estimated distance to be it; for our latitude by meridian altitude at noon to-day, was 75° 12′ 50″ N., and longitude by chronometer 1° 00′ 31″ 5 W. of Winter Harbour*:

* The variation of the compass at this place was found to be 125° 01′ 52″ E.

and the hill in question was always judged to be between six and seven miles from the ships. After we had pitched our tents, and got every thing that was on the cart down to them, we supped and lay down to rest until the evening, when we began to make preparations for resuming our journey. All the provisions, tents, and indeed every article of public property, were weighed, and equitably distributed amongst the officers and men, according to their supposed strength. I am sorry to say, however, that, notwithstanding the necessity there was on this occasion, for every person to take some share of the public burden, there was one amongst us who did not offer to carry a single article but his own private property; his name I forbear to mention, nor would I indeed notice the circumstance at all, were it not in justice to the rest of the party to say of them, that, instead of showing any inclination to imitate such a glaring instance of a want of public spirit, it appeared to stimulate them to emulate one another in their exertions.

Monday, 12th. — We struck the tents at two o'clock this morning, every thing else being by this time packed up that we intended to take with us. What we left indeed were things of very little use, such as empty canteens, and meat-cases, in which we used to carry water, and wash in; some spare ammunition was also left, and a few other things that were deemed useless. The pole of the cart was set up against the side of a wall that we built yesterday to shelter the tents from the wind, and at the foot of this pole we deposited the tin-cases and canteens, and indeed every thing else that was left.* We began our journey at half-past two o'clock, and about three reached the shore of the gulf, or lake before mentioned, our route was from this time until five o'clock along the foot of the mountains that bound the north-western side of it at this place. During this part of our march we saw several ptarmigans, two or three of which we shot, and on a pool of open water, close to the beach, we saw a couple of geese of the same kind as those that we saw on the north side of the island. A raven was also seen in the course of the morning and some bank swallows. The rocks that we came along the foot of this morning were composed of sandstone, but different in character from that which we met with in the ravines that we have been passing for some days past, for it existed in large blocks. At five o'clock we came to a low point, from which we had a good view of the extent and direction of the gulf, or lake, as it extended inland. Of its extent, indeed, we could form no certain judgment, as we could not see the termination of it; but with respect to its direction we found that it ran to the northward and eastward, or rather between north-east and east. After having seen that going round the top or north-east end of it, would take us very much out of our way, it was determined to venture directly across it from this point; but as we had already been nearly three hours on the march,

* We deposited a cylinder here which contained a piece of parchment, on which was written the same information as on those that we left at the different places already mentioned.

it was deemed to be too great an exertion to attempt crossing it without halting, the distance at the narrowest part being estimated to be at least six or seven miles, and as this could not be done conveniently on the ice, our only alternatives were to rest where we were, or to go to the island mentioned yesterday, which we considered to be about halfway across, and not lying much out of the direction that we wished to go. We therefore started for the island a few minutes after five o'clock, and arrived there at seven. A few minutes after we landed there, we discovered that this large sheet of water, which we were hitherto in doubt whether it was a lake or an arm of the sea, is actually the latter, for one of us which happened to take up a pot-full of water out of a pool on the ice close to the beach, found that it was very brackish, which decided the point quite to our satisfaction; very little doubt, indeed, remained on our mind respecting it before, for we found as we came along hummocks of ice thrown up in different places on the shore, a thing which we could hardly suppose would happen if it was a lake. We found the island to be composed, like the adjacent hills, of sandstone, and very barren. It is about three-quarters of a mile in length, from north north-west to south south-east; and nearly of the same breadth. It rises perpendicularly from the sea on the west side to the height of six or seven hundred feet, and the ascent to it, indeed, on every other side is pretty steep. From the top of it there was a very good view of the gulf to the westward, or, in other words, towards its mouth, for it runs nearly east and west. The two capes that form the entrance of it are, I understand, to be called Cape Beechey, and Cape Happner, after the two officers of these names belonging to the expedition. The distance between these capes and the island was estimated to be from six to seven leagues, and the average breadth of the gulf beyond the island to the westward between four and five leagues. The gulf itself is to be named Liddon's Gulf, in compliment to the commander of the Griper; and a bold promontory on the north side of it is to be called Cape Edwards, after the principal medical officer of the expedition; and the island is to be named Hooper's Island, after the officer of that name belonging to the Hecla. In speaking of the mineralogy of Hooper's Island, I omitted to mention that we found several pieces of crystallised carbonate of lime on it, small pieces of quartz and felspar were also met with, and it is probable that if we had time to examine it more minutely we should meet with many other varieties; and it is not in minerals only, that it promised to be an interesting place; it seemed to be a great resort for birds, for we saw several ptarmigans on it, and a great many of the geese so often mentioned in the course of our journey, were seen on the pools of water that lay off it. Of these birds we managed to shoot four during our stay, and found them to be brent geese (*Anas Bernicla*, Lin.) They weighed about four pounds each, at least that was the weight of the first one that we shot, and the rest appeared to be about the same size. The latitude of the place where the tents were pitched was found by meridian altitude to be 75° 05′ 08″ N., and longitude by chronometer 1° 08′ 03″ W. of Winter Harbour. * We left the island at half-past six, and directed our course to the nearest part of the land on the south-east side of the gulf, where we arrived at half-past eight.

On reaching the shore we saw two reindeer, and some ptarmigans, but we could not, nor indeed did we try much to get near them, for the ice where we crossed it this morning was so deeply covered with snow, that every person appeared to be pretty well fatigued by the time we landed. The land on this side of the gulf, we found to be, comparatively speaking, low, and less covered with snow than on the opposite side. After crossing a piece of rising ground near where we landed, we entered into a fine open valley leading to the south-ward and eastward. In the N. W. side of it there was a lagoon, about three quarters of a mile in circumference; it communicated with the gulf by a channel about fifty yards in breadth, across which we travelled. On the top of a small eminence, about thirty feet above the level of the sea, and close to the entrance of the lagoon, we found a piece of fir wood about two feet long, and at the thickest end about the same circumference. We found the skeleton of a musk-ox here also, and several reindeer's horns were seen as we came along. There was every appearance indeed of this valley being very much frequented by these

* The variation of the compass on this island was found to be 122° 59′ 37″ E.

animals, for their tracks were very numerous, and even without these indications it might be inferred that it is a place likely to be resorted to both by deer, and musk-oxen, for it afforded the best pasturage of any place that I have yet seen on this island. At eleven o'clock we pitched our tents, and dined.

Tuesday, 13th. — Instead of resuming our journey this morning, as usual after dinner, it was determined not to start until the evening, in order to employ the forenoon in examining the valley and the shore of the gulf, in this neighbourhood, more particularly, as being places where we were likely to meet some objects of interest; and the sequel will show that our anticipations were realized, and consequently that our delay was amply repaid. Our success in the sporting way was not indeed so great as we expected, for a few ptarmigans and a golden-plover were all that we killed; but we had the satisfaction of finding, that much more may be done, for we saw no less than thirteen deer in one herd, and a musk-ox was also seen for the first time this season; but what is still more interesting, we found that this island had been inhabited at some period or other: for we found the remains of six Esquimaux huts, at the distance of two hundred and fifty, or three hundred yards from the beach, on a stony eminence on the southeast side of the valley. They resembled, in every respect, the ruins that we met with, and were described on the 28th of last August, as also the Esquimaux huts that we saw the year before in Baffin's Bay; being composed of rough stones, and of a rude oblong figure, about eight feet long, and five or six feet broad, besides a place about two feet square, at the end of each, which I have been told, is the place where the Esquimaux keep their provisions. Detached from the huts, we found a square place between two and three feet each way, which we supposed to have been the cooking place of the whole party. At a little distance from this there was another rectangular place, the use of which we could form no idea of; it was about three feet long and one foot broad, and filled to the depth of six or seven inches with ptarmigans' dung. How long it is since these huts were inhabited, it is impossible to say, but it must have been many years ago, for the flags with which they were paved were covered with moss, and the exposed sides of the stones that composed the walls were all covered with lichen. But whatever the length of time may be since they were inhabited, it is probable that those who did inhabit them were not strangers to this coast, for they certainly chose the most eligible spot for game that we have seen in this country. The geographical site of these huts was *nearly* as follows, viz. lat. 75° 2′ 37″ N., and longitude, by chronometer, 48′ 48″ west of Winter Harbour; I have said nearly, because the observations from which these results were obtained were made at the tents, which were about half a mile inland of the huts. The variation of the compass was found here to be 126° 1′ 48″ easterly. Every object that we had in view at this place, being at length accomplished, we packed up, and resumed our journey at six o'clock in the evening, the weather being at the time hazy, with a fresh breeze of wind from the S. S. E. We had not been above an hour on the march, when it came on to snow; we continued on our way, however, until nearly eight, thinking that the weather would, perhaps, clear up; but, on finding then that there was no appearance of it, we pitched our tents to secure a dry spot before it was too late.

Wednesday, 14*th*. — The weather having cleared up about four o'clock, we began immediately to prepare for our journey, and in rather less than twenty minutes we were again on the march. About five o'clock, the weather became fine and clear, so that we had an excellent view of the rocky precipices on the north side of Liddon's Gulf; and shortly after we saw Table Hill, which we kept in sight, and towards which we directed our course until we stopped at eight o'clock. The surface of the country that we passed over this this morning, was, generally speaking, even, but not level, for it rose gradually as we went along to the southward and eastward. A very considerable portion, I think, indeed, nearly one half the surface of the land, is now clear of snow.

This has been one of the finest days that we have had this summer, for it was for some part of the time warmer than we could wish it. Our latitude, to-day, at noon, was 74° 53′ 55″ N., and with respect to our longitude, it is not an object worth being mentioned now, for we are so near Table Hill, that we expect to reach it in our next journey. We started again a little before six o'clock in the evening, and directed our course, as before, towards Table Hill, which we reached about twenty minutes before ten, and pitched our tents at the foot of it. Our route was, during this march, over ground of the same nature as that which we passed in the forenoon, with this difference, however, that it was much more difficult to travel over, for it is so completely saturated with water, that we frequently sank into it up to the ankle, and sometimes farther, and even in the driest parts of it we went down an inch or two; in short, we avoided the black ground to-day as much as we sought it ten days ago. We observed, during this day's march, a considerable difference in the mineralogical character of the country, for instead of the whitish sandstone that prevailed so abundantly from Liddon's Gulf to the north side of the island, we found to-day, that the kind of stone we generally met with had a greenish tinge, and of a loose or disintegrated texture, like the sandstone in the ravines near Winter Harbour. Small pieces of granite, quartz, and felspar, were pretty frequently met with to-day, and when we got within a couple of miles of Table Hill, we began to meet limestone. Vegetation is now in a very flourishing condition, the sorrel is very far advanced, and there is a species of saxifrage (*oppositifolia*) beginning to blossom.

Thursday, 15*th*.—After taking a few hours' rest, we all turned (at two o'clock) to build a monument on the top of Table Hill*, which we finished

* As this hill is a conspicuous object at a very considerable distance, its geographical position deserves to be mentioned.

by six. It is of a circular form, ten feet in diameter at the base, and about eleven feet high. In the centre of it we deposited an empty Donkin's meat-canister, containing a slip of parchment, on which was written the same brief notice that was on the pieces that we left at the other places that I have already mentioned, viz. "This was deposited here by a party from his Majesty's ships Hecla and Griper, who wintered on this island in 1819 and 1820." In building it we left also a small passage, leading on an inclined plane from the outside to the centre, through which it is intended to convey a cylinder (that is to be sent out from the ship*), in which will be a paper giving a more detailed account of our stay, and object in visiting these regions, &c. As it was apprehended that we should find it disagreeable to travel in the heat of the day, instead of setting off to the ships after we had finished the monument, we retired, as usual, to rest. We broke up our encampment again, for the last time, at a quarter after three o'clock in the afternoon, and got on board by seven

---

It was obtained from observations made at the monument that we erected on the top of it, viz.

Latitude by meridian altitude	74° 48′ 33″	N.
Longitude by chronometer -	23 04	W. of the ships.
Variation of the compass	123 16 01	E.

* This cylinder was sent out after our return; and in the entrance of the hole through which it was conveyed, there was fixed a copper-plate, on which was punched the names of the ships, and the date of the year. I may remark, also, in this place, that a similar plate was fixed on the south-west side of the pile that was erected on North-East Hill, near Winter Harbour.

in the evening, where we were received with every demonstration of a hearty welcome ; after having performed a journey of at least one hundred and eighty miles, for, by the most moderate computation, I think that we must have averaged twelve miles a-day. In giving the account of this journey, I am perfectly aware that I have been more minute in many instances than the subject that I was treating deserved ; but I thought that, by attempting to cull it, I might omit some circumstances that deserved to be mentioned. I have, therefore, given the whole almost *verbatim* from the notes that I made at the time on the spot.

Friday, 16th. — Nothing occurred on board worthy of particular notice during the time we were away ; getting the ballast in, and re-stowing the holds, were, I believe, the principal things done during our absence. A very great difference however, hastaken place in the state of the country around Winter Harbour, for those parts that were covered with snow when we went away, are now abounding with plants of various kinds beginning to blossom ; in fact, the aspect of the country is so much changed, that, were we not so thoroughly acquainted with every place in this neighbourhood, we should hardly recognise some parts of it again. The ice in the harbour has got considerably thinner, but there is no part of it open yet, nor is there any appearance indeed of its breaking up for some time. As there is no immediate prospect, therefore, of our leaving this place for some time, it is intended to send a party from each ship with ten or twelve days' provisions, in order to try what they can do in the way of procuring game for the use of the expedition. Each party are to take tents with them of the same kind as we had on our late journey, so that they can easily remove them from one place to another, according as they find game more or less abundant in different situations. The party from the Hecla are to consist of three officers and three men, and as I am appointed to be one of it, my narrative of the events that may happen on board, must be again interrupted until our return. We started from the ship at half past eleven o'clock in the evening, accompanied by an officer and three men, who were sent to assist us in carrying the tents and provisions, &c. We directed our course to the eastward, for we learnt from a party that went out on an excursion in that direction some days ago, that they saw a great many geese on some lakes on the west side of what is commonly called Bounty Cape.* We got out there between five and six o'clock next morning, and pitched our tents on the top of a dry eminence, which we estimated to be from eight to nine miles from the ships. A regular diary of all the circumstances that occurred from this period until our return again on board, would be so crowded with repetitions about things of so little interest, that even the reading of it would be more apt to be considered a tedious task, than a source of pleasure or information. Under this

* This name was first given by the men to that remarkable headland that is situated near the 110th degree of longitude, in consequence of that meridian being that for which the first reward is given; and, I understand, from the name being so very appropriate, that it is to be confirmed.

impression, therefore, I shall deviate from my former plan of giving the occurrences of every day separately, in the order in which they happened, and endeavour to comprise and arrange every thing worthy of notice under different heads, in regular succession. In the first place, then, with respect to the country, although we were out here only ten days, it was surprising to see the great change that took place, for on first going out we found the greatest part of the low land covered with snow, and the streams of water that flowed from it, had not then formed into any regular channels, but were spread all over the plains near the coast, making them as it were one entire swamp. Before we came in, however, these swamps had in a great measure been drained of their water, which formed three or four streams (within the space of five or six miles) that we used generally to distinguish them by the name of rivers, and one or two of them indeed were of such magnitude for some time, as not to be altogether undeserving the appellation. These streams passed through many small lakes, which appeared generally to be very shallow. We saw two or three lakes, however, amongst the mountains, which, from the character of the land around them, we had reason to suppose were of considerable depth; and I remarked this difference between them, that the lakes on the low land were clear of ice, whilst those amongst the hills were almost entirely covered with it. Vegetation was very far advanced indeed by the time that we returned, for some spots where there was moisture and good soil, the grass was from two to three inches long; and the sorrel was so abundant that we used in a few minutes to collect enough to make a sallad every day to our dinner. With respect to the mineralogical character of those parts that we traversed over, I observed nothing different from that seen in the immediate neighbourhood of Winter Harbour, viz. sandstone, composing the whole of the fixed rocks, and the greatest part of the loose stones also; granite, limestone, and small pieces of red felspar were frequently met with, but these formed but a very small proportion indeed, when compared with the quantity of sandstone that was seen. Having thus taken a cursory review of the mineral and vegetable pro uctions that we had an opportunity of seeing, my next object is to notice the different kinds of animals that we saw. The deer were not so numerous as we expected to find them, for two dozen, or thirty at most, were as many as we saw the whole time we were out, and of these we only succeeded in killing two; this we attributed in a great measure to the shyness of the does, for they were so careful of their young, that there was no possibility of getting near them. The two deer that we killed were very lean, for although they appeared to be full-grown, the first one weighed only 54 lbs. when skinned and cleaned, and the other which we got about a week after 64 lbs. Their horns were not above nine or ten inches in length; they were covered with a soft skin, which had a fine downy coat; their tips were flexible, but if bent much, were easily broken; the substance of the horns were very porous, and full of blood. The colour not only of these two, but indeed of all the deer we saw, was white, with the exception of a light ash-coloured patch on their back; but the fawns appeared to be entirely of that colour. The next animals I ought to mention, if I take them according to their size, are a couple of wolves which we saw one afternoon; but as we had but a distant view of them, I can say nothing about them. We had also a distant view, two or three times, of some foxes; the only thing in which they appeared to differ from those that were caught during the winter was, in their having a black patch on their sides a little before their hind quarters.

We saw several hares during the time we were out, of which we killed four; their average weight was from seven to eight pounds; they were perfectly white, with the exception of the tips of their ears, which were black. These were all the varieties of quadrupeds that we saw, and of the feathered tribe the number was not much greater. Brent geese, king ducks, and long-tailed ducks, arctic and glaucous gulls, comprised the whole of the aquatic birds that we saw; and a few ptarmigans, plovers, sanderlings, and snow-buntings, were all the land birds that were seen. The geese were, the first two or three days after we went out, pretty numerous, but, on finding themselves disturbed, most of them went away, and those that remained secured themselves by keeping in the middle of two or three large lakes, where our shot would not reach them; we succeeded, however, in killing a dozen of them during the time we were out. The ducks were not numerous, so that our success in that way was very trifling. With respect to the ptarmigans, I believe all were killed that were seen, viz. fifteen; and, if fifty times the number had been seen, I believe we might have killed them all, for they are as stupid as any birds I ever saw. These are all the circumstances that occurred during our ten days' excursion, that deserve to be mentioned; and I am not sure, indeed, that they are of sufficient importance to claim so much notice as I have taken of them. As soon as we returned on board, another party was sent out for the same purpose as we were on, with ten days more provisions.

Tuesday, 27th. — With respect to the events that occurred on board during the time we were away, they have been of so little consequence that they do not deserve to be noticed. The ice on the harbour has decayed indeed, very considerably during these ten days past; it is covered now with pools of water along shore, and at the places where the streams of water from the ravines discharge themselves into the harbour, it is quite detached from the beach. The land is now completely clear of snow, with the exception of what there is in the ravines, and that is dissolving very rapidly indeed; for the torrents of water that run down them, exceed any thing of the kind that we have seen in these regions before. The surface of the country now presents a very pleasing appearance; some parts of it, in particular, abound with such abundance of purple-coloured saxifrage in blossom, that even persons accustomed to a better climate than we have been for some time past, could not help admiring it; but to us, who experienced, and who have so recently emerged from the dreary scene of an arctic winter, it will naturally appear more delightful. The sorrel is, however, the only vegetable production from which we derive any benefit; but from it we have a very abundant supply of a most useful, and very palatable article of diet. All the men are sent on shore twice a-week, viz. on Sunday and Thursday, to gather it, and what they collect, after being mixed with vinegar, is served out to them regularly.* Notwithstanding every attention has been paid to the different seeds that were sown in the gardens, I believe that we shall receive but very little benefit from the produce of them, for their growth is very tardy indeed.

Friday, 30th. — At two o'clock this morning departed this life, William Scott, boatswain's mate, who had been ill for some months past, first with scurvy, and afterwards with diarrhœa, and general debility. He was considered a very good and quiet man, and I am told an excellent seaman; but, unfortunately, it is said that he was rather addicted to spirits. Whether a consciousness of this failing preyed on his mind or not, I cannot pretend to say; but he was often observed to be very low-spirited, which amounted sometimes, during his illness, to hypochondriasm.

Sunday, July 2d. — Immediately after divine service this forenoon, his body was taken on shore, and interred on a plain between two and three hundred yards from the beach. Almost the whole of the officers and men of both ships attended on

* As a considerable quantity of the lemon-juice has been, as I have already remarked, destroyed by the frost during the winter, it has, of course become an object of importance to economise what remains, and as the sorrel that is gathered is considered to be a good substitute for it, the serving of it out has for the present been suspended.

this occasion, to perform this last duty that we owe one another; we all walked two and two, in regular procession, and in the order which is always observed on these occasions. *

Friday, 7th.—The weather has been remarkably fine since the beginning of this month, the ice on the harbour is now full of holes in the neighbourhood of the ships, and along shore it is detached from the land entirely at high water; we found the thickness of it in several places where we measured it this evening, to vary from a foot, to eighteen inches. In the course of the afternoon a large flock of loons flew across the harbour, going to the westward, from which we are inclined to think, that there is some open water in that direction, and we have reason to suppose, that we shall soon have that here also. A few days ago we picked up on the surface of the ice, between the ships and the shore, three fish, between ten inches and a foot long each, which answered to the character given by Linnæus of the pouting whiting. We supposed that they got on the surface

* On a slab of schistose sandstone about three feet long, and two feet broad, there was cut the following inscription:

"To
The Memory of
Wm. Scott, Seaman,
His Britannic Majesty's ship
Hecla;
Obiit June 30th, 1820.
Æt. 33 years."

This stone was placed at the head of the grave, with its front facing to the westward; and the grave itself was covered with stone, in order to prevent its being disturbed by wolves, or any other animals.

of the ice, at the time that it was overflowed by the stream tides in the winter. In speaking of tides, it reminds me that I have hither omitted to mention, that we have been for nearly these two months past, observing regularly every day, the rise and fall of the tide in this harbour. * And we found, from the result of these observations, that the greatest rise and fall is only four feet two inches, and that occurred only once, viz. at eight o'clock in the forenoon, on the 13th of May last.

Friday, 14th. — Nothing of any importance has occurred for this week past. The ice has now got very thin, but it has not yet broke up any where except along the shore. It is expected, however, that the first strong breeze of wind we have will break it up ; and, in order to be able to avail ourselves of the first opportunity that may offer for getting away, every thing is now ready, I believe, for taking our departure. Among other mementos that we have left to indicate our stay at this place, is a large pile of stones, or monument, as it is called, that we erected yesterday, on the most conspicuous hill in this neighbourhood, situated about two miles to the north-east of where the ships lay, and from thence usually termed North-East Hill. This pile is about ten feet in diameter at the base, and between ten and eleven feet high. In the centre of it we deposited a tin cylinder, containing some silver coins, and a paper giving an account of our stay, and object in visiting these regions. On the south end of a large

* See Appendix.

stone, situated between two and three hundred yards from the beach, on the south-west side of the entrance of the harbour, we cut the following words so deeply, that I imagine some traces of them will be legible for some centuries to come. The words in question are these: — "His Britannic Majesty's ships, Hecla and Griper, commanded by W. E. Parry, and M. Liddon, wintered in the adjacent harbour, 1819-20." I may remark also that the inscription on the tomb-stone of the late William Scott will be another lasting monument that will show the place near which we have now passed the best part of a year. Besides these, many other relics will be left, that would identify Winter Harbour for some ages; but, what is more unperishable than all these marks, which time will destroy, we have determined its geographical position with such precision, I presume, that if any future navigator should hereafter visit this coast, he will have no difficulty in finding this port, at least as far as its situation will be concerned.

The latitude of the spot where the ship lay since the 26th of September, 1819	74° 47′ 15″ N.
Longitude of ditto, by lunar observations	110° 48′ 30″ W.
Variation of the compass, as found on shore, clear of the ship's attraction	128° E.

Although we are now in perfect readiness, and, I may say, indeed, in daily expectation of leaving this place, it is intended to keep parties out shooting until we have an immediate prospect of setting off. My diary of the occurrences on board must, therefore, be again suspended for a while, as I am appointed to be one of the party that is to go out this evening to relieve those that are at the tents. We left the ships at ten o'clock at night, and arrived at the tents at four o'clock next morning.

Tuesday, 25th. — My account of all the circumstances that came under our observation, from that period, until our return, may be comprised in very few words. It would, indeed, be little better than a mere tautology of the events of our first *shooting excursion*, if I were to relate those that occurred at this time. With respect, therefore, to the animals that we met with, I have to observe only, that they were of the same kind as those we saw before; but much fewer in number, owing, no doubt, to their being so much chased and disturbed for these six weeks past. The face of the country is very much improved, as far as regards its being much drier, and consequently better adapted for travelling; but with respect to its appearance, it has lost very considerably in this point, for almost the whole of the flowers that adorned it, about a fortnight or three weeks ago, have now run into seed, and their petals fallen off, so that the land has begun again to look naked. The lakes and streams that were so numerous, and some of considerable size, when we were out about the middle of last month, are now almost entirely dried up; even those streams that we then dignified with the name of rivers, are now so small, that we crossed them on our return to-day without wetting our feet. The exhalation from these lakes is almost incredible, considering the nature of the climate ; for the vapour that rises from them sometimes appears at a little distance, as thick as if it rose from the surface of hot water. During our excursions, lately, we observed another curious circumstance, peculiar, I imagine, to this climate, at least to the extent that we saw it. The thing I allude to is, that in several places along the sides of the hills, we observed where pieces of ground, from fifty to sixty yards in length, and between thirty and forty in breadth, had started from their place, and slided down these hills to the distance of sixty or seventy yards, forming, where they had stopped, large heaps of earth, and in other places spreading over the face of these hills. The depth of the chasms that were left by the removal of these pieces of ground was, in general, about two feet ; the surface of the ground in them was firmly frozen, whilst the ground that slided away was so soft, that a person would sink into it.

How far these casual circumstances may operate in changing the face of this country, I do not pretend to say, but there is one thing certain, that it has undergone a very considerable change, and that too at no very distant period of time ; for we found the jaw-bones of a whale on a plain, at the distance of a mile, at least, from the sea, and a crown-bone of a whale was picked up about the same distance from the shore, near Winter Harbour. And, in both these cases, the bones were, I think, too heavy for wolves or bears to drag them that distance inland ; and, if that be admitted, I do not see any other way in which the thing can be accounted for, except by supposing that the coast has extended its former limits. But my object being that of stating facts, I shall avoid entering any farther into these conjectures, in case of drawing wrong conclusions. On returning to the tents this morning, we found an officer and three men there, who were sent out to assist us in taking the tents, &c., on board, there being hopes, at length, of leaving Winter Harbour; for all the ice on it is now broke up, and drifting about from one side to the other, according to the direction of the wind. We started at three o'clock in the afternoon, and got on board by eight o'clock in the evening.

Wednesday, 26th. — The wind being from the southward this forenoon, all hands were employed warping the ships out towards the mouth of the harbour, where we anchored, the entrance being as yet choked up with ice; but, as we know that there is clear water along shore outside, this obstruction, we may reasonably expect, will soon be removed by the first fresh breeze of northerly wind that we have.

Friday, 28th. — We are still detained by the ice above-mentioned, which has been thrown up, by the late southerly wind that we have had, into large hummocks on the reef, at the south-east side of the entrance of the harbour. Our passage, indeed, is not over that reef, but the ice that has grounded on it, seems to offer obstruction in its passage outward, to that which is in the harbour. We saw a large seal on the ice to-day, but he lay so near the edge of the piece that he was on, that he succeeded in getting into the water before we got to him, although he was severely wounded with balls.

Tuesday, August 1st. — The first of August appears to be a lucky day in the events of this voyage, for it was on this day last year that we entered Lancaster's Sound, and at twenty minutes after one o'clock this afternoon we made sail out of Winter Harbour, after having been part of every month in the year in it, and, consequently, upwards of ten calendar months. Our anxiety, for some time past, to recommence our labours after so long a period of inactivity, and the pleasure that we felt on finding that long-wished-for period at length arrived, may be more easily conceived than expressed; for, notwithstanding the several plans that were adopted to keep both body and mind employed, we could not help occasionally reflecting, that much of our time was idly spent, whilst a great deal yet remained to be done, before the object of the expedition would be accomplished. On getting out of the harbour to-day, however, the prospect before us gave us every reason to hope that, notwithstanding the shortness of the season, much might be done; for, as far as we could see to the westward, there was a channel of open water, three or four miles in breadth, along the land. To the eastward, this channel appeared to be still wider, but that not being our way, we paid but little attention to what lay in that direction. The weather was extremely fine to-day; but the wind being for most part of the time against us, we made no great progress.

Wednesday, 2d. — The wind being still adverse, our advance to the westward was, as yesterday, but very slow; and in the afternoon it veered round to the southward, and, consequently, soon set the ice in with the land, so that we were obliged, at four o'clock, to make fast to a hummock of ice, aground near the shore.

Thursday, 3d.—The weather was foggy most part of this day; and, the ice being close in with the land, we have not moved from the place where we brought up yesterday. It has been observed, since we made fast here, that the flood-tide comes from the westward, and that the time of high-water corresponds with that in Winter Harbour.

Friday 4th.—The wind having veered round to the N. W. this forenoon, the ice soon began to drive off from the land, and by one o'clock in the afternoon we cast off and made sail. As we advanced to the westward, we found the channel to be gradually widening, so that, about midnight, we found as great a space of clear water as we ever observed before off this part of the island, and, in the opinion of some, more, indeed, than we found last year; for the ice was estimated to-night to be, at least, four miles and a half, or five miles, off the coast; and as to the extent of this channel to the westward, we had the pleasure of seeing no end to it in that direction, and, to add to this, we had a fresh breeze of wind in our favour, and fine clear weather. About midnight we got abreast of the place where we were stopped so long by the ice, at the time the Griper's party lost their way, in the month of September last.

Saturday, 5th. — We got this forenoon abreast of the high land, where we were stopped by the ice last autumn; the wind having failed us about noon, a party went ashore to make observations, &c. They found the rocks here to consist of sandstone, as on all other parts of this island, where we have yet landed. The sorrel, and other plants that were brought on board, were considerably larger than those of the same kind that we found about Winter Harbour, most probably owing to the more favourable situation in which they grew; being well sheltered from the northerly wind by the high land, and having a southerly aspect. It appears that this part of the coast is well stocked with hares, for they saw four during the short time they were on shore; a glaucous gull, and a raven were also seen. At six o'clock in the evening we got to the edge of a loose stream of heavy ice; but as we advanced into it, it became closer, and at a quarter before nine it was found to be so compact that there was no possibility of getting through it. We therefore made fast to some hummocks of ice, about twenty yards from the beach, in from seven to nine fathoms' water. We had not been above an hour or two fast, when we found the ice had closed in with the land, both to the eastward and westward. Our situation, therefore, was not deemed to be by any means safe; for the ice was driving to the westward with considerable velocity, and our only protection against it was a low point of land, that lay to the eastward of us. Whilst the ice ran to the westward, however, this point sheltered us very well; but, in the event of its returning by the wind or tide in the contrary direction, or from the southward, we must be completely exposed to it; circumstances may, however, become more favourable before such a change takes place.

Sunday, 6*th*. — After we made fast last evening, some of us went ashore, and, in the course of the night, killed fourteen hares, and a number of glaucous gulls, which were found with their young on the top of an insulated rock, about thirty feet high, situated near the mouth of a ravine, about five miles to the eastward. The coast here is very bold and precipitous, rising abruptly from the sea to the height of about eight hundred and fifty feet. At the foot of the rocks there is, indeed, in some places, a slope from forty to fifty yards in breadth, covered generally with the loose fragments of stone that fall from them. These rocks consist entirely of schistose sandstone, and a kind of slate-clay, of a light green colour. Along the face, and pretty near the top of these precipices, there are a number of insulated columns, or rather insulated masses, that resemble, in some measure, when viewed a little way off, the turrets of a dilapidated building; but, when viewed more closely, that is, from the foot of the precipices, their natural structure is seen to great advantage; and, as far as lofty and rugged cliffs can be said to be picturesque, some of those in question were eminently so. Nor is this romantic scene confined only to the rocks that faced the sea; on the contrary, some of the ravines that ran inland, contained some that excelled the former, if possible, in the variety of their fantastic shapes. There is one of these ravines near the ship, that is particularly interesting in this way. I remarked that all these rocks were invariably stratified horizontally. The surface of the country is, generally speaking, plain, and, if viewed from the sea, would come under the denomination of table-land.

Monday, 7th. — From the top of the hills abovementioned, land was seen to-day, extending from S. to W. S. W., and supposed to be about fifty miles off. Whether this is the continent of America, or an island lying off it, is certainly a question that our present knowledge is inadequate to decide; I shall therefore not offer an opinion on the subject. From the same elevated situation that this land was seen, we had also a good view of the sea to the westward, or rather, I am sorry to say, of the ice; for, as far as we could see, in that direction, as well as to the southward, and even to the eastward, it was covered with ice. There were here and there, indeed, small pools, and lanes of open water, but no continuous opening. The ice that lay close in with the land was in general broken up, into what might, comparatively speaking, be termed small pieces; but, beyond this, that is, to seaward, it appeared to consist of immense floes, some of them several miles in diameter. We find also that the ice here is much heavier than any that we saw before, and is at the same time quite of a different character; for, instead of its presenting an even surface, like the ice in Baffin's Bay, it is completely covered with hummocks, resembling what I understand the Greenland ice to be. Since we came here we have observed another circumstance that deserves to be mentioned, when speaking of the ice off this part of the coast: the circumstance that I allude to is, a ledge of ice that is firmly attached to the land, and extends from it in general no more than fifteen or twenty yards. The surface of this icy girt is covered with five or six feet water, and its outer edge is so steep, that from six to seven fathoms are found immediately alongside of it.

Wednesday, 9th.—The ice has been almost constantly in motion during these two days past; sometimes it is drifting to the eastward, and at other times in a contrary direction, but it never leaves a clear space of any extent in either way. We had an opportunity of observing this evening an instance of the violent pressure that takes place occasionally by the collision of this heavy ice; for two pieces that happened to come in contact close to us pressed so forcibly against one another, that one of them, although forty-two feet thick, and at least three times that in length and breadth, was forced up on its edge on the top of another piece of ice. But even this is nothing when compared with the pressure that must have existed to produce the effects that we see along the shore, for not only heaps of earth and stones, several tons' weight, are forced up, but hummocks of ice from fifty to sixty feet thick are piled up on the beach. It is unnecessary to remark that a ship, although fortified as well as wood and iron could make her, would have but little chance of withstanding such overwhelming force; and, from a conviction of this, we consider our present situation, as I have already said, a very precarious one. But to dismiss this subject for something more interesting, I have to notice, in the first place, that a whale was seen two nights ago, for the first time this season; and, on the same day, we shot a fawn, which weighed thirty-eight pounds. A few hares and glaucous gulls have also been killed within these two days, but our success to-day, in the sporting way, deserves most notice, for we shot a musk-ox. When first seen, he was going along the beach to the eastward; and, from the nature of the ground, was obliged to pass so close to us, that he was fired at from the ship. We thought at first that he was wounded on this occasion; but we soon had reason to alter our opinion, for he galloped off at greater rate than an animal of his shape could be supposed capable of going. The nature of the ground was, however, as I have already remarked, very favourable for our purpose; for he was hemmed in by the sea on one side, and steep cliffs, which he could not ascend, on the other. When he found, therefore, that he was assailed in such a way that there was no possibility for him to escape, he immediately put himself in a posture of defence, by taking up a position in front of a large stone, where he could not certainly be attacked by any other animal, except under a great disadvantage; but to the means that we had, he could offer no resistance, and consequently fell.

His weight and dimensions were as follows: viz. —

	Feet.	In.
Length from the snout to the end of the tail -	6	10
Length of the tail - - - - -	0	3
Height from the sole of the fore-hoof to the top of the hunch - - - - -	4	8
From ditto to the knee-joint of the fore-leg -	1	1
From the hoof to the second joint, (*i. e.* the length of the fore-leg) - - - - -	2	3
Length of the fore-hoof - - - - -	0	$4\frac{3}{4}$
Breadth of ditto - - - - -	0	5
Circumference of the fore-leg below the knee -	0	7
Length from the sole of the hind-hoof to the hock	1	5
Length of the hind-leg - - -	2	9
Length of the hind-hoof - - - -	0	4
Breadth of ditto - - - - - -	0	$4\frac{1}{4}$
Circumference of the hind-leg below the hock -	0	$6\frac{1}{2}$
Height from the sole of the hind-hoof to the top of the back - - - - - -	4	2
From the end of the snout to the fore-shoulder -	2	5
From ditto to the upper part of the root of the horns - - - -	1	10

	Feet.	In.
From the end of the snout to the eyes - -	1	0½
From the root of the horns to the top of the hunch	2	0
Between the tips of the horns - - -	2	0
Circumference of the horns as low as could be measured - - - - -	1	0½
Base of the horns longitudinally - - -	0	11½
Length of the ears (which were pointed and situated close behind the horns) - -	0	6
Circumference of the neck close to the head -	3	8
Incisores (lower jaws) six in number, and molares in both jaws twenty-four, viz. twelve in each		
Length of the nostrils - - - -	0	3
Breadth between the nostrils (upper end) - -	0	4
Breadth between the eyes - - -	0	11
Length of the longest hair on his rump - -	2	5

Weight of the carcase when skinned and cleaned - - - - -	lbs. 421
Weight of the head, skin, and feet -	134
Estimated weight of the entrails and blood, &c. - - - -	160
Total weight -	715

The hair on different parts of the body was of different lengths, and of various colours, the prevailing colour, however, was black, and the longest hair was, as above stated, on the rump and hind quarters. He had a thick mane extending from the head to the top of the hunch; the colour of it was of a pale russet. Immediately behind the hunch there was a saddle, or bed, of short hair, of a yellowish white colour, about a foot and a half in length, along the ridge of the back, and nearly of the same breadth. The legs, as far as the knee-joint, were of a dirty white colour, and the hair on them this far was no longer than that on an English ox. At the root of the long hair, there was a finer kind of an ash colour, which was indeed as fine as any wool, and would certainly, if manufactured, make as fine cloth as any English wool. Mr. Pennant, indeed, mentions, in his description of the musk-ox, that a man of the name of Jeremie had stockings made of the wool, or hair, of that animal, which were equally as fine as any silk stockings. It would seem, that the animal casts this fleecy covering annually, for in the thick part of the mane, and on each side of the neck, there was a layer of this wool quite detached from the body of the animal, and only prevented from falling off, from being interwoven amongst the long hair. The hair on his forehead was all matted into small lumps with earth, and the roots of the horns were also covered with it, from which it would appear, that he was in the habit of tearing up the ground with his head; of this, indeed, we were ourselves eye-witnesses in one instance, for after we had surrounded him, so as to prevent his escape, he began rubbing his head against the ground, as if threatening us with destruction if we approached nearer, and I have no doubt, that to any animal that inhabits these regions he would be a formidable antagonist, not excepting the bear itself. His flesh tastes a good deal of musk, but not so much so as to be disagreeable; on this point, however, I ought to pay some deference to the opinion of a few persons amongst us who think differently. With regard to the heart and liver, it was agreed by all parties that they were not very palatable; and those who ate the kidnies say, that they tasted more musky than any other part. To conclude the subject, I have no doubt that people living a little more affluently than we have been for some time past, would not relish the best part of it very much at first, but it is a taste which, like many others, I think might easily be acquired.

Friday 11*th.* — Nothing has occurred during these two days past worthy of particular notice. The ice, as I have already remarked, drives one time to the eastward and at another time to the westward, according to the set of the tide or direction of the wind; but it never leaves a clear space of any magnitude in either way, so that we have as little prospect of getting on as we had the first day we made fast here.

Monday, 14*th.* — I formed a piece of floe-ice to-day (taken indiscriminately from a long side) into a cube whose sides measured one foot, two inches seven-tenths, which, when put into salt-water at the temperature of 34° and of the specific gravity 1.0105, one inch and eight-tenths of it remained above the surface of the water, or rather more than one-eighth of the whole mass. Judging therefore of the thickness of the floes in this neighbourhood, from the proportion of them above the surface of the water, we are led to conclude that their average thickness is from forty to fifty feet, and many of them much more.

Tuesday, 15*th.* — The ice having been observed early this morning to clear off the coast for a little way to the westward, we got under weigh at five o'clock, A. M., and ran about two miles along shore, when we were obliged to make fast again at six, the ice being close in with the land. Although we gained but little ground on this occasion, we have benefited very considerably by getting the ships into a much more secure place than that which we left; for we have got into a creek formed by large hummocks of ice aground within twenty yards of the beach; in fact, we lie so close to the shore, that we step almost immediately on it from the ship. In the course of the day I took a walk of five or six miles along shore to the westward, during which excursion I shot nine hares, and saw a great many tracks of reindeer, and musk-oxen. The land is of the same character, as far as I could see, as that which I described where we had been lying for this week past. The coast now begins to trend very much to the northward, as nigh as I can judge about north-west, for the place that we left this morning was in latitude 74° 25′ 24″ N. and longitude by chronometer 113° 42′ 30″ W., and that where the ships now lie is in latitude 74° 26′ 06″ N. and longitude by the mean of three sets of sights for chronometer 113° 46′ 05″ W.* With respect to the state of the ice, I could perceive no material difference in it to-day, from what it has been for this week past: close in with the land it is broken up, as I have already mentioned, into small pieces; but at the distance of a mile (or two at the farthest) from the coast, commence a line of floes that extend to the westward and southward, as far as the eye can

* These last results, viz. latitude 74° 26′ 06″ N., and longitude 113° 46′ 05″ W., were obtained from observations made on the 16th instant, although mentioned amongst the events of the 15th.

penetrate from the most elevated situation in this neighbourhood, and leaving no clear space except a few pools, and small lanes as I remarked some days ago.

Wednesday, 16*th*. — Without digressing much from the subject of my narrative, I may remark in this place, that the reason generally given, why so much heavy ice should lay off this part of the coast, is, because we are near the west end of this island, so that the ice which comes from the northward lodges here. The land that we see to the southward and westward may be considered also another locality that tends to keep this place always hampered with ice. In consideration of these circumstances, the advanced period of the season, and perhaps other reasons which it is neither my business nor intention to enquire into, the object of prosecuting our voyage to the westward, in this parallel of latitude, has to-day been abandoned. And by a general order to the officers who keep watch, it appears that our object now is to endeavour to get to the southward, for they are required to keep a good look-out for any opening that may appear amongst the ice in that direction. We therefore cast off from the ice at half past two o'clock in the afternoon, and made sail to the eastward, not without some feelings of regret and disappointment, at being at length obliged to abandon our hopes of a passage, where we had at one time so much reason to expect our endeavours to be crowned with success. I am fully persuaded, however, that every person who will take the trouble of making himself acquainted with the events of our voyage, will be perfectly convinced that our retrograde movement to-day is neither an inconsiderate, nor a precipitate measure; on the contrary, I believe, the annals of navigation will produce but few, if any instance of such perseverance as we have manifested in our attempts to get to the westward along this coast, for it is now within a few days of twelve months since we made the east end of this island, a distance of very little more than one hundred miles. But to leave the subject for others to judge, I shall proceed to give an account of any occurrences that may happen during our return to the eastward. The wind being light, we made no great progress this afternoon, and about midnight we were stopped altogether by the ice; we therefore made fast as usual to some hummocks of it that were aground within a few yards of the beach.

Monday, 21st.—These four or five days past have been very barren of events worthy of notice; we are still detained at the place where we made fast on the night of the 16th, and if we had not had one year's experience of the length of the summer season in these regions, we might be apt to suppose that the winter had already set in, for what little space there was of clear water when we made fast here, is now covered with young or bay-ice, as it is called, which is in general about an inch thick; but in those places along shore where it is overshadowed by the hummocks of ice along the beach, it is considerably thicker, for in those places it does not dissolve during the heat of the day.

Wednesday, 23d.—A breeze of wind sprung up this forenoon from the westward, which, in a short time, drove the ice a little way off the land, or rather slackened it, for it did not open a clear passage. We availed ourselves however of the opening, such as it was, for at half-past twelve, A. M. we cast off, and made sail to the eastward; but we were obliged to make fast again at seven o'clock in the evening, the ice being close in with the land. Abreast of where we made fast this evening, we found the large piece of ice that was mentioned on the 9th instant, as having been pressed up on its edge, from which circumstance it would appear, that there is a current, or prevailing tide setting to the eastward along this coast, for this piece of ice has come about twenty miles to the eastward within these sixteen days past, the difference of longitude alone being upwards of a degree.

Thursday, 24th.—We cast off and made sail again at ten o'clock this forenoon, but the ice was so close that we made but little progress, and at noon we were stopped by it altogether, and again made fast to a hummock of ice aground in nine fathoms' water. Soon after we made fast, we observed a herd of seven musk-oxen at the foot of a hill, at the distance of about two miles from the beach. We prepared immediately to go after them, but the eagerness of one or two who wished to be foremost set them off before we got sufficiently near them; by following them, however, we succeeded in getting one of them, which was a bull, and apparently the largest in the herd. Among those that got away there were two calves, and all the rest, with the exception of one, appeared to be cows. In the course of the evening, another musk-bull was shot, which was found by itself, and therefore supposed not to be one of the herd just mentioned. It would be quite unnecessary to enter into a description of these two animals, as they differed in no respect from the one that we killed on the 9th instant, except in being a little smaller, or rather lighter, for the first one that was shot to-day weighed only three hundred and fifty-nine pounds, and the other three hundred and sixty-eight pounds. This difference appeared to be chiefly owing to the one that we killed some time ago, being in better condition than these, for they did not seem to differ much in size. At the foot of the hill where we saw these musk-oxen to-day, and along a plain that lay between it and the sea, we passed so many skulls and skeletons of musk-oxen, that I am inclined to alter my opinion respecting their migrating to the coast of America during the winter, for if they only visit this country in the summer-time, it is somewhat strange that so many should die here during such a favourable part of the year. Besides, they are so well provided by nature for enduring the rigour of the climate, that the necessity for their leaving this island does not appear to be altogether so indispensable, as a person would at first sight be inclined to believe. This, however, is a subject on which much might be said for or against the question, but as I am not particularly interested, on my own part, to establish the point, whether they migrate or remain here, I shall forbear saying any more about the matter, any farther than that we know that wolves and foxes pass the winter here, and neither of them appeared to be better provided for withstanding the cold, than the musk-ox; and with respect to food, there is certainly much more grass in the valleys in this vicinity, than they will destroy this season.

Friday, 25th.—We made an attempt again this evening, to get to the eastward, but from want of wind, and the closeness of the ice, we were obliged to make fast again, without having gained above a mile, after several hours' labour. I made a cube of ice to-day, from a piece that was thrown up on the hummock to which we were fast; its sides measured two feet, and when put into salt water with that side of it uppermost that the piece of ice from which it was made had up at the time, three inches and a half remained above the surface of the water, but when the opposite side was up only three inches appeared above the water. This was no doubt owing to one side of the cube being denser, and consequently heavier than the other; in making it, indeed, I remarked, that the side that was uppermost of the piece of ice was more porous than the other. Although the weather is still remarkably fine, we have many indications of the approach of winter; the young ice continues to increase in thickness, some of it was measured to-day that was three inches thick; stars have also been seen about midnight for this week past, and many other things might be mentioned that tend to show that the close of this season is not very far distant.

Saturday, 26th.—A fresh breeze sprang up

from the northward and westward this morning, which soon opened a passage along shore; we, therefore, got under weigh at six o'clock, and made sail to the eastward. We were a good deal hampered with ice during the forenoon; but in the afternoon we got into a clear sea, so that by six in the evening we were abreast of Winter Harbour. We saw very plainly as we went along the pile of stones on North East Hill with the naked eye, although it was estimated that we passed at the distance of seven or eight miles from it. The monument on Table Hill was also in sight during most part of the afternoon, in fact every hill that we passed this afternoon was recognised; and although I believe none regretted taking this last farewell view of the ground that we had so often trod, yet it was impossible to look at it with the same indifference as at other parts of the coast; for every hill reminded us of some circumstance or other that happened during our perambulations these eleven months past. In the evening we got into such a wide space of clear water that no ice could be seen even to the southward, except from the mast-head.

Sunday, 27th. — We had a fine run to-day to the eastward, for we were in the evening off the east end of Melville Island. As this is the first time that I have made use of this name, it may be necessary to mention that the island off or on which our exploits have been performed for these twelve months past, is named after the nobleman who presides as first lord of the admiralty; and I understand that it, and all the islands that lie in its neighbourhood to the eastward, are to be called, in honour of our sovereign, the North Georgian Isles. The various other names that have been given to islands, capes, points, bays, and inlets, that we have discovered during our voyage are so numerous that it would be too tedious to mention them all in this place, nor would the mentioning them be of any use, unless I was to refer to the chart (on which they are laid down), and even such a reference would be rather out of place if made at this time. I cannot omit noticing, however, that the magnificent opening or passage, that leads from what was formerly called Lancaster Sound into these seas, is named Barrow's Straits, after the well-known gentleman of that name, whose clear judgment foresaw the existence of this passage, and whoze zeal and influence had been so instrumental in fitting out the expedition for its discovery, even when doubts were entertained and propagated against the probability of its success. But I must leave this subject to those who are much better able to discuss it, and resume my diary of the rest of the events of the day.

After divisions this morning, Mr. Parry addressed the officers and ship's company in words to the following effect, viz. that it was his opinion, and that of the senior officers of the expedition, that the farther prosecution of our voyage to the westward in this parallel of latitude would be useless; therefore, that our present object was to endeavour to get to the southward, and if that should be found impracticable, that it would be necessary to return to England:

and finally he informed them, that whenever this last resolution should be determined on, that they should be again put on full allowance of provisions.

Monday, 28th. — Our progress to the eastward still continues to be very rapid; we were to-day at noon in latitude 74° 58′ N. and nearly in longitude 100° W. The sea is quite open to the eastward, but to the southward it is completely covered with ice. This ice, and all what we have passed indeed on this side of Winter Harbour, has been, compared to that to the westward, very light, and in other respects quite of a different character; for its surface is perfectly smooth, and appears to be one continued floe altogether, or, more properly speaking, one extensive field; for, if I am not mistaken, the distinction between the two terms is, that a floe may be seen over, but if it should be of such a size as not to be seen across, it is called a field. If this definition is correct, then the ice that we have been passing during these two days comes under the latter denomination, for we have never seen water beyond it.

All the land that we have passed to-day is completely covered with snow that looks to have fallen lately, for near the shore it appears to be but very thinly covered.

Tuesday, 29th. — We passed last night and during this forenoon several islands that we had not seen before, owing to our being obliged, on account of the ice, to keep more to the northward than we did when going to westward last year. Some of these islands are of considerable extent, and all of them were, like those mentioned yesterday, covered with snow. In their general character they resembled those that we saw in this neighbourhood last year, that is, low, and even surfaced. This description does not, however, apply to them all, for some of those that we saw this forenoon were high, and, in many places, rugged. It was so dark last night that we were obliged to lay to for three hours; we have made considerable progress to-day, however, for we got in the evening to the west end of Burrow's Straits. We have in the course of the day seen a number of mallemucks, which, as far as I remember at present, are the first birds of the kind that we have seen for these twelve months past.

Wednesday, 30*th*. — The blank space where we saw no land last year, from 91° to 92° of west longitude, owing to the distance we were from it, we found last night to be a continuous line of coast, having a kind of large open bay in it, facing to the northward. Early this morning we got to the entrance of Regent's Inlet *, which I understand was full of ice, consequently no attempt was made to get into it. This being the easternmost inlet or opening that we know of, leading to the southward, the object of making any further attempts to go in that direction, appears to be at length abandoned, or rather it seems that it is now

* This being, I believe, the first time that I have used this name, it may be necessary to remark, that the place called Regent's Inlet, is that large opening leading to the southward and westward, into which we sailed the second week of August last year.

determined to return to England. Mr. Parry therefore, made this determination publicly known to the officers and ship's company this morning, and, according as he promised in his address to them on the 27th instant, full allowance of provisions is now ordered to be issued; and in the afternoon a suit of warm clothes, furnished by government, gratis, was given to every person on board.

Thursday, 31*st.* — After passing Regent's Inlet, we continued our course to the eastward, keeping as near the south side of Barrow's Straits as the ice would allow us. The distance we were from the coast, was generally from seven to eight miles, and this space was completely filled up with ice; however, as the weather was clear, there was no necessity for our going any closer to the land, as we could see it very plainly. Indeed, the nature of the land was such, that it might be seen very distinctly at three times the distance we were off, in such weather as we had to-day; for the land on the north side was seen as we came along, and that opposite to it on the south side of the straits, is exactly similar to it in character, and I believe also in height, being, I imagine, from eight or nine hundred, to a thousand feet high, bold, and composed of horizontal strata, that looked at a distance like gigantic steps rising one above another. The land on both sides was completely covered with snow, and that on the south side apparently very deeply. Between us and the north land there appeared to be no ice. From two to four o'clock this morning, we were passing the mouth of a spacious inlet, from four to five leagues in breadth, that ran to the southward. The entrance of it was, like Regent's Inlet, full of ice. It is to be named, I understand, Admiralty Inlet. From the east side of this inlet, the character of the land is very much changed, for here the stratification ceases; and the land, instead of rising abruptly from the sea, ascends gradually as it recedes from the coast, so that the highest part of it, or that which terminated our view, was a long way inland. About eight leagues to the eastward of the above inlet, is the opening that was called in our former voyage, Barrow's Bay; but from the view that we had of it this morning, we have strong reasons to doubt of its being a bay, for we were much nearer to it than we had ever been before, and we could see no land at the bottom of it. The space that was open did not appear indeed, to be very wide; but wherever the continuity of land is not actually seen, I think that it would be presumption to say, that there is no passage, especially in regions like these, that have never been explored. This bay, or inlet, or whatever it may be termed, was like that which we passed in the morning, full of ice; at the entrance of it there appeared to be two low islands, and at the bottom of it, and nearly in the middle of the opening, there appeared to be another small, round-topped island; but this last was so far off, that we were in doubt whether it might not be the top of a distant hill. In the course of the afternoon we passed a large bear swimming, at the distance of two miles at least from the land; a boat was dispatched after him, but there was so much sea on at the time, that we never got sight of him after leaving the ship. A whale was also seen this evening, for the first time since we returned to the eastward. I may also remark, that we passed some icebergs to-day, for the first time since we left this place last year.

Friday, September 1*st.* — We passed Possession Bay last night, and have been running all this day to the southward, within a few leagues of the coast. At three o'clock in the afternoon we came abreast of an opening, which agrees in its situation with Pond's Bay on the chart. We stood in towards it until we were stopped by the ice, which lay off this part of the chart. It was estimated that we were at this time, from eight to ten leagues from the entrance of this inlet; but, notwithstanding we were that distance off, we are certain that if it is a bay, it must be a very deep one, for we could see nothing like land at the bottom of it. The capes that formed the entrance of it, and the land indeed on both sides of it, as far in as we could see, were bold and very high. The angle that the capes subtended, measured 8° 44′, which, if the distance we were off be properly estimated, would make the entrance of it about six miles wide.

Saturday, 2*d.* — We were running to the southward all day along the land, and generally between ten or twelve miles distant from it. The space was, for most part of the way, covered with ice, but the land being high, we had no occasion for going any nearer to it, for the purpose of a general survey, such as we are taking. In the course of the forenoon, we passed a place where there appeared to be a large harbour. In two or three places along this part of the coast, we saw some large glaciers, one of them that we passed this morning was estimated to be at least two miles long. A great number of icebergs were also seen in the course of the day: most of them lay between us and the land, and several of them appeared to be aground, for the tide-mark on them was at one time five or six feet above the surface of the water. We sounded several times as we were passing them, and found from sixty to seventy fathoms' water. During these two days past, a great number of mallemucks, and several of the various other aquatic birds that frequent these seas have been seen, viz. glaucous, and ivory gulls, loons, ratges, and the black-diver, commonly called dovekey, or Greenland dove.

Sunday, 3d. — The wind being very light, and what little there was of it being against us, a party of us landed this forenoon on a part of the coast situated in latitude 71° 30′ N., and longitude 71° 15′ W. Near where we landed, there was an island about three miles long, situated in a sort of bay, and separated from the mainland by a channel about two miles broad. The east end of this island, or that end which faced the sea, terminated in a very remarkable cliff, which was estimated to be from three to four hundred feet high, and rose quite perpendicular from the sea; in one point of view, indeed, it overhung a little. The whole of the coast of this island, as far as we saw, was so precipitous as to be perfectly inaccessible. On the mainland, also, about this place, there are some of the most remarkable piked mountains I ever saw, for some of them are so pointed, that they look at a distance not unlike the spires of a ruined building. The land is mountainous, and exceedingly rugged, and is covered with snow down to the sea side. The rocks are composed entirely of granite and gneiss, the former of the kind that is termed, by geologists, the oldest granite, that is, consisting of large crystals of the different component parts, particularly the felspar. Fragments of beautiful white quartz were also very abundant here. Of the vegetable productions of this place we could say but very little, for the land was, as I have already said, covered with snow, besides it is too late in the season to collect plants in this climate. Of the animal kingdom we also saw but few specimens; of these few, however, were two red-throated divers that we shot, which are the only birds of the kind that we met with this voyage. Two flocks of Brent geese, some glaucous gulls, and a few snow-buntings, were all the animals, I believe, that were seen here. We saw, however, the tracts of bears, wolves, and foxes, in considerable numbers, and the track of some cloven-footed animal was also seen; we supposed it to be that of a musk-ox, but it was much larger than any that we had seen before. We met also with bones of a whale, that had been thrown up on the beach, and not far from the same place were found indications of some people (probably Esquimaux) having been here, for a piece of whale-bone that they had cut was picked up, and, as a proof that it had not been driven there by the sea, the chips that had been cut off it were lying there. It was low water at three o'clock, and from that time until half-past five, it had risen twelve inches: it set to the southward.

Monday, 4th. — We made no great progress to-day, owing to there being but little wind for a considerable part of the time; our course has been the same as for some days past, along shore, and about the usual distance from it, that is, between three and four leagues. In the course of the afternoon we crossed two banks lying about the distance just mentioned from the coast. The soundings on them varied from twelve and a half to eighteen fathoms; coarse sand with black and red specks. Between the two banks, the water deepened to fifty-six fathoms; nature of the bottom the same as above. Whilst we were on these banks, it was remarked that a tide or current was drifting us very fast to the southward; but, on getting into deep water, we tried to ascertain its rate, but, to our surprise, could not find either tide or current. There were a great many icebergs aground about the edges of these banks, and there was also a considerable quantity of loose ice in the same neighbourhood, no doubt owing to its being retained there by these bergs. At one o'clock we were a little surprised to see a strange ship bearing N. E. of us, and distant between seven and eight miles; in the course of the afternoon three more sails were seen, from which we immediately concluded that they must be whale-ships. Although we are all anxious to hear the news, yet, as we are on our way home ourselves, I believe the general wish is, that we should avoid falling in with these vessels, in order that we may be the bearers of our own news; but two of them lie so directly in our way, that, without altering our course, we must pass very close to them, and as our wish to avoid them does not go so far as to induce us to go out of our way, it is probable that we shall speak them to-morrow morning.

Tuesday, 5th.—In the course of the forenoon we passed close to one of the ships that were seen yesterday, and found her to be the Lee, of Hull; having thirteen fish on board. We learnt from her, that King George the Third, and His Royal Highness the Duke of Kent are dead, and several other pieces of information of minor importance; among others, that riots and tumults have been stirred up in different parts of the country by disaffected people, but that all of them, however, have been happily suppressed, without much violence. They also told us that no less than eleven ships were destroyed in this country by the ice last year, and as nothing was heard of us after that catastrophe, some unfavourable opinions were entertained by many people respecting the fate of our expedition. After remaining for a short time in company with her, we sent some letters on board, in the event of her getting to England before us; but if they follow the plan they seem to have in view at present, it is probable that we shall be home first ourselves, for they intend going as far north as the latitude of 72°, in order to get round a barrier of ice, which they say extends from the land a little way to the southward of us, that is, between the 69th and 70th deg. N. as far as the parallel just mentioned. But as we ran down along this coast two years ago, at the same part of the season, without meeting with any ice to obstruct our progress; and as the avoiding of ice is not so much our object as that of surveying the coast, it is intended, I believe, to continue our course along the land, running all hazards of whatever obstacles we may happen to meet with. Therefore, after parting company with the Lee, we resumed our former course, but keeping rather closer in with the land, in order to see a small party of Esquimaux, which, they told us, lived near the shore on the north side of a bay, about twenty miles to the southward. In the course of the afternoon we fell in with another whaler, called the Friendship, of Hull, having seventeen fish on board. We received no news of any importance from her, except what is above mentioned. I ought not to omit mentioning, however, that this ship and another, (the Truelove, of Hull,) were, this summer, at the top of Baffin's Bay, and looked into Sir Thomas Smith's Sound, which they found to be like another of the Sounds of Baffin, a Sound without bottom. They informed us also, that some of the whale-ships entered Lancaster's Sound this summer, and, among others, the Alexander, of Aberdeen, one of the ships employed on the former voyage of discovery to these seas.

Wednesday, 6th. — As we were standing in this evening towards the place where the Lee told us the Esquimaux lived, four canoes were observed paddling towards us. While they were yet at a considerable distance off, we could hear them making a great noise, which they continued to do as they approached us. They came alongside without the least hesitation, and one of our boats being there, our people assisted them in getting out of their canoes, which were all hoisted on board, and helped them up the side. On getting on board, they evinced no signs either of fear or astonishment: on finding themselves in security, their first act was to turn to, to dance; if turning round, jumping, and other wild gesticulations deserve that appellation. At the same time that they were showing us their accomplishments in the dancing way, they gave us a specimen of their vocal talents also; but to call the two or three monotonous ejaculations that they uttered, a song, would certainly be a misapplication of the word, for the whole of their melody consisted only of these three words, viz. "hey yey yagh," which they repeated with great rapidity, and with vehemence, in proportion to the movements of the body; these were at first very violent, but by degrees became more moderate, from being unable, I imagine, to continue such fatiguing exertions. After due time was allowed them to exhibit all their elegant acquirements, we made signs to them to go below, to which proposal they readily assented, and, in order to entertain them in return for their exhibition on deck, two or tree tunes were played on the hand organ. Whether they were cheered by the music, or considered it necessary to continue to amuse us, I cannot say for certain; but they skipped about, and hey yey yagh'd more furiously than ever. We have reason, however, to think, that all this proceeded more from a desire to please us than from any pleasure they had in it themselves; for one of them, who was an older man than any of the rest, on its being signified to him to sit down in order to have his picture taken, he immediately sat down very composedly, whilst the others were displaying all their antic feats. This old man appeared to be of a very facetious

disposition, and a very great adept at mimickry; for now and then, when his attention was drawn off to view the surrounding objects, it was signified to him the necessity of maintaining a steady posture; and in doing so, he used to imitate, with an air of the most complete buffoonery and good humour, the attitude of the person who was showing him the posture that it was wished he should keep himself in.

This man appeared to be between fifty-five and sixty years of age, for his hair and beard were quite grey. His visage differed materially from that of the rest, particularly in being much narrower. He was also considerably shorter than any of them, for he measured only four feet eleven inches and a half, and the shortest of the others was five feet four inches and a half; the remaining two were nearly of the same height, one measured five feet five inches and a half, and the other five feet six inches. The two last appeared to be also nearly about the same age, that is, between five-and-twenty and thirty; the young man did not look to be above one or two and twenty. The Esquimaux countenance has been so often, and so accurately described, that it would be quite unnecessary to enter into a lengthened detail respecting the features of these people, as they differed in no respect from the numerous accounts already given; viz. a broad and flat countenance, high-cheek bones, small and deep-sunk eyes, short pug nose, large mouth, thick lips, coarse black and straight hair, and a thin black beard, both on the chin and upper lip, and the colour of the skin somewhat of a light tawny-brown, and greasy. With regard to their clothes, they differed but little also from that worn by the Esquimaux of Greenland. The jackets, or rather frocks, of the three young men, were made of of white dog or wolf skin, having the fur-side in, or next their body: they came down as far as the hip-joint; and their lower border was straight all round, with the exception of a small slit in the front: they all had hoods to them, which served for a head-covering. Their breeches were also made of the same kind of skin, but having the fur-side out; and their boots, which came up to the knee, were likewise made of the same material, and had the fur-side in. The old man's dress was made entirely of seal-skin, but in its shape it differed in no respect from that of the others: it had this peculiarity, however, that his frock had the fur-side of the skin out. Their canoes were made of seal-skin, and of the same shape as those of the Greenlanders, but rather larger, and not near so neat, probably owing to the latter having better instruments to execute their work with. The frames of their canoes were made chiefly of fir-wood, as were also their paddles, which were about nine feet and a half long, double-headed, and the rim of the blades very neatly edged with bone. Their spears were from four to five feet long, and were made of narwhal's horns: most of them were headed with sharp-pointed pieces of bone; but one of them had a lance-pointed piece of iron fitted on to the end of his spear; and the old man had a piece of wood, about the same length as their spears, near one end of which there was a sharp iron hook, made apparently of a nail. They had a scimetar-shaped knife each, made of the tusks of the walrus, or sea-horse; and on each canoe there was a large inflated bladder, which I suspect to be that of the same animal. These implements, a few seal-skins, and two or three spare jackets, were all the articles they had, and with all of them they very soon parted; for, after they had pretty well tired themselves jumping and bawling, they turned to, to barter, and in a very short time disposed of every thing they had, except their canoes, and before they went away, they bartered one of them also. As there was no intention to impose upon them, nothing was offered them except such things as were deemed would be useful to them, such as knives, scissars, needles, nails, gimblets, and pieces of wood; and for the canoe they, or rather the man it belonged to, received four boarding pike-staves, and the heads of five or six of them, several pieces of wood, a handkerchief, a pair of mittens, and a piece of red cloth. One of our men made them a present of a hand-saw, and another gave one of them a red shirt; beads, looking-glasses, and a number of other things of little value were also given them, but, as I have already remarked, not in exchange for what they had, but merely as donations. They showed a great deal of intelligence and probity in their dealings; for they evinced no great desire for beads, or any other baubles, and they never attempted to take any thing except what was given them. We remarked, that every thing they received they immediately touched with their tongue, apparently to show that it was then legally their property. From what we saw of them, they appeared to be perfectly honest, a virtue which has seldom been found amongst uncivilized people. It may be said, indeed, in this instance, that they had no great opportunity for pilfering, if they were so disposed; but if such a disposition existed, it is probable that some symptoms of it would be detected; but as there were none discovered, it is but a piece of justice due to them to consider them honest, whilst nothing to the contrary can be said against them. We understood, from the people of the Lee, that when they fell in with them, they could hear nothing from them but the word "Pillitey," which signifies, I believe, in the Esquimaux language, Give me something. Of this begging expression, however, they made very little use whilst on board of us, most probably owing to the commercial system that was adopted, from which they soon learned that they had the means of procuring what they wanted, without humbling themselves to beg for it. We endeavoured to learn a few words of their language, or rather we tried to ascertain if it is the same as that spoken by the Esquimaux in other parts of these regions, and as far as our means of deciding this point went, we have reason to suppose that it is. The method that was adopted to ascertain this, was by showing them specimens, and drawings, of the different animals that we had reason to think they must be acquainted with.

Immediately the head of the rein-deer was shown them, they called it "tooktook," and according to Mr. Chappell's account of the Esquimaux in Hudson's Straits, they call the deer "muck-tu." A drawing of a bear, and others of some other animals being shown them, they appeared to know very well what they were intended to represent;

but they talked so much, that it was impossible to say for certain what their names for them were.

With respect to the musk ox we are not sure that they are acquainted with him, and if they are, it is doubtful what their name for him is; for although a good drawing, and, afterwards, a head of one of these animals were shown them, they said nothing that appeared to be expressive of his name, until some person pointing to the head, said, umimack, which word they immediately repeated, but pronounced it as if spelt oomingmack. It is doubtful, therefore, whether they understood that we were informing them, that umimack was our name for the animal, or that they were telling us that oomingmack was their name for him. There is one circumstance, however, which may be mentioned, that tends to strengthen the latter opinion, which is, that the tribe of esquimaux we fell in with near the top of Baffin's Bay two years ago, told Saccheuse (our Esquimaux interpreter) that a large animal, which they called umimack, frequented that country. They described it as having a horn on its back, but this would be so extraordinary a thing, that it is more reasonable to suppose that they meant a hunch, although from the paucity of words in their language they might not have a term to express it. But this is a subject which our present knowledge does not enable us to say much about, with any degree of certainty; though I think we may take it for granted, that all the Esquimaux tribes that are scattered along the shores of Greenland, North America, and its adjacent islands, are the same race of people, and, as far as our observations go their appearance, dress, manners, mode of living, as well as their language, tend to confirm this point. With regard to their origin, most of the writers who have written about them suppose them to be of Samoeid or Tartar descent; but on this point I have no pretensions to offer an opinion.

After our visitors had bartered every thing they had to dispose of, and we had obtained from them all the information that was possible to be learnt, they were assisted into their canoes again, and a boat was sent with them to land the man that sold his canoe. On leaving the ship they made no signs indicative of taking farewell, but they went away apparently very much pleased with the reception they met with, and the bargains they had made. On the way going ashore our boat tried for a little while to pull against them, but our people soon found that they were no match for them, especially the two young men, for the old man either could not, or did not, exert himself much on the occasion. During this trial an opportunity occurred for observing how quickly they noticed any thing that was said when they could make out the meaning of it; for on hearing the officer who had charge of the boat tell the men to "pull away," they immediately comprehended, from the exertions that were made, that this was an injunction to the men to increase their efforts, and by way of jocosely showing their own dexterity, they used to go on a-head of our boat, and call out "Pull away, pull away." Immediately they landed, another of them sold his canoe to the officer that went in the boat, for his dirk, a Flushing-jacket, a shawl that he had about his neck, a knife, and some beads. It being dark at the time they landed, our people did not see their huts, but they judged afterwards that they were at no great distance from them; for about a quarter of an hour after they left the shore, on their return, they heard great shouts, apparently of rejoicing; and amongst them they could distinguish the voices of women and children, or at least voices that they considered to be such.

Thursday, 7th. — We stood in this morning towards the fiord, or inlet, where the Esquimaux landed last night, and when we got close in, a boat went ashore to see their habitations, which they found to consist of two huts made of seal-skins, and situated close to the beach. The inhabitants of these huts they found to be the four men who visited us last night, four women, and nine children. One of the women was very old, and was on that account supposed to be the wife of the old man already mentioned. Two of the others were judged to be about thirty years of age, and they were supposed to be the mothers of all the young family: one of them was pregnant. The fourth damsel appeared to be too young to be yet living a conjugal life; and there was another circumstance remarked with regard to her, that was considered as a mark that she had not yet arrived at the happiness of a matrimonial life. The circumstance alluded to is, that the other three were tattooed, whilst she was not, from which it was supposed, that this barbarous decoration was the distinguishing badge of a married woman. This honourable, and no doubt in their estimation, ornamental piece of artificial beauty, consisted of two curved lines, extending from the outer corner, or angle of the eyes, down to the upper lip. The convex side of these lines pointed backwards, and their junction at their lower end formed an acute angle. The chin and lower lip were also tattooed, by straight lines, which diverged from the mouth downwards. Whether it was owing to her being free from these barbarous scars, or not, I do not pretend to say, but they who saw her, speak of the young girl, comparatively, as a great beauty; whilst they describe the old dame as the picture of ugliness. With respect to their dress, the women seem to have been habited nearly in the same manner as the men, namely, in leather-jackets, boots, and breeches. Their huts were about the same shape and size, as the ruins of those that we met with on Melville Island; but the square place at the end of them, which was supposed, at that time, to be the place where they kept their provisions, appears to be their fire-place. They did not find them so filthy inside, as the Esquimaux huts are generally described to be; but it must be recollected that these were their summer-huts. They found that they lived in a state of great affluence, at least as much so as people, living as they do, could be expected, for they had several stores of sea-horses' flesh, covered with stones, along the beach. And as another proof that they cannot be badly off for provisions, they had no less than fifty or sixty dogs, which alone would require no small quantity of food. Although it is probable that they derive the chief part of their sustenance from the sea, it is probable that they also occasionally manage to kill deer; for they showed one of the gentlemen that went on shore the skin of one, and made signs to him that the animal had been killed by an arrow, pointing to the hole that the arrow had made. The only bow found amongst them, however, was a small one made of whalebone, that appeared to be intended as a play-thing to one of their children; but the advantages of such an instrument, and the very ordinary ingenuity and means required to make it, render it probable that they are acquainted with the use of the bow and arrow. It may be mentioned, indeed, as a proof of this, that the arrow belonging to the small bow just spoken of was feathered, a circumstance which can hardly be supposed to have been accidentally done to adorn a toy. With respect to their fishing implements, none were seen that differed much from those that they brought on board last night. Some articles were found amongst them, however, which evidently show that they had intercourse, either directly, or through the means of others, with Europeans, for they had a piece of a file set into a bone handle, in such a way as to resemble an adze in miniature; they had also some beads, different from any that we had given them when they were on board. This place appears, however, to be at present their permanent residence; for one of the officers who went up a little way into the bay, or inlet where they lived, in order to sound, found their winter-huts there. And certainly, as far as appearances go, they could not get a more eligible situation for their abode in this country; for the inlet is full of small islands, which, I should imagine, to be places likely to be very much resorted to by walruses, and in the breeding season, by the different birds which frequent these regions. How far this inlet goes inland, it is impossible for us to say, as we could see nothing like a termination to it: if we were to judge of its extent by the depth of the water in it, we might suppose it to be very considerable; for we found one hundred and eighty fathoms water within the entrance of it, and not above a mile from the shore. It appeared to be from four to five miles in breadth, as far in as we went. But to return again to the natives of this inlet, I have only further to say of them, that from what I can learn, they all displayed the same spirit of cheerfulness, contentment, and good humour, that they evinced in so eminent a degree on board; and if they had reason at that time to be well pleased with the bargains they had made, I understand that they had equally as good a cause to be satisfied with their traffic to-day; for they got a hatchet, five brass-kettles, several knives, nails, pieces of wood, beads, and various other things, in exchange for another of their canoes, a sledge, (made of bones,) fourteen dogs, (most of them puppies,) two stone troughs, made of *lapis allaris*, or potstone, and one or two spears. The stone troughs are exceedingly well made, considering their means; the one was nearly a foot long, and about half that in breadth and depth; the other was considerably larger; the former served them to cook their victuals in, and the latter to hold the oil or grease that they burnt, to cook them with. The head of one of the spears, which was also made of stone, (clay-slate,) was remarkably well executed; in fact, when we consider that the only instrument they were seen to possess, that could be of any use in making the different articles they had, was the piece of file above mentioned, it is surprising how well they finished every thing. Judging, therefore, from these circumstances, we have reason to hope, that with the means we afforded them, they will benefit very considerably for many years to come. Among the occurrences of this day, I omitted to mention, that the sun was beautifully eclipsed from eight to nine o'clock this morning.

Saturday, 9*th*.—Nothing of any importance occurred during these two days past; our course has been, along the land, to the southward; but as we have had but light winds for most part of the time, we have made no great progress. We were at noon to-day about the latitude of 69½° N. The character of the land at this place differs very materially from that to the northward, for it is, comparatively speaking, low, and even-surfaced. Along the coast, indeed, for about a degree to the northward from this, the land is low near the sea; but inland it is backed by a range of high hills; here, however, no high land is visible even in the interior, as far as we can see.

Sunday, 10*th*. — We had a strong breeze of wind to-day from the north-west, by compass, so that we had, or rather might have had, a good run to the southward, but most part of the forenoon was occupied in examining a large bay that we crossed. At the bottom of it there are six or seven high, round-topped islands, one of which is remarkable from its being of a reddish colour. When we were abreast of these islands, it blew very fresh indeed off the land, from which I am inclined to think that another inlet runs in here, similar to that where we found the Esquimaux the other day.

Tuesday, 12th. — We have made very little progress during these two days, owing to there being very little wind, we have also been impeded a good deal by the young ice which forms during the night. The land here is of the same high and rocky character as that to the northward. We passed a rock yesterday which was very remarkable, for the front of it that faced the sea was at least four hundred feet high, and quite perpendicular, and in the front of it there were several white streaks running up and down, which looked at the distance we were from it, columns of the rock. Along this part of the coast there are several small islands, particularly at the entrance of the inlets, or harbours, which abound here in such numbers.

Wednesday, 13th. — The Aurora Borealis was seen last night, streaming very beautifully from west to south-east; in the latter direction its motions were very rapid, and its colours were also very brilliant: the prevailing colour was a light yellow; but the outer edge of those coruscations that streamed towards the zenith appeared at different times of a light purple hue. We came this morning to a barrier of ice, extending from the land to the northward and eastward as far as we could see. Our only alternative was, therefore, to return to the northward, and endeavour to get across the north end of it. Our progress in this retrograde movement, to-day, was very slow, chiefly for want of wind, and being also very much impeded by the young ice. A number of whales have been seen to-day, and for several days past.

Saturday, 16*th*. — The weather has been so thick during these two days past, that we have been obliged to make fast to a floe, in order to wait for its clearing up to see which way to go; for we are so surrounded with ice, that by attempting to run at present, we might only hamper ourselves by running into the middle of a pack. We sounded to-day in eight hundred and ten fathoms, soft mud: the temperature of the water at this depth was ascertained by the self-registering thermometer to be 27°, that of the surface, at the same time, being 30½°. By way of experiment, four pieces of wood were fastened to the sounding line on this occasion, which when they came up, were, as might naturally be expected, very much saturated with moisture, from the great pressure of the water at such a depth. The pieces of wood were, one of oak, another of elm, the third of ash, and the fourth of fir; and they were, as might also be presupposed, saturated in proportion to their density; that is, the weight of the piece of oak was least, and that of the piece of fir most increased, by the quantity of water forced into them.

Sunday, 17*th*. — The weather having cleared up a little this morning, we prepared to cast off; the only preparation, indeed, necessary on the occasion, was to endeavour to get on board one of the

Esquimaux dogs, that had been on the ice for these three days past; but, notwithstanding most of the ship's company were sent after him, he was so wild that it was impossible to get hold of him; rather, therefore, than leave him to starve, he was shot.

Monday, 18th. — The weather still continues foggy, and we meet with a considerable quantity of floe ice, some of which is heavier than any that I remember having seen in Davis's Straits before. In order to avoid danger, we therefore make fast during the night. We sounded to day in eight hundred and ninety seven fathoms; no bottom.

Friday, 22d. — Nothing of any importance has occurred during these four days past: the weather has been generally foggy; and our progress to the southward has been very much impeded by the ice, which, as I have already remarked, is heavier than we have been accustomed to meet with in these seas; for several of the floes that we have passed lately were from two to three feet above the surface of the water, which, from the different experiments that we have made on the specific gravity of ice, would make the thickness of these floes, from fifteen to twenty feet. We had an eclipse of the moon this morning; but from the impossibility of observing the immersion or emersion, with any degree of correctness on board of ship, nothing was deduced from it in the way of determining our longitude. We spoke the ship Ellison of Hull, during the night, with fifteen fish on board.

Saturday, 30th. — This week past has been as

barren of incidents worthy of notice as any period of equal length, for some time past. We crossed the Arctic circle on the 24th inst.; and for most part of the time since that, we have had generally coarse weather; we have now, however, got clear of the ice, and we have kept at such a distance from Cape Farewell, that there is nothing to apprehend whatever way the wind may blow. Our latitude, to-day, at noon, was 58° 44′ 51″, and longitude by chron. 53° 12′ W.

Monday, October 2d. — We have had a gale of wind during these two days past, which moderated considerably in the course of this afternoon. We lost sight of the Griper about six o'clock this morning: she appeared at the time that we last saw her to be lying to. We ran, however, until nine o'clock, at which time the wind began to abate a little, we, therefore, brought to, and waited for her until two in the afternoon; but as she had not made her appearance, although the weather had by that time cleared up, there was reason to suppose that she had taken a different course from that which we came, and had probably passed us before th› weather cleared up; we, therefore, made sail, keeping rather to the northward of our course, in hopes of falling in with her.

Tuesday, 3d. — A vigilant look-out has been kept all day for the Griper, but nothing has as yet been seen of her; so that we now begin to suspect that we shall not see her again until we meet at Shetland, which, I understand, is the appointed place of rendezvous in case of separation.

The Aurora Borealis appeared very beautifully

from nine till eleven o'clock this evening, forming an arch extending from east to west across the zenith; almost the whole of the south side of the hemisphere was indeed illumined by it, but it was not seen to the northward except near the zenith. It presented at different times a beautiful display of some of the prismatic colours, particularly the red, orange, yellow, and green; lake was also a predominant colour in some parts occasionally. With respect to the different forms that it assumed, and its various movements, I consider it impossible to give a correct idea of them by words. It appeared sometimes in immense sheets of light, moving rapidly along the surface of the sky, and at other times it darted in straight columns from different parts of the sky towards the zenith. The most remarkable appearance, however, that it presented, was a sort of serpentine motion that it had at one time from west to east, across the zenith. The electrometer was tried, but it was not affected, nor did we hear any noise such as has been said to be produced by this phenomenon. Whether the Aurora Borealis dims the light of the stars or not, I can hardly pretend to say, but I can affirm this much, that I could see very plainly, in the thickest part of it, the four small stars forming the diamond-shaped figure in the constellation of the Dolphin, from which I imagine that a great part of the dimness that appears to be occasioned, is owing to the stars and Aurora Borealis being nearly of the same colour.

Wednesday, 11*th*. — We picked up this afternoon a piece of pine three feet eleven inches in length, and seven inches in diameter; it appeared to have been a considerable time in the water; there was no axe-mark, or that of any other tool, to be seen upon it, so that it is probable that it had been drifted to this place from the coast of America. Our latitude at noon was 61° 8′ N., and longitude, when sights were taken for chronometer in the forenoon, 34° 44′ W. Several land-birds, namely, hawks, and wheat-ears, have been seen about the ship at different times for some days past.

Monday, 16*th*. — A heavy gale of wind commenced very suddenly at nine o'clock in the forenoon of Saturday last, and continued to blow very violently from that time until noon to-day, and heavy squalls occurred indeed occasionally until three o'clock in the afternoon. During the first night of the gale our stern-boat was carried away by a sea, which struck her. That, however, was a loss that hardly deserves to be mentioned, when compared with what we sustained to-day, for at half-past one o'clock this afternoon, we carried away our bowsprit, fore-mast, (about two feet above the deck,) and main-top-mast, a little above the cap. Our best bower-anchor was also obliged to be cut away, in consequence of some of the wreck getting entangled with it. Notwithstanding the bustle and confusion that were unavoidably occasioned by this accident, and the boisterous state of the weather, the ship was cleared of the wreck, and the remaining masts secured without any person being hurt.

Wednesday, 18*th*. — All hands have been busily employed during these two days fitting the rigging, and preparing to get jury-masts up: a jury fore-mast was got up indeed to-day, and the main-top-mast is ready for going up to-morrow morning. We saw a strange sail a few miles astern of us in the afternoon, but the weather being thick at the time, we could not make out what she was, and, as the wind was light at the time, she did not come up with us in the course of the evening.

Thursday, 19th. — Nothing more has been seen of the vessel just mentioned, whether she steered a different course during the night in order to avoid falling in with us from seeing the state we were in, I cannot pretend to say: but, be that as it may, we are now in a state that does not require her assistance even if she was to appear, for we have got a jury-bowsprit rigged, and top-masts up to-day. The wind and weather is still, however, rather unfavourable for us, for the sea has not yet gone down, and the wind is from the southward and eastward.

Friday, 27th. — Nothing occurred for this week past worthy of any notice; the wind has been for most part of the time rather against us, and we have had ever since the last gale of wind a heavy swell. We saw three vessels yesterday, one of which showed Prussian colours. Soon after day-light this morning land was descried, which we knew from our latitude to be Fula or Foul Island, one of the Shetland Islands. Our longitude by the chronometers agreed with that in which this island is laid down within three or four miles, which shows the great utility of these machines, if such a proof was wanting; but their use in navigation is too well known to require any comment of mine.

Saturday, 28th. — We have been running to the southward to-day between Fair Island and Ronaldsha, both of which were in sight for most part of the day.

Sunday, 29th. — When the weather cleared up at noon to-day, we saw Mormond Hill in Banffshire, bearing W. S. W. by compass, and distant five or six leagues. I must here conclude my narrative, as an order has been issued to-day, requesting all logs and journals, &c. that have been kept by any person during the voyage to be sealed up, and sent to Mr. Parry, in order to be transmitted to the Lords Commissioners of the Admiralty.

In concluding this journal, I may remark that although we have not actually discovered the north-west passage, yet we have so far proved its existence, that I presume no person can henceforth be so sceptical as to doubt it; and I am even in hopes, indeed, to see the day, when its actual existence will be proved beyond a doubt.

APPENDIX.

No. I — *A List of the Officers and Ships' Companies of the Expedition.*

HECLA.

Names.	Rank or Quality.	No.
William Edward Parry, -	Lieut. and Command.	1
Frederick William Beechey, -	Lieutenant, - -	1
John Edwards, - -	Surgeon, - -	1
William H. Hooper, - -	Purser, - -	1
Edward Sabine, - -	Captain R. A., -	1
Alexander Fisher, - -	Assistant Surgeon,	1
Joseph Nias, - -	Midshipman, -	1
William J. Dealy, - -	Ditto, - -	1
Charles Palmer, - - -	Ditto, - -	1
James C. Ross, - -	Ditto, - -	1
John Bushnan, - - -	Ditto, - -	1
James Halse, - -	Clerk, - -	1
John Allison, - - -	Master Pilot,	1
George Crawford, - -	Mate, - -	1
James Scallon, - - -	Gunner, - -	1
Jacob Swansea, - -	Boatswain, - -	1
William Wallis, - - -	Carpenter, -	1
Seamen, - - -	Petty Officers, & A. B.	33
Marines (including a serjeant),	Serjeant & Privates,	6
A serjeant and private of artillery,	Artillery-men, -	2
	Total -	58

GRIPER.

Names.	Rank or Quality.	No.
Matthew Liddon, - -	Lieut. and Command.	1
H. P. Hoppner, - -	Lieutenant -	1
Charles J. Beverley, - -	Assistant Surgeon,	1
Andrew Reid, - -	Midshipman, -	1
A. M. Skene, - - -	Ditto, - -	1
William A. Griffiths, - -	Ditto, - -	1
Cyrus Wakeham, - - -	Clerk, - -	1
George Fyfe, - -	Master Pilot, -	1
Alexander Elder, - - -	Mate, - -	1
Seamen, - - - -	Petty Officers, & A.B.	22
Marines, - - -	Corporal & Privates,	5
	Total -	36

No. II.—*A List of Nautical, Astronomical, Meteorological, and other Instruments supplied to the Expedition. The Numbers in the right-hand column refer to the portion of the different Articles supplied to the Griper, and consequently those in the middle column to the number kept on board the Hecla.*

Instruments supplied to the Expedition.		Hecla.	Griper.
Astronomical clocks and stands ...	2	2	
Altitude instruments	4	2	2
Artificial horizons	6	3	3
Azimuth compasses	8	4	4
Anglometers	4	2	2
Barometers (marine)	4	2	2
Ditto (mountain)	4	2	2
Beam compasses........................	2	1	1
Brass scales	2	1	1
Chronometers			
Compasses (steering)	4	3	1
Circular protractors	2	1	1
Cyanameters	2	1	1
Charts, boxes of	2	1 box	1 box
Drawing instruments, cases	2	1 case	1 case
Dip sectors	2	1	1
Dipping needle	1	1	
Dip-steering needle.......................	1	1	
Electrometers	2	2	
Electric chains	2	2	
Gunter scales..............................	2	1	1
Hydrometers	2	1	1
Hygrometers	2	2	
Hydrophorus	1	1	
Instrument for magnetic force	1	1	
Micrometer..................................	1	1	
Parallel rulers	4	2	2
Portable observatory	1	1	
Repeating circle	1	1	
Thermometers	20	10	10
Ditto (register)	1		1
Theodolites, (one small and the other 7-inch)	2	1 7-inch	1 small
Transit instrument	1	1	
Telescopes (2 feet)	6	4	2
Variation transit	1	1	
Ditto needle............................	1	1	
Water bottles..............................	3	2	1

No. III. — THE Maximum, Minimum, and Mean Temperature of the Air in the Shade, and the Maximum, Minimum, and Mean Height of the Barometer; together with the Latitude and Longitude at Noon every Day, from the 11th of May, 1819, to the 30th of September, 1820.

Day of the Month.	Temperature of the Air.			Height of Barometer.			Latitude at Noon.			Longitude at Noon.		
	Max.	Min.	Mean.	Max.	Min.	Mean.	Mer. Alt.	2d Alt.	D. R.	Lunar.	Chron.	D. R.
1819.	°	°	°	Inches.	Inches.	Inches.	° ′ ″	° ′ ″	° ′ ″	° ′ ″	° ′ ″	° ′ ″
May 1								In the river Thames				
2												
3												
4												
5												
6												
7												
8												
9												
10												
11	64	58	61	30.19	30.14	30.15	Nore Light N. E. one mile					
12	63	54	58	30.11	30.01	30.08	Kazenland N. W. by N., Lowestoff N. ½ E.					
13	60½	51	55	30.05	30.00	30.01	At anchor, Cromer Light-house N. W. by W.					
14	62	51	55	30.10	30.05	30.07	Winterton Light-house W. two miles					
15	56	50	53	30.08	30.01	30.05	At anchor in Yarmouth Roads					
16	56	49	53	30.08	29.95	30.02	Blakeney Church W. Cromer S. W. by S.					
17	55½	51	53	29.95	29.65	29.82	South side of Robin Hood's Bay W. by N. ½ N. 13 miles					
18	55	49	52	29.60	29.60	29.60	56 47 25 N.	—	57 0 53 N.	—	46 40	1 6 0 W.
19	54	48	51	29.60	29.56	29.58	58 56 23	—	59 2 0	—	1 21 35	1 45 30
20	52	47	50	29.83	29.61	29.72	59 17 1	—	Fair Island E. 12 miles		—	—
21	49	47½	48	29.97	29.87	29.94	—	—	59 27 0	—	3 43 0 W.	—
22	51½	48	50	30.06	29.95	30.01	59 5 18	—	59 13 42	—	6 47 37	6 29 54
23	51	49	50	30.16	30.06	30.11	58 34 17	—	58 40 36	—	10 20 19	10 19 56
24	52	48	50	30.21	30.17	30.19	57 51 53	—	58 4 39	—	13 36 0	13 34 59
25	51	49	50	30.24	30.21	30.22	57 8 46	—	57 23 33	—	16 59 34	16 55 30
26	50½	47	49	30.30	30.26	30.27	—	—	57 2 58	—	—	20 44 40
27	51	47	49	30.29	30.29	30.29	56 51 51	—	56 59 34	—	23 59 50	23 44 22
28	49	47	48	30.18	30.07	30.13	57 26 16	—	57 13 27	—	25 5 43	25 1 8
29	49	47	48	29.94	29.58	29.80	—	—	57 38 58	—	25 48 21	25 46 27
30	49	45	47	29.28	28.99	29.11	—	—	57 46 10	—	—	29 9 0
31	48½	45	46	29.10	28.86	28.97	—	—	58 12 46	—	30 19 39	30 43 48
	64	45	51	30.30	28.86	29.91	Range and Mean for May, 1819.					

Day of the Month.	Temperature of the Air.			Height of Barometer.			Latitude at Noon.			Longitude at Noon.		
	Max.	Min.	Mean.	Max.	Min.	Mean.	Mer. Alt.	2d Alt.	D. R.	Lunar.	Chron.	D. R.
1819.	°	°	°	Inches.	Inches.	Inches.	° ′ ″	° ′ ″	° ′ ″	° ′ ″	° ′ ″	° ′ ″
June 1	45½	41	43	28.95	28.86	28.92	58 6 53 N.	—	57 45 52 N.	—	—	33 30 48 W.
2	43	41	42	29.32	28.97	29.14	57 0 38	—	57 14 51	—	34 30 52 W.	34 13 39
3	41	39	40	29.59	29.37	29.46	55 57 51	—	56 17 50	—	34 33 53	34 54 13
4	45½	40	42	29.78	29.60	29.68	55 0 33	—	55 7 21	—	35 43 0	35 22 0
5	43½	41	42	29.86	29.68	29.76	—	—	55 2 59	36 11 39 W.	36 0 34	36 16 15
6	45	41	43	29.76	29.72	29.73	55 22 21	—	55 21 41	—	37 13 45	37 34 30
7	45½	39	42½	29.77	29.48	29.61	55 51 13	—	55 48 27	—	36 59 15	36 50 55
8	42	39	40½	28.81	29.25	29.51	56 26 57	—	56 27 17	—	—	37 34 25
9	42½	39	41	29.84	29.75	29.79	55 54 35	—	55 56 7	—	37 23 47	37 35 31
10	42	40	41½	29.82	29.70	29.78	55 57 20	—	56 9 47	—	37 45 43	37 42 31
11	44	39½	42	29.60	29.48	29.51	56 29 50	—	56 24 32	—	39 48 20	40 0 58
12	42½	39½	40	29.78	29.43	29.65	57 23 9	—	57 20 44	—	40 16 4	40 6 53
13	42½	40	41	29.84	29.70	29.77	—	—	57 48 27	—	—	40 41 49
14	42	37½	40	29.97	29.87	29.92	57 36 43	—	57 41 3	—	41 30 4	41 41 21
15	41	37	38	29.92	29.51	29.67	—	—	57 25 44	—	42 43 42	42 50 0
16	41	37	39	29.80	29.52	29.68	58 12 43	—	58 33 46	—	47 29 11	46 48 8
17	40	36½	38	29.75	29.75	29.76	58 29 56	—	58 58 55	—	48 9 24	48 22 5
18	37	34	35	29.91	29.84	29.88	59 8 21	—	59 44 41	—	—	47 28 48
19	43	32½	36	29.84	29.80	29.82	59 48 26	—	59 48 35	—	47 47 36	47 50 4
20	52	35	41½	29.63	29.42	29.55	60 17 18	—	60 10 38	—	49 45 51	49 45 42
21	42½	38	40	29.60	29.48	29.54	61 16 0	—	61 8 36	—	53 48 11	53 20 54
22	39	34	37	29.76	29.60	29.67	—	—	62 8 18	—	57 52 31	57 44 39
23	39	28	34	29.93	29.80	29.88	62 43 9	—	62 53 36	—	61 17 4	60 36 19
24	38	32	35	30.06	29.92	29.98	63 34 24	—	63 29 57	—	61 18 24	61 37 51
25	37	30	34	29.82	29.70	29.74	60 0 0	—	64 3 45	—	—	61 8 32
26	34	30	31½	29.66	29.57	29.61	63 59 29	—	—	—	61 26 10	—
27	34	28	31	29.48	29.32	29.40	63 46 50	—	—	—	61 39 33	—
28	37	30½	33	29.42	29.33	29.38	63 39 4	—	—	—	61 46 58	—
29	34½	31	33	29.80	29.43	29.64	—	—	63 31 40	—	—	62 17 0
30	39	32	36	29.84	29.82	29.83	63 25 0	—	—	—	62 17 0	—
	52	28	38½	30.06	28.86	29.64	Range and Mean for June, 1819.					

Day of the Month.	Temperature of the Air.			Height of Barometer.			Latitude at Noon.			Longitude at Noon.		
	Max.	Min.	Mean.	Max.	Min.	Mean.	Mer. Alt.	2d Alt.	D. R.	Lunar.	Chron.	D. R.
1819.	°	°	°	Inches.	Inches.	Inches.	° ′ ″	° ′ ″	° ′ ″	° ′ ″	° ′ ″	° ′ ″
July 1	+39	+34	+36	29.83	29.78	29.80	64 11 54 N.	—	64 12 36 N.	—	60 41 10 W.	61 2 42 W.
2	37½	35½	36	29.78	29.70	29.75	65 18 32	—	—	—	58 34 36	—
3	35	30	33	29.61	29.10	29.30	—	—	66 26 8	—	—	57 42 36
4	33	30½	31½	29.42	29.35	29.38	—	—	66 50 47	—	—	57 22 26
5	33	29	31	29.48	29.35	29.40	66 56 38	—	66 59 11	—	57 3 39	57 33 11
6	38	31	34	29.54	29.42	29.50	67 44 5	—	67 32 32	—	58 1 46	58 24 49
7	46	34	40	29.59	29.51	29.55	68 24 52	—	68 22 17	—	57 16 57	57 22 31
8	40	34	38	29.68	29.60	29.62	68 30 1	—	68 36 52	—	57 38 43	57 48 22
9	34	30	32	29.74	29.69	29.72	68 45 53	—	68 57 37	—	—	58 17 13
10	32	28	30	29.80	29.75	29.78	69 4 28	—	69 14 17	—	58 26 51	58 50 3
11	32	26	29½	29.77	29.73	29.76	—	—	69 24 40	—	—	58 27 27
12	33½	28	30½	29.66	29.63	29.63	69 42 44	—	61 51 4	—	—	58 2 34
13	32	31	32	29.90	29.72	29.82	—	—	69 59 38	—	57 50 54	57 34 37
14	36½	28½	32	29.90	29.84	29.87	70 17 43	—	70 31 32	—	58 41 19	58 30 54
15	31	28	30	29.91	29.81	29.87	70 27 43	—	70 31 43	—	59 29 33	59 37 24
16	36	27	33	29.90	29.76	29.85	70 56 16	—	70 31 43	—	59 48 32	59 46 38
17	34	31	33½	29.84	29.71	29.78	—	—	72 0 27	—	60 4 48	59 59 52
18	33	30½	32	29.90	29.79	29.82	—	—	72 11 57	—	—	59 17 37
19	34	29	31	29.93	29.90	29.91	72 31 58	—	72 27 57	—	59 22 30	59 9 7
20	30	27	28½	29.84	29.70	29.79	—	—	72 57 31	—		58 56 3
21	42	27	38	29.63	29.56	29.58	72 58 13	—	73 5 13	—	59 1 17	58 54 20
22	45	34	40	29.62	29.58	29.60	73 13 23	—	73 12 13	—	60 32 12	59 46 41
23	36	29	31½	29.70	29.62	29.66	73 4 10	—	73 9 2	—	60 28 45	60 52 52
24	37	31	34	29.83	29.60	29.75	72 59 30	—	—	—	60 27 45	—
25	40	32	35	29.89	29.84	29.87	72 56 37	—	—	—	60 33 32	—
26	35	28	32	29.85	29.82	29.83	73 2 17	—	—	—	60 32 16	—
27	35	33	34	29.90	29.74	29.84	—	—	73 5 56	—	—	60 42 51
28	33	33	33	29.71	29.53	29.61	—	—	73 26 15	—	—	62 32 33
29	37	33	34	29.52	29.49	29.50	—	—	73 51 17	—	—	68 2 15
30	38	33	36	29.54	29.51	29.52	74 1 57	—	74 4 17	—	75 23 29	74 15 51
31	43	35	37	29.51	29.50	29.50	73 40 24	—	—	—	77 15 16	—
	+46	+26	+33½	29.93	29.10	29.68	Range and Mean for July, 1819.					

Day of the Month.	Temperature of the Air.			Height of Barometer.			Latitude at Noon.			Longitude at Noon.		
	Max.	Min.	Mean.	Max.	Min.	Mean.	Mer. Alt.	2d Alt.	D. R.	Lunar.	Chron.	D. R.
1819.	°	°	°	Inches.	Inches.	Inches.	° ′ ″	° ′ ″	° ′ ″	° ′ ″	° ′ ″	° ′ ″
Aug. 1	+36	+33½	+34½	29.60	29.51	29.54	73 55 18 N.	—	—	—	77 40 0 W.	—
2	41	33	37	29.73	29.59	29.66	74 30 3	—	—	—	78 1 0	—
3	38	33	35½	29.70	29.50	29.63	74 25 31	—	—	—	80 4 30	—
4	37½	33½	35	29.51	29.45	29.48	74 15 53	—	—	—	86 30 30	—
5	35	33½	34	29.51	29.48	29.49	—	—	74 14 30 N.	—	89 31 40	89 18 40 W.
6	35	33	34	29.56	29.51	29.53	73 52 20	—	—	—	89 27 0	—
7	36	31	34	29.60	29.53	29.56	72 45 4	—	—	—	89 48 12	—
8	35	30	33	29.65	29.59	29.62	72 13 25	—	—	—	90 3 9	—
9	39½	30½	34	29.67	29.62	29.65	72 47 31	—	—	—	90 5 0	—
10	36	31	33	29.55	29.52	29.54	—	—	72 53 0	—	—	90 1 0
11	35	33	33	29.66	29.49	29.56	—	—	72 57 15	—	—	89 57 0
12	35	30	32½	29.85	29.80	29.82	72 59 40	—	—	—	—	90 4 0
13	40	30	37	29.86	29.72	29.81	73 13 25	—	—	—	89 22 23	—
14	42	34	37	29.76	29.61	29.71	73 35 30	—	—	—	89 1 20	—
15	39	32	35	29.63	29.61	29.62	73 39 36	—	—	88 36 20 W	—	—
16	36	33	34	29.68	29.61	29.64	73 45 10	—	—	—	—	88 30 30
17	35	32	33	29.66	29.63	29.65	—	—	73 48 20	—	—	88 14 3
18	36	32½	34	29.64	29.60	29.62	73 50 56	—	—	—	88 9 2	—
19	33	32	33	29.55	29.53	29.54	—	—	74 20 30	—	—	87 30 0
20	36	33	34	29.63	29.57	29.61	—	—	74 26 30	—	—	88 7 0
21	36	.33	35	29.66	29.62	29.65	74 29 15	—	—	—	90 19 0	—
22	38	33	36	29.76	29.67	29.72	—	—	74 33 15	—	—	91 41 30
23	36	32	34	29.76	29.66	29.71	74 20 52	—	—	—	94 43 15	—
24	39	28	29½	29.66	29.61	29.63	—	—	74 23 0	—	—	97 56 0
25	32	30	30½	29.87	29.64	29.75	—	—	74 40 30	—	98 30 30	—
26	35	30	32	30.07	29.95	30.01	74 48 47	—	—	—	99 1 15	—
27	34	30½	32½	29.96	29.80	29.90	75 1 51	—	—	—	101 31 1	—
28	34	30	32	29.70	29.60	29.65	75 3 12	—	—	—	103 44 37	—
29	32	31	32	29.57	29.40	29.48	74 58 6	—	—	—	—	103 54 42
30	34	30	32	29.36	29.31	29.33	—	—	74 57 15	—	—	104 5 42
31	34	31	32	29.59	29.39	29.51	—	—	74 58 0	—	—	104 17 15
	+42	+28	+33½	30.06	29.31	29.63	Range and Mean for August, 1819.					

Day of the Month.	Temperature of the Air. Max.	Min.	Mean.	Height of Barometer. Max.	Min.	Mean.	Latitude at Noon. Mer. Alt.	2d Alt.	D. R.	Longitude at Noon. Lunar.	Chron.	D. R.
1819.	°	°	°	Inches.	Inches.	Inches.	° ′ ″	° ′ ″	° ′ ″	° ′ ″	° ′ ″	° ′ ″
Sept. 1	+36	+31½	+33	29.99	29.63	29.77	74 59 35 N.	—	—	—	106 7 36 W.	—
2	36	31	33	30.31	30.05	30.21	74 55 55	—	—	—	106 59 0	—
3	37	31	34	30.42	30.31	30.37	None	—	74 54 30	—	—	107 25 0 W.
4	35	28	32	30.37	30.31	30.34	74 54 49	—	—	—	108 31 44	—
5	32	28	30½	30.31	30.21	30.24	—	—	74 42 45	—	—	110 24 30
6	30	25	28	30.18	30.14	30.15	At anchor in Coppermine Road					
7	30	25	28	30.12	30.10	30.11	—	—	74 32 15	—	—	111 7 30
8	31	28	30	30.09	30.07	30.08	—	—	74 29 0	—	—	111 37 30
9	32	29	31	30.11	30.04	30.07						
10	32	30	31	30.10	30.01	30.07						
11	30	26	28	29.95	29.86	29.89						
12	30	28½	29½	29.80	29.73	29.76	—	—	74 30 15	—	111 43 30	—
13	29	15½	26	29.62	29.41	29.53						
14	17	9	14	29.77	29.57	29.71						
15	21½	16	19	29.80	29.72	29.76						
16	24	17	21	29.70	29.57	29.64	—	—	74 23 25	—	112 29 30	—
17	22	16	20	30.07	29.72	29.89	74 22 15	—	—	—	—	112 51 9
18	29	20	24	30.00	29.90	29.95	—	—	74 29 30	—	—	111 54 45
19	25	19	22	29.75	29.47	29.61	—	—	74 31 0	—	—	111 38 0
20	21	10½	17	29.46	29.36	29.41	Same Station as above		—	—	—	—
21	19½	10	16	29.60	29.43	29.51	Ditto		—	—	—	—
22	23	17	20	29.62	29.54	29.58	74 39 18		74 41 30	—	—	110 41 20
23	23	20	22	29.80	29.66	29.74	At the entrance of Winter Harbour					
24	24	9	20	30.04	29.80	29.93	Cutting into Winter Harbour					
25	17	7	14	30.14	30.04	30.10	Ditto	Ditto				
26	8	−1	5	30.19	30.17	30.17	Ditto	Ditto				
27	21	+5	15	30.14	30.04	30.09	74 47 15	—	—	110 48 30	—	—
28	23	10	17	29.98	29.88	29.92						
29	14	8	11	29.82	29.76	29.78						
30	7	4	6	29.87	29.70	29.78						
	+37	−1	+22½	30.42	29.36	29.90	Range and Mean for September, 1819.					

Day of the Month.	Temperature of the Air. Max.	Min.	Mean.	Height of Barometer. Max.	Min.	Mean.	Latitude at Noon. Mer. Alt.	2d Alt.	D. R.	Longitude at Noon. Lunar.	Chron.	D. R.
1819.	°	°	°	Inches.	Inches.	Inches.	° ′ ″	° ′ ″	° ′ ″	° ′ ″	° ′ ″	′ ″
Oct. 1	+ 9	+ 6	+ 7	29.76	29.73	29.86	74 47 15 N.	—	—	110 48 30 W.	—	—
2	17½	9½	13	29.77	29.	29.74						
3	10	6	9	29.59	29.68	29.75						
4	16	5	10	29.71	29.17	29.39						
5	13	− 7	3	29.81	29.10	29.44						
6	8	8	1	29.26	29.50	29.73						
7	15	0	+ 6	29.	29.20	29.22						
8	1	8½	− 3	30.00	29.46	29.80						
9	0	5	2	30.00	29.93	29.95						
10	5	3	+ 2	29.83	29.68	29.75						
11	10	+ 2	4½	29.69	29.60	29.63						
12	7	− 8	− 4	29.63	29.44	29.53						
13	16	+ 3	+ 7	29.57	29.43	29.49						
14	5	− 6	− 2	30.00	29.44	29.71						
15	13	0	+ 6	29.62	29.30	29.42						
16	−12	−12½	− 5	29.91	29.49	29.74						
17	10½	16	13	30.20	29.93	30.09						
18	2	14	6	30.22	30.18	30.19						
19	7	14	11	30.20	29.98	30.12						
20	13½	17½	15	30.00	29.93	29.95						
21	7	14	10½	30.21	30.00	30.10						
22	3	14	7	30.32	30.27	30.30						
23	+ 6	9	0	30.13	30.03	30.07						
24	1	6	− 3	30.06	30.01	30.04						
25	5	+ 2	+ 4	30.16	30.05	30.11						
26	4	− 8	− 1	30.11	30.06	30.09						
27	− 4	15	10	30.02	29.87	29.95						
28	17	23	20	29.79	29.72	29.77						
29	20	28	24	29.73	29.69	29.71						
30	25	27½	26	29.73	29.70	29.71						
31	4	28	12	29.91	29.70	29.84						
	−17½	−28	− 3½	30.32	29.10	29.84	Range and Mean for October, 1819.					

Day of the Month.	Temperature of the Air.			Height of Barometer.			Latitude at Noon.			Longitude at Noon.		
	Max.	Min.	Mean.	Max.	Min.	Mean.	Mer. Alt.	2d Alt.	D. R.	Lunar.	Chron.	D. R.
819.	°	°	°	Inches.	Inches.	Inches.	° ′ ″	° ′ ″	° ′ ″	° ′ ″	° ′ ″	° ′ ″
Nov. 1	− 2	− 3	− 1	29.89	29.81	29.87	74 47 15 N.	—	—	110 48 30 W.	—	—
2	5	0	+ 3	29.90	29.81	29.86						
3	6	0	4	30.02	29.93	29.97						
4	6	+ 5	5	30.17	30.07	30.12						
5	+ 6	− 7	− 0½	30.30	30.21	30.27						
6	− 8	18	14	30.32	30.27	30.29						
7	6½	16	11	30.08	30.00	30.03						
8	5	13	10	29.93	29.93	29.93						
9	11	15	13	29.98	29.87	29.92						
10	6½	15	9½	30.07	30.00	30.04						
11	13	26½	18½	30.07	30.02	30.03						
12	24	32	28½	30.13	30.02	30.07						
13	24	34	28½	29.95	29.86	29.92						
14	25	32	26	29.81	29.79	29.80						
15	21	40	31	29.95	29.73	29.79						
16	36	42	40	30.20	30.04	30.14						
17	30	40	35½	30.21	30.09	30.15						
18	34	37	36	30.07	29.97	30.04						
19	38	47	43	30.20	30.12	30.16						
20	40	47	43½	30.14	29.96	30.05						
21	20	40½	28	29.81	29.72	29.76						
22	21	25	23	29.72	29.72	29.72						
23				30.20	29.92	30.06						
24				30.11	29.83	29.98						
25	5	18	12	29.81	29.73	29.77						
26	20	28	25	29.70	29.67	29.69						
27	13	28½	18	29.67	29.63	29.65						
28	24½	32	28	29.80	29.68	29.75						
29	31	32½	32	29.75	29.72	29.74						
30	32	34	33½	29.73	29.66	29.69						
	+ 6	−47	−20½	30.32	29.63	29.94	Range and Mean for November, 1819.					

Day of the Month.	Temperature of the Air.			Height of Barometer.			Latitude at Noon.			Longitude at Noon.		
	Max.	Min.	Mean.	Max.	Min.	Mean.	Mer. Alt.	2d Alt.	D. R.	Lunar.	Chron.	D. R.
1819.	°	°	°	Inches.	Inches.	Inches.	° ′ ″	° ′ ″	° ′ ″	° ′ ″	° ′ ″	° ′ ″
Dec. 1	−25	−34	−30	29.60	29.58	29.58	74 47 15 N.	—	—	110 48 30 W.	—	—
2	28	36	32½	29.60	29.52	29.57						
3	9	23	16	29.46	29.40	29.43						
4	26	34	31½	29.42	29.36	29.39						
5	27	35	31	29.46	29.36	29.39						
6	23	34	27	29.51	29.45	29.47						
7	19	26	22	29.67	29.53	29.59						
8	15	22	19½	29.80	29.67	29.73						
9	17	21	18½	29.89	29.83	29.86						
10	18	21	19	29.90	29.89	29.89						
11	4	20	11	29.80	29.65	29.71						
12	9	20	14	29.74	29.67	29.70						
13	7	14	10½	29.92	29.79	29.86						
14	7	10	8	30.40	30.04	30.23						
15	7	15	11½	30.30	30.33	30.35						
16	8	18	13	30.31	30.13	30.24						
17	0	9	4	30.00	29.85	29.90						
18	3	11	5	29.90	29.84	29.88						
19	9	24	17	29.95	29.94	29.94						
20	19	25	22½	29.96	29.93	29.94						
21	19	25	23	30.11	30.00	30.07						
22	27	35	31	30.06	30.05	30.05						
23	30	37	33½	30.10	30.03	30.06						
24	24	34	31	30.01	29.71	29.84						
25	23½	30	26	29.69	29.59	29.64						
26	5	34	16	29.35	29.10	29.22						
27	17	32	24½	29.94	29.47	29.71						
28	34	39	36½	30.33	30.01	30.16						
29	34	40	37	30.71	30.40	30.56						
30	30	43	38½	30.75	30.62	30.68						
31	+ 6	28	7	30.39	29.80	30.09						
	+ 6	−43	−21½	30.75	29.10	29.86	Range and Mean for December, 1819.					

Day of the Month.	Temperature of the Air. Max.	Min.	Mean.	Height of Barometer. Max.	Min.	Mean.	Latitude at Noon. Mer. Alt.	2d Alt.	D. R.	Longitude at Noon. Lunar.	Chron.	D. R.
1820.	°	°	°	Inches.	Inches.	Inches.	° ′ ″	° ′ ″	° ′ ″	° ′ ″	° ′ ″	° ′ ″
Jan. 1	− 2	−28	−18	29.93	29.72	29.81	74 47 15 N.	—	—	110 48 30 W.	—	—
2	19	29	24	29.71	29.63	29.67						
3	29	42	34½	30.00	29.73	29.87						
4	34	44	40	30.24	30.03	30.13						
5	28	35	32	30.22	30.20	30.20						
6	22	33	28½	30.16	30.09	30.11						
7	32	40	37	30.10	30.03	30.06						
8	33	38	35½	30.11	29.87	30.02						
9	33	35	34	30.31	30.10	30.22						
10	32	43	36	30.35	30.34	30.34						
11	42	46	44	30.33	30.25	30.28						
12	42	47	44½	30.24	30.10	30.16						
13	40½	47	45	30.33	30.26	30.28						
14	32	40	35	30.20	30.18	30.19						
15	34	39	35	30.51	30.20	30.33						
16	34	39	37	30.77	30.65	30.70						
17	16	34	24	30.59	30.29	30.43						
18	5	15	10	30.25	30.15	30.20						
19	8	28	17	30.25	30.19	30.22						
20	16	31	24	30.13	30.10	30.11						
21	16	23	19	30.09	30.01	30.06						
22	22	29	26	30.15	30.06	30.10						
23	18	26	22	30.11	30.06	30.09						
24	20	28	24½	29.87	29.59	29.69						
25	23	30	26	29.69	29.66	29.67						
26	26	36	31	29.75	29.67	29.70						
27	32	36	33½	29.90	29.75	29.82						
28	35	39	37	30.14	29.94	30.05						
29	19	33	26	30.11	29.94	30.04						
30	19	20	19	29.93	29.90	29.90						
31	22	28	24	29.85	29.83	29.84						
	− 2	−47	−30	30.77	29.59	30.07	Range and Mean for January, 1820.					

Day of the Month.	Temperature of the Air.			Height of Barometer.			Latitude at Noon.			Longitude at Noon.		
	Max.	Min.	Mean.	Max.	Min.	Mean.	Mer. Alt.	2d Alt.	D. R.	Lunar.	Chron.	D. R.
1820.	°	°	°	Inches.	Inches.	Inches.	° ′ ″	° ′ ″	° ′ ″	° ′ ″	° ′ ″	° ′ ″
Feb. 1	−17	−26	−20½	29.88	29.82	29.85	74 47 15 N.	—	—	110 48 30 W.	—	—
2	27	38	31½	29.92	29.88	29.90						
3	35	44	39½	30.01	29.92	29.96						
4	37	41½	39½	30.02	29.97	30.00						
5	20	37	29	29.89	29.75	29.81						
6	18	23	20½	29.69	29.64	29.65						
7	20	30	24½	29.75	29.75	29.75						
8	27	32	28	29.81	29.75	29.78						
9	23	28	25½	29.68	29.57	29.61						
10	26	40	31½	29.64	29.50	29.56						
11	38	42	39½	29.70	29.47	29.60						
12	39	44	42	29.34	29.32	29.33						
13	37	46½	41½	29.45	29.32	29.38						
14	38	48	46	29.69	29.53	29.62						
15	32	50	40½	29.75	29.69	29.72						
16	29	36	32	30.02	29.75	29.88						
17	26	39	33	30.08	30.04	30.05						
18	24	28	26	29.96	29.87	29.92						
19	19	24	21	29.77	29.60	29.68						
20	23	26	24	29.58	29.53	29.55						
21	25	37	30	29.80	29.59	29.72						
22	34	41	36½	29.93	29.83	29.90						
23	35	41	37½	29.93	29.89	29.90						
24	39	43	40½	29.99	29.91	29.95						
25	30	38½	34½	29.82	29.72	29.75						
26	20	29	26	29.72	29.70	29.70						
27	24	32	27½	29.73	29.67	29.70						
28	25	32	29	29.97	29.75	29.87						
29	27	37	29½	30.15	30.02	30.10						
	−17	−50	−32	30.15	29.32	29.76	Range and Mean for February, 1820.					

Day of the Month.	Temperature of the Air.			Height of Barometer.			Latitude at Noon.			Longitude at Noon.		
	Max.	Min.	Mean.	Max.	Min.	Mean.	Mer. Alt.	2d Alt.	D. R.	Lunar.	Chron.	D. R.
1820.	°	°	°	Inches.	Inches.	Inches.	° ′ ″	° ′ ″	° ′ ″	° ′ ″	° ′ ″	° ′ ″
March 1	−25	−40	−31	30.16	29.80	30.05	74 47 15 N.	—	—	110 48 30 W.	—	—
2	17	33	25	29.63	29.52	29.57						
3	26	37	31	29.68	29.55	29.62						
4	24	33	27½	29.62	29.50	29.57						
5	9	26	16½	29.41	29.30	29.37						
6	+ 2½	8	2½	29.12	29.00	29.05						
7	2	15	6	29.27	29.03	29.17						
8	−16	22	18	30.15	29.32	29.76						
9	3	14	8½	30.13	29.88	29.98						
10	+ 1	14	4½	29.78	29.62	29.69						
11	6	11	2	29.63	29.30	29.47						
12	−19	29	24	29.96	29.62	29.82						
13	18	27	22½	29.97	29.82	29.90						
14	12	24	17½	29.83	29.62	29.75						
15	10	23	16	29.76	29.50	29.60						
16	13	26	21½	29.88	29.76	29.82						
17	12	24	17½	29.87	29.83	29.85						
18	5	16	8½	29.99	29.78	29.88						
19	10	18	13½	30.00	29.91	29.96						
20	8	18	11½	29.89	29.75	29.85						
21	12	24	15½	29.78	29.63	29.69						
22	8	22	13½	29.88	29.72	29.78						
23	17	26	22	30.05	29.91	29.99						
24	18	27	21½	30.06	29.95	29.99						
25	22	30	26½	29.94	29.92	29.92						
26	21	29	25½	30.14	29.93	30.00						
27	19	33	26	30.19	30.03	30.13						
28	16	29	24	30.26	30.19	30.22						
29	17	28	23½	30.19	30.14	30.16						
30	12	28	20	30.25	30.14	30.21						
31	3	27	11½	30.18	29.89	30.00						
	+ 6	−40	−18	30.26	29.00	29.80	Range and Mean for March, 1820.					

Day of the Month.	Temperature of the Air.			Height of Barometer.			Latitude at Noon.			Longitude at Noon.		
	Max.	Min.	Mean.	Max.	Min.	Mean.	Mer. Alt.	2d Alt.	D. R.	Lunar.	Chron.	D. R.
1820.	°	°	°	Inches.	Inches.	Inches.	° ′ ″	° ′ ″	° ′ ″	° ′ ″	° ′ ″	° ′ ″
April 1	0	−16	− 6	30.02	30.01	30.01	71 47 15 N.	—	—	110 48 30 W.	—	—
2	− 2	25	8	30.02	29.89	29.95						
3	9	26	18½	29.81	29.79	29.79						
4	8	26	14½	29.86	29.83	29.84						
5	5	24½	16½	30.00	29.86	29.90						
6	15	25	18½	30.01	29.96	29.98						
7	13	26	21	30.00	29.89	29.94						
8	13	29	20	29.87	29.84	29.85						
9	14	30	21½	29.88	29.83	29.85						
10	12	32	22½	29.80	29.70	29.73						
11	12	27	19½	29.68	29.57	29.62						
12	11	29	20	29.64	29.52	29.56						
13	15	31	22½	29.85	29.67	29.76						
14	14	29	19	29.95	29.89	29.93						
15	+ 6	17	7	29.72	29.40	29.54						
16	− 5	19	12	29.90	29.57	29.77						
17	5	21	13½	30.26	29.94	30.12						
18	1	15	8	30.32	30.23	30.28						
19	+ 2	13	4	30.23	29.92	30.05						
20	4	9	2	29.78	29.67	29.69						
21	3	10	3	29.96	29.70	29.83						
22	0	12	4½	30.00	29.97	29.98						
23	+13	5	+ 4	29.89	29.63	29.75						
24	14	+ 4	10	29.71	29.67	29.69						
25	14	− 7	4½	30.20	29.70	29.97						
26	11	12	− 1	30.55	30.25	30.38						
27	9	12	0	30.86	30.66	30.80						
28	15	5	+ 4½	30.79	30.46	30.60						
29	22	+ 3	12	30.66	30.43	30.55						
30	32	6	20	30.67	30.34	30.50						
	+32	−32	− 8	30.86	29.40	29.97	Range and Mean for April, 1820.					

Day of the Month.	Temperature of the Air.			Height of Barometer.			Latitude at Noon.			Longitude at Noon.		
	Max.	Min.	Mean.	Max.	Min.	Mean.	Mer. Alt.	2d Alt.	D. R.	Lunar.	Chron.	D. R.
1820.	°	°	°	Inches.	Inches.	Inches.	° ′ ″	° ′ ″	° ′ ″	° ′ ″	° ′ ″	° ′ ″
May 1	+17	0	+ 8½	30.48	30.31	30.34	74 47 15 N.	—	—	110 48 30 W.	—	—
2	11	− 1	6	30.46	30.39	30.41						
3	15	+ 2	9	30.42	30.39	30.40						
4	16	0	7½	30.41	30.38	30.39						
5	20	+ 2	11½	30.36	30.26	30.31						
6	8½	− 2	3½	30.24	30.09	30.15						
7	5	4	½	30.06	29.98	30.00						
8	8	2	3	29.99	29.98	29.98						
9	9	1	4½	30.03	29.93	29.98						
10	10	+ 1	5½	30.07	30.00	30.02						
11	10	− 1½	4	30.14	30.08	30.11						
12	18	1	8½	30.19	30.15	30.16						
13	17	1	7½	30.34	30.19	30.26						
14	17	3	7½	30.41	30.36	30.39						
15	19½	1	9	30.28	30.26	30.31						
16	24	2	12½	30.23	30.19	30.20						
17	29	+ 7	18½	30.24	30.21	30.22						
18	24	10	18	30.31	30.23	30.27						
19	25	10	17½	30.27	30.24	30.25						
20	25	10	16½	30.20	30.10	30.16						
21	29	6	18½	30.11	29.99	30.02						
22	32	12	23	30.21	30.02	30.10						
23	34	20	27	30.30	30.00	30.19						
24	38	25	32½	30.12	29.77	29.89						
25	40½	32	36	29.99	29.74	29.87						
26	36½	30	33	30.20	30.00	30.12						
27	47	32½	39	30.02	29.23	29.98						
28	37	33	34½	29.81	29.27	29.58						
29	33	24	26½	29.60	29.27	29.40						
30	38	24	31	29.96	29.70	29.86						
31	35	27	30½	29.98	29.89	29.93						
	+17	− 4	−16½	30.48	29.25	30.10	Range and Mean for May, 1820.					

Day of the Month.	Temperature of the Air.			Height of Barometer.			Latitude at Noon.			Longitude at Noon.		
	Max.	Min.	Mean.	Max.	Min.	Mean.	Mer. Alt.	2d Alt.	D. R.	Lunar.	Chron.	D. R.
1820.	°	°	°	Inches.	Inches.	Inches.	° ′ ″	° ′ ″	° ′ ″	° ′ ″	° ′ ″	° ′ ″
June 1	+40	+31	+36	30.00	29.88	29.94	74 47 15 N.	—	—	110 48 30 W.	—	—
2	36	31	34	30.00	30.00	30.00						
3	43	29	35	29.98	29.74	29.86						
4	39	31½	35½	29.70	29.50	29.50						
5	40	30	34½	29.58	29.52	29.55						
6	37	28	32	29.68	29.60	29.64						
7	31	28	29½	29.64	29.50	29.55						
8	36	28	32	29.60	29.55	29.59						
9	38	30	33½	29.69	29.60	29.63						
10	33	32	32	29.73	29.62	29.69						
11	36	33	33½	29.84	29.76	29.79						
12	34	30	32	29.94	29.86	29.89						
13	37	29½	33	29.93	29.75	29.89						
14	37	32	34½	29.73	29.65	29.70						
15	39	29	34½	29.80	29.74	29.38						
16	37	29	33½	29.90	29.85	29.87						
17	43	30	34½	30.00	29.29	29.94						
18	43	31	37	30.13	30.00	30.06						
19	40	34	37½	30.13	30.08	30.11						
20	39	34	36	30.07	29.97	30.02						
21	42	35	38	29.96	29.93	29.94						
22	51	36	44	30.04	29.94	30.00						
23	45½	38	42	30.00	29.93	29.97						
24	41	33	37	29.94	29.79	29.84						
25	41½	34	37	29.80	29.76	29.79						
26	47	33	40	29.90	29.81	29.85						
27	43	36	39	29.96	29.87	29.90						
28	44	32	37	29.81	29.74	29.78						
29	46	39	41	29.79	29.75	29.76						
30	48	37	43	29.80	29.59	29.67						
	+51	+28	+36	30.13	29.50	29.81	Range and Mean for June, 1820.					

Day of the Month.	Temperature of the Air.			Height of Barometer.			Latitude at Noon.			Longitude at Noon.		
	Max.	Min.	Mean.	Max.	Min.	Mean.	Mer. Alt.	2d Alt.	D. R.	Lunar.	Chron.	D. R.
1820.	°	°	°	Inches.	Inches.	Inches.	° ′ ″	° ′ ″	° ′ ″	° ′ ″	° ′ ″	° ′ ″
July. 1	+44	+36	+40½	29.60	29.56	29.57	74 47 15 N.	—	—	110 48 30 W.	—	—
2	45	36	40½	29.70	29.62	29.65						
3	53	34	43½	29.73	29.71	29.72						
4	45	37	39½	29.77	29.73	29.74						
5	52	37	44	29.83	29.75	29.77						
6	51	43	47½	29.83	29.75	29.78						
7	55	41	47	29.90	29.83	29.86						
8	55	43	48½	29.90	29.86	29.88						
9	49	40	43½	30.01	29.77	29.90						
10	48	43	45½	29.83	29.70	29.76						
11	49	41	43	29.90	29.80	29.84						
12	49	40	43½	29.80	29.78	29.79						
13	55	40	46	29.82	29.76	29.79						
14	56	42	48	29.76	29.66	29.72						
15	47	38	43	29.79	29.68	29.71						
16	49	36½	42½	29.76	29.72	29.75						
17	60	41	51	29.81	29.75	29.79						
18	48	34	43	29.84	29.69	29.78						
19	50	36	43	29.75	29.69	29.72						
20	43	38	40	29.70	29.60	29.62						
21	45	33	40	29.64	29.60	29.62						
22	50	37	45	29.69	29.66	29.67						
23	43	34	39	29.70	29.67	29.69						
24	49	36	41½	29.71	29.60	29.67						
25	50	35½	43	29.59	29.31	29.45						
26	42	34	36½	29.27	29.13	29.17						
27	37	32½	34½	29.44	29.26	29.38						
28	42	34	37	29.39	29.30	29.33						
29	38	32	34½	29.52	29.34	29.45						
30	42	32	37	29.55	29.52	29.53						
31	40	34½	36½	29.52	29.44	29.48						
	+60	+32	+42	30.01	29.13	26.66	Range and Mean for July, 1820.					

Day of the Month.	Temperature of the Air.			Height of Barometer.			Latitude at Noon.			Longitude at Noon.		
	Max.	Min.	Mean.	Max.	Min.	Mean.	Mer. Alt.	2d Alt.	D. R.	Lunar.	Chron.	D. R.
1820.	°	°	°	Inches.	Inches.	Inches.	° ′ ″	° ′ ″	° ′ ″	° ′ ″	° ′ ″	° ′ ″
Aug. 1	+43	+32	+36	29.83	29.69	29.76	At anchor at the entrance of Winter Harbour					
2	38	32	34	29.84	29.70	29.79	74 36 33 N.	—	—	—	—	110 59 0 W.
3	39	33	35½	29.70	29.57	29.64	74 36 6	—	—	—	—	Ditto
4	38½	33	35½	29.69	29.65	29.67		—	—	—		
5	41	30½	34	29.79	29.69	29.73	74 21 49	—	—	—	112 45 35 W.	111 15 29
6	36	33	33½	29.76	29.59	29.67						
7	38	31	34½	29.62	29.56	29.59						
8	39	33	36	29.64	29.60	29.61						
9	40	31	34½	29.60	29.46	29.51						
10	34	30	31½	29.60	29.54	29.57	74 25 36	—	—	—	113 42 13	—
11	33	30	31½	29.64	29.53	29.59	Mean of 6					
12	38	30½	34	29.70	29.48	29.54	Mer. Alts.					
13	45	31	36½	29.87	29.76	29.82						
14	38	27	33	29.81	29.71	29.76						
15	37	29	33	29.85	29.76	29.80	74 26 25	—	—	—	113 46 43	—
16	34	29	32	30.01	29.83	30.94	Ditto	—	—	—	113 46 43	—
17	36	28	31½	30.03	29.96	29.00						
18	36	30	33	29.90	29.79	29.84						
19	40	28	33½	29.87	29.79	29.82						
20	36	27	31½	29.91	29.85	29.88	74 24 50	—	—	—	112 38 55	—
21	37	26	30½	29.84	29.69	29.76						
22	37½	29	31½	29.69	29.64	29.66						
23	35	30	31½	29.79	29.71	29.74						
24	34	30	31½	29.83	29.71	29.79	—	—	74 27 0	—	112 14 0	—
25	38	27	32	29.85	29.83	29.84	74 27 19	—	—	—	112 13 12	—
26	34	25½	28½	29.81	29.68	29.73	—	—	74 28 50	—	—	111 56 20
27	31	22½	27½	29.92	29.72	29.84	—	—	75 2 0	—	105 14 20	—
28	31	22	28	29.86	29.72	29.78	74 58 28	—	—	—	—	100 46 45
29	30	28	29	29.66	29.61	29.64	74 27 5	—	—	—	—	95 7 45
30	33	28	30	29.65	29.62	29.63	74 12 18	—	—	—	—	88 43 25
31	34	29	31½	29.75	29.63	29.67	—	—	73 53 50	—	—	80 25 30
	+45	+22	+32½	30.03	29.46	29.73	Range and Mean for August, 1820.					

Day of the Month.	Temperature of the Air.			Height of Barometer.			Latitude at Noon.			Longitude at Noon.		
	Max.	Min.	Mean.	Max.	Min.	Mean.	Mer. Alt.	2d Alt.	D. R.	Lunar.	Chron.	D. R.
1820.	°	°	°	Inches.	Inches.	Inches.	° ′ ″	° ′ ″	° ′ ″	° ′ ″	° ′ ″	° ′ ″
Sept. 1	+ 33	+ 30	+ 31½	29.83	29.75	29.80	—	—	72 55 0	—	—	75 19 15
2	33	31	31½	29.89	29.82	29.86	—	—	72 9 52	—	73 57 55	73 58 0
3	38	32	33½	29.83	29.73	29.80	74 24 0	—	—	—	70 58 40	—
4	36	31	33½	29.71	29.63	29.68	71 2 42	—	—	—	70 19 25	—
5	41	31	36	29.69	29.63	29.65	—	—	70 45 0	—	68 57 19	—
6	32	29	30½	29.76	29.64	29.70	—	—	70 47 12	—	—	67 57 46
7	36	29	31½	29.73	29.62	29.67	70 17 0	—	—	—	68 29 0	—
8	32	26	28½	29.61	29.56	29.58	70 13 55	—	—	—	—	67 24 10
9	34	27	31	29.76	29.59	29.69	69 24 37	—	—	—	—	67 8 20
10	35	31	32½	29.81	29.73	29.77	—	—	68 56 57	—	66 56 57	—
11	35	30	32½	29.69	29.50	29.58	68 19 25	—	—	—	66 5 58	—
12	36	26	31	29.52	29.47	29.50	68 15 20	—	—	—	66 51 30	—
13	33	29	31	29.73	29.62	29.68	—	—	68 15 0	—	—	65 36 0
14	35½	30	31½	29.82	29.73	29.77	68 22 59	—	—	—	65 12 28	—
15	35	24	31	29.74	29.59	29.66	—	—	68 24 18	—	—	63 32 42
16	36	23	30½	29.72	29.50	29.62	—	—	68 29 49	—	—	63 48 0
17	36	28	31	29.56	29.49	29.53	—	—	68 30 8	—	64 21 0	63 45 46
18	32	26	29	29.48	29.25	29.35	—	—	68 24 3	—	—	63 8 12
19	33	28	31	29.49	29.32	29.41	—	—	67 54 28	—	—	62 2 9
20	31½	29	30	29.62	29.50	29.57	—	—	68 12 11	—	—	60 50 19
21	32	29	30	29.60	29.55	29.57	—	—	67 45 30	—	—	60 0 42
22	34	29	30½	29.57	29.55	29.56	67 37 34	—	—	—	58 54 57	59 26 4
23	34	30	31	29.72	29.49	29.55	—	—	—	—	58 47 28	58 50 25
24	36	30	32	29.77	29.46	29.64	—	—	—	—	58 52 54	59 0 23
25	35	30½	32½	29.50	29.33	29.44	66 13 14	—	—	—	—	58 5 38
26	31	28	30	29.35	29 05	29.22	—	—	65 41 9	—	59 9 24	58 6 38
27	32	30	31	29.38	29.00	29.22	64 29 37	—	—	—	56 38 59	55 59 14
28	34	31	32	29.56	29.44	29.50	—	—	62 37 17	—	55 27 35	55 29 17
29	38	32	34½	29.66	29.57	29.61	60 19 43	—	—	—	54 17 45	54 28 56
30	43	34	36½	29.49	29.31	29.41	58 45 51	—	—	—	58 1 51	53 19 9
	+ 43	+ 23	+ 31½	29.89	29.00	29.59	Range and Mean for September, 1820.					

No. IV.—A DIAGRAM,

Exhibiting a Series of Azimuths taken on every second point of the Compass, for the purpose of determining the Deviation on board His Majesty's ship Hecla, July 24th, 1819, in latitude 73° 00′ N. long. 60 26′ W.

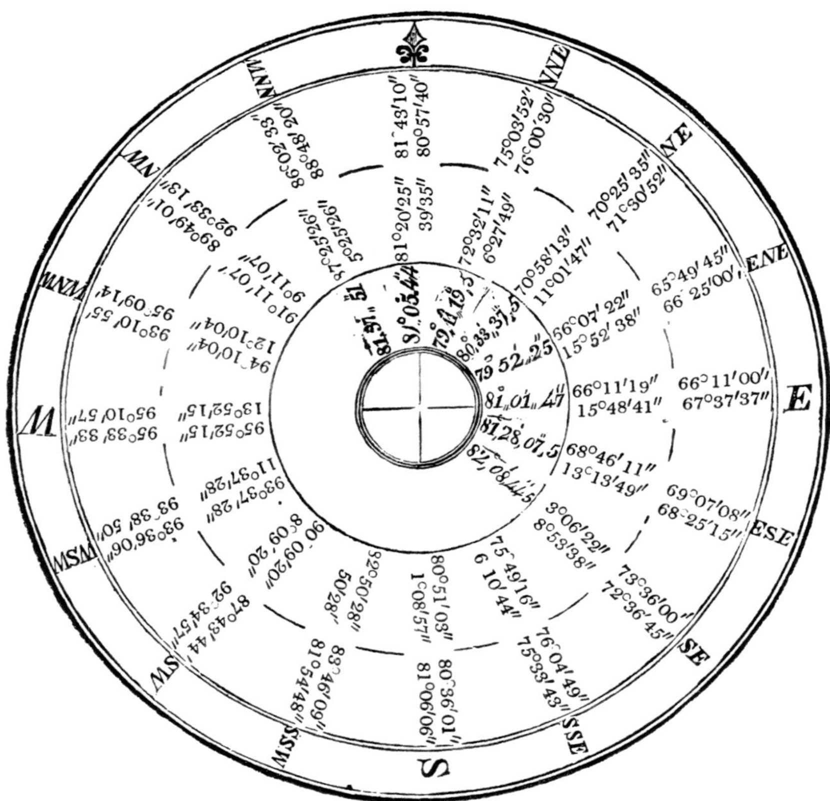

In the above diagram, the letters contained in the outer circle represent the direction of the ship's head when the azimuths were taken; the circle next to it shews the amount of the variation observed on each direction of the ship's head: the figures on the left side * of the rhumb-lines being taken by one of Kater's azimuth compasses, and those on the right side of the same lines, by a card of Mr. Jennings (placed on the stand of Walker's azimuth compass), having two magnetic needles placed at right angles to one another. The figures on the left side of the rhumb-lines in the next circle, are the mean of the two observations, which is taken as being likely the nearest approximation to the truth: the figures on the right side of the rhumb-lines in this circle, shew the difference between the mean variation observed on each direction of the ship's head, and the true variation, as observed on the ice, which, by the mean of twenty-six azimuths, was found to be 82° W. The figures in the inner circle are the sum of the two opposite points, which is presumed to be the true variation on these points; finally, the mean of all the observations, when summoned up, were 80° 48′ 39″ 37‴ W.

* As this term may, in the present instance, be misunderstood, it is necessary to observe, that the figures on the left side of the rhumb-line, North, are 81° 43′ 10″, and on the right side 80° 57′ 40″, and so on.

No. V. — A DIAGRAM,

Shewing the deviation of the compasses on board His Majesty's ship Hecla, at Northfleet, May 6th, 1819. The magnetic dip, or vertical inclination of the magnetic needle, being 74° 35′. The manner in which the experiment was performed, is thus: — the true magnetic bearings of some distant object on shore was obtained, which, in this instance, was the steeple of a church, bearing E. 6° 30′ N. The inner circle shews the bearings of the steeple, with the ship's head on each of the rhumb-lines, except west,

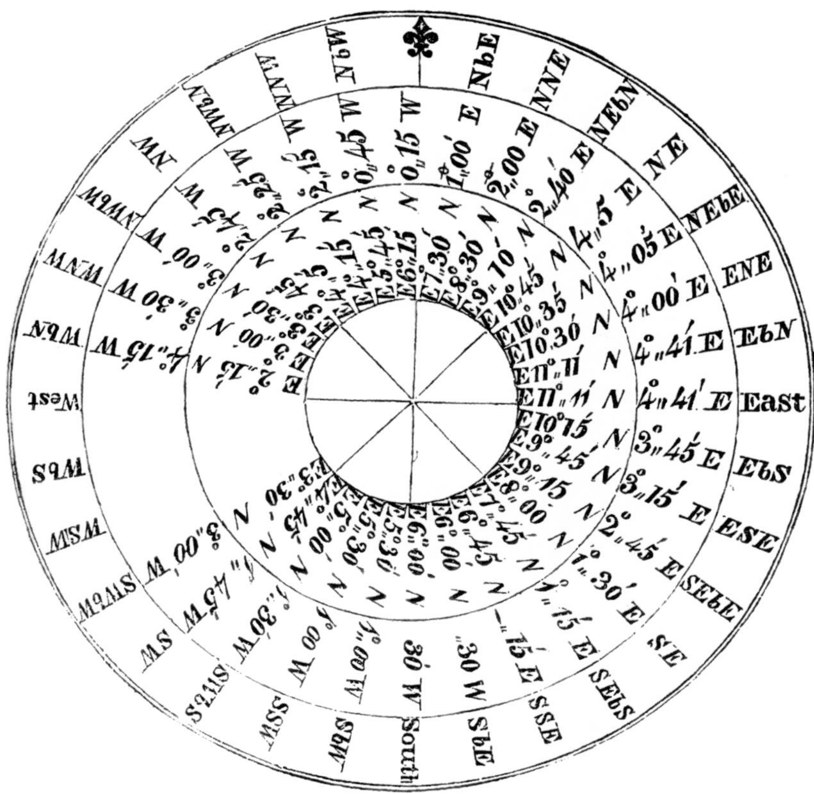

W. by S. and W. S. W.; and the middle circle contains the amount of the deviation on those points, which is equal to the difference between the true magnetic bearings of the steeple; and its bearings with the ship's head on the different rhumb-lines marked in the outer circle.

No. VI. — *Copy of the Paper contained in the Bottle thrown overboard, May 22d*, 1819.

"His Majesty's Ship Hecla, at two o'clock P.M., on the 22d of May, 1819, latitude 59° 4′ N., longitude 6° 55′ W., light breezes and fine weather, wind East, Griper in company. All well. Temperature of the air, 51½°. Sea water, 48½."

(Signed) W. E. PARRY, Lieutenant and Commander

☞ "Whoever finds this paper, is requested to forward it to the Secretary of the Admiralty, London, with a note of the time and place at which it was found."

☞ "Quiconque trouvera ce papier, est prié d'y marquer le tems et lieu ou il l'aura trouvé, et de le faire parvenir au plutôt au Secretaire de l'Amirauté Britannique à Londres."

☞ "Quienquiera hallàra este papel, está pedido de enviarlo al Secretario del Almirantazgo, a Londrés, con una nota del tiempo y del lugar en los quales se halló el dicho papel."

☞ "Enhver som finder dette papür, anmodes at insende samme unfortövet til Regjeringen i Tuöbenhavn eller i Stockholm, eller til Secretairen af det Brittiske Admiralitet i London, med bemærkning angaaende tiden naar, og stedet hvor papiret er fundet."

☞ "Een ieder die dit papier mogt vinden, wordt hiermede verzogt, om het zelve, ten spoedigste, te willen zenden, aan den Heer Minister van de Marine der Nederlanden in 'S Gravenhage, of evel aan den Secretari der Britsche Admiraliteit, te London, en da by te voegen eene nota, inhoudende de tyd en de plaats alwaar dit papier is gevonden geworden."

☞ “ No. VI. — *continued*.

Каждый кто найдетъ сей листъ, имѣетъ доставить оный безъ потери времянiи въ Санктъ Петербургъ Господину Министру военныхъ Морскихъ силъ, или въ Лондонъ Секретарю Аглинскаго Адмиралтейства, означивъ на семъ листѣ время когда, и мѣсто гдѣ, оный былъ найденъ.” —

No. VII. — Copy of a TIDE-TABLE kept on board His Majesty's Ship Hecla, from the 4th of May to the 21st of June, 1820, in Winter Harbour, Melville Island.

Time.			Rise of the Tide from last low Water.		Fall of the Tide from last high Water.	
Day of the Month.	Hour and Minute.	A. M. or P. M.	Feet and Inches.		Feet and Inches.	
	h. m.		ft.	in.	ft.	in.
May 4th, 1820.	5 45	P. M.				
	Mid.				1	5
May 5th	6 0	A. M.	2	3½		
	0 30	P. M.			2	2
	6 45	P. M.	1	1½		
May 6th	0 45	A. M.			1	1
	7 20	A. M.	2	1		
	2 0	P. M.			1	11
	8 0	P. M.	0	11½		
May 7th	2 30	A. M.			0	11½
	9 0	A. M.	1	11½		
	4 0	P. M.			2	1¾
	11 0	P. M.	1	5		
May 8th	4 0	A. M.			1	5½
	10 45	A. M.	2	5		
	5 45	P. M.			2	7½
	11 15	P. M.	2	1½		
May 9th	5 30	A. M.			1	11½
	Noon		2	9		
	5 45	P. M.			3	3½
May 10th	0 12	A. M.	2	11½		
	6 20	A. M.			2	10
	12 20	P. M.	3	2		
	6 15	A. M.			3	9
May 11th	1 0	A. M.	3	8		
	7 15	A. M.			3	4
	1 0	P. M.	3	6½		
	7 0	P. M.			3	8½
May 12th	1 15	A. M.	3	8½		
	7 30	A. M.			3	6½
	1 30	P. M.	3	7		
	8 0	P. M.			3	10
May 13th	1 45	A. M.	4	1		
	8 0	A. M.			4	2
	2 10	P. M.	3	9½		
	8 15	P. M.			3	7½
May 14th	2 15	A. M.	3	9½		
	8 45	A. M.			3	8½
	3 0	P. M.	3	3		
	9 0	P. M.			3	3
May 15th	3 20	A. M.	3	10		
	9 30	A. M.			3	8
	3 30	P. M.	3	0		
	9 30	P. M.			3	1

TIDE TABLE — *continued.*

Time.			Rise of the Tide from last low Water.		Fall of the Tide from last high Water.	
Day of the Month.	Hour and Minute.		A. M. or P. M.	Feet and Inches.		Feet and Inches.	
	h.	m.		ft.	in.	ft.	in.
May 16th, 1820.	3	30	A. M.	3	8		
	10	0	A. M.			3	1
	4	0	P. M.	2	3		
	10	25	P. M.			2	6½
May 17th	4	0	A. M.	2	9½		
	10	50	A. M.			2	7
	4	45	P. M.	2	0		
	11	0	P. M.			2	0
May 18th	5	15	A. M.	2	6		
	11	30	A. M.			2	2½
	5	45	P. M.	1	3½		
	Mid.					1	3
May 19th	6	0	A. M.	2	0		
	12	15	P. M.			1	10½
	6	30	P. M.	1	2		
May 20th	0	30	A. M.			1	0½
	7	0	A. M.	1	7½		
	1	0	P. M.			1	7½
	8	15	P. M.	1	0		
May 21st	2	0	A. M.			0	10
	8	30	A. M.	1	9		
	2	25	P. M.			1	8
	9	0	P. M.	1	1		
May 22d	3	15	A. M.			1	0
	9	30	A. M.	1	6		
	4	10	P. M.			1	11
	10	30	P. M.	1	6		
May 23d	4	45	A. M.			1	4½
	11	0	A. M.	1	6		
	5	0	P. M.			2	2½
	11	45	P. M.	2	1½		
May 24th	6	0	A. M.			1	5½
	Noon			2	0		
	6	30	P. M.			1	11½
May 25th	0	15	A. M.	2	3½		
	6	45	A. M.			2	2
	12	20	P. M.	2	3½		
	6	30	P. M.			2	11½
May 26th	0	40	A. M.	2	8½		
	7	15	A. M.			2	7½
	1	0	P. M.	2	7¼		
	6	30	P. M.			3	1¼
May 27th	1	25	A. M.	2	5½		
	7	30	A. M.			3	1
	1	45	P. M.	2	11		
	7	30	P. M.			3	2½

TIDE TABLE — *continued.*

Time.			Rise of the Tide from last low Water.		Fall of the Tide from last high Water.	
Day of the Month.	Hour and Minute.		A. M. or P. M.	Feet and Inches.		Feet and Inches.	
	h.	m.		ft.	in.	ft.	in.
May 28th	2	0	A. M.	3	7		
	8	0	A. M.			3	0
	2	10	P. M.	3	0		
	8	25	P. M.				
May 29th	2	30	A. M.	3	10		
	9	0	A. M.			3	7
	3	0	P. M.	3	3		
	9	0	P. M.			3	6
May 30th	3	0	A. M.	3	0		
	9	15	A. M.			3	1
	3	0	P. M.	2	7½		
	9	30	P. M.			3	1½
May 31st	3	50	A. M.	3	7½		
	10	15	A. M.			3	3½
	3	30	P. M.	2	7		
	10	0	P. M.			2	7
June 1st	4	15	A. M.	3	4		
	4	45	A. M.			3	4
	4	30	P. M.	2	2½		
	11	0	P. M.			2	3
June 2d	5	10	A. M.	3	0		
	11	30	A. M.			2	10½
	6	0	P. M.	1	8		
	Mid.					1	10½
June 3d	6	0	A. M.	2	9		
	0	45	P. M.			2	6½
	7	0	P. M.	1	9		
June 4th	1	15	A. M.			1	7½
	7	30	A. M.	2	9		
	2	0	P. M.			2	2½
	8	0	P. M.	1	6		
June 5th	2	30	A. M.			1	8
	8	30	A. M.	2	7		
	3	5	P. M.			2	5½
	9	15	P. M.	1	10½		
June 6th	3	45	A. M.			1	8
	9	40	A. M.	2	5		
	4	30	P. M.			2	10
	10	30	P. M.	2	4		
June 7th	4	40	A. M.			2	1½
	10	30	A. M.	2	6½		
	5	0	P. M.			2	6½
	11	0	P. M.	2	6½		
June 8th	5	30	A. M.			2	9
	Noon			2	10		
	6	10	P. M.			2	10

TIDE TABLE — *continued.*

Time.				Rise of the Tide from last low Water.		Fall of the Tide from last high Water.	
Day of the Month.	Hour and Minute.		A. M. or P. M.	Feet and Inches.		Feet and Inches.	
	h.	m.		ft.	in.	ft.	in.
June 9th	0	30	A. M.	2	10½		
	6	40	A. M.			2	11½
	0	45	P. M.	3	0½		
	6	50	P. M.			3	1½
June 10th	0	55	A. M.	3	4		
	7	10	A. M.			3	3
	1	15	P. M.	2	11		
	7	15	P. M.			3	1½
June 11th	1	40	A. M.	3	6½		
	8	0	A. M.			3	7
	1	50	P. M.	2	11		
	8	0	P. M.			3	1
June 12th	2	45	A. M.	3	6		
	8	35	A. M.			3	5
	2	50	P. M.	3	0		
	9	0	P. M.			3	4
June 13th	3	30	A. M.	3	8½		
	9	40	A. M.			3	6½
	3	15	P. M.	2	11		
	9	25	P. M.			2	11½
June 14th	3	40	A. M.	3	7		
	10	0	A. M.			3	1½
	4	0	P. M.	3	0		
	9	45	P. M.			3	2
June 15th	4	30	A. M.	3	5		
	10	30	A. M.			3	1
	4	35	P. M.	2	3		
	10	40	P. M.			2	10
June 16th	4	50	A. M.	3	3		
	11	0	A. M.			2	10
	4	30	P. M.	2	0		
	11	0	P. M.			2	1
June 17th	6	15	A. M.	2	10		
	1	0	P. M.			2	7
	7	15	P. M.	2	0½		
	Mid.					2	4
June 18th	6	0	A. M.	2	6½		
	0	45	P. M.			2	4
	7	0	P. M.	1	6		
June 19th	1	0	A. M.			1	5
	7	30	A. M.	1	10		
	1	45	P. M.			2	0½
	8	0	P. M.	1	8½		
June 20th	2	0	A. M.			1	8
	8	0	A. M.	2	0		
	3	0	P. M.			1	4

TIDE TABLE—*continued*.

Time.			Rise of the Tide from last low Water.		Fall of the Tide from last high Water.	
Day of the Month.	Hour and Minute.		A. M. or P. M.	Feet and Inches.		Feet and Inches.	
	h.	m.		ft.	in.	ft.	in.
June 20th	10	0	P. M.	2	0		
June 21st	4	0	A. M.			1	11
	10	0	A. M.	1	7		
	4	0	P. M.			1	9
	9	30	P. M.	1	8		

THE END.

Printed by A. and R. Spottiswoode,
Printers-Street, London.

CPSIA information can be obtained at www.ICGtesting.com
Printed in the USA
LVOW13s1051030614

388278LV00001B/28/P